INNOCENCE
AND WAR

FULL-DRESSED TOURIST.

INNOCENCE AND WAR

Mark Twain's Holy Land Revisited

Ian Strathcarron

DOVER PUBLICATIONS, INC.
MINEOLA, NEW YORK

Bibliographical Note

This Dover edition, first published in 2012, is an unabridged republication of the work originally published by Signal Books Ltd., Oxford, in 2012.

Library of Congress Cataloging-in-Publication Data

Strathcarron, Ian Macpherson, Baron, 1949–
    Innocence and war : Mark Twain's Holy Land revisited / Ian Strathcarron. — Dover ed.
        p. cm.
    Originally published by Signal Books Ltd, Oxford, in 2012.
    Includes index.
        ISBN-13: 978-0-486-49040-3
        ISBN-10: 0-486-49040-8
        1. Middle East—Description and travel. 2. Twain, Mark, 1835–1910. Innocents abroad. 3. Strathcarron, Ian Macpherson, Baron, 1949– —Travel—Middle East. I. Title.

DS44.98.S77 2012
818'.403—dc23
[B]
                                                                2012021190

Manufactured in the United States by Courier Corporation
49040801
www.doverpublications.com

Contents

To Karen Armstrong and Larry David
for services to sanity on board *s/y Vasco da Gama*

Preface to THE INNOCENTS ABROAD, OR THE NEW PILGRIMS' PROGRESS.

This book is a record of a pleasure trip. If it were a record of a solemn scientific expedition, it would have about it that gravity, that profundity, and that impressive incomprehensibility which are so proper to works of that kind, and withal so attractive. Yet notwithstanding it is only a record of a pic-nic, it has a purpose, which is to suggest to the reader how he would be likely to see Europe and the East if he looked at them with his own eyes instead of the eyes of those who traveled in those countries before him. I make small pretense of showing anyone how he ought to look at objects of interest beyond the sea—other books do that, and therefore, even if I were competent to do it, there is no need.

I offer no apologies for any departures from the usual style of travel-writing that may be charged against me—for I think I have seen with impartial eyes, and I am sure I have written at least honestly, whether wisely or not.

Mark Twain. San Francisco.

Preface to INNOCENCE AND WAR: MARK TWAIN'S HOLY LAND REVISITED

Mark Twain and I first met in Compendium Books in Athens, Greece. I was researching my book about Lord Byron's Grand Tour, Joy Unconfined!; Mark Twain was hiding towards the end of an anthology called Travelers' Greece. The editors had chosen Chapter 32 from The Innocents Abroad, recalling the full moon quarantine-breaking visit to the Parthenon. The chapter sparkled with clarity and fresh eyes and the next day I ordered The Innocents Abroad. Three days later the die was cast for me to sail down to Syria and rejoin him there the following spring.

I wish I could also say that this book is a record of a pleasure trip but it is not; rather I hope it shares with its inspiration an open interpretation of events as they were seen and shares with the reader an idea of what it is like to be drawn into that most unholy land, the Holy Land.

Ian Strathcarron. www.strathcarrons-ahoy.com

Prologue
Mark Twain Before the Holy Land

Mark Twain was born on 3 February 1863; he was twenty-seven years and two months old at the time. Up until then he had been masquerading under the *nom de vie* of Samuel Langhorne Clemens, but on that February day in 1863 for the first time he ended a newspaper piece with the name "Mark Twain". That same piece started with the words: "I feel very much as if I had just awakened from a long sleep."

His twenty-seven-year long sleep as a poor white Presbyterian Missouri home boy, apprentice typesetter, Mississippi River boat pilot, Civil War fugitive and failed Nevada and California silver mine prospector only ended when he stumbled into journalism through a happenstance of desperation and nepotism, a happenstance which also confirmed his faith in Providence. But once Providence had decided to let loose Mark Twain's way with words on the world he launched himself, as if making up for the lost years, into a frenzy of written creativity and lecturing performance. He was the first American writer to give all of his post-War country a voice of its own, in a tone pitched perfectly between old world cynicism and new world optimism, and in a style that satisfied the linguistic probity and conventions of the East Coast and the limitless opportunities for spontaneous self-expression in both the mild or Wild West. Ernest Hemingway later declared that "all modern American literature comes from Huckleberry Finn".

It was not always thus. Born two months prematurely and in the most fragile health in the tiny hamlet of Florida in the middle of Nowhere, Missouri, he followed his earnest and unlucky father around various failed business ventures until they settled in Hannibal, Missouri, when the still often bed-bound Sam was only four years old. He grew up in material poverty in a land of plenty, yet not uncomfortably in a society where bartering, self-sufficiency and good neighborliness were their own currencies, and extended families their own welfare.

Maintaining respectable membership of the Presbyterian* congregation was as important as maintaining a respectable number of slaves. As he was later to recall in his autobiography: "When I was a boy everybody was poor but didn't know it; and everybody was comfortable and did know it. There were grades of society—people of good family, people of unclassified family, and people of no family. Everybody knew everybody and was affable to everybody and nobody put on any visible airs; yet the class lines were quite clearly drawn."

Although poor they were "people of good family". His father could, and did, boast that one of his Clemens ancestors was part of the court that tried and found guilty King Charles I of England. His mother's family, the Lamptons, was of even more ancient origin having shared a nine hundred years lineage—albeit somewhat tentatively by the nineteenth century—with the Earldom of Durham. For the young Sam his Clemens father was austere, stiff, cold, pious and proud—and, in retrospect, born under an unlucky star. The Lampton side was the opposite: big-hearted, wholehearted, frail in body but full in soul. His father died aged forty-four, when Sam was eleven, from shame and pneumonia after being swindled on a business deal and forcing the family to fall from poor to dirt poor. The only time Sam saw a family kiss was when his father drew his sister down to him, kissed her and said, as his last words, "let me die". Sam's mother survived, indeed flourished, and lived with her large heart and kind spirit for a further fifty years.

His father did leave an inheritance, 100,000 acres in Jamestown, Tennessee, but even that proved unlucky. He was convinced that it contained coal, copper, iron, timber, and oil and that one day the railroad would go straight through it. His father said "whatever befalls me, my heirs are secure; I shall not live to see these cares turn to silver and gold but my children will." But, as they say, "where there's a will there's a relative" (funnily enough not one of Mark Twain's aphorisms) and from the moment of his father's death the inheritance was squandered away bit by bit by family squabbles, short term expediency, sibling politics and general inertia. Twain's observation on it all was: "We were always going to be rich next year—no need to work. It is good to begin life rich; it is good to begin life poor—these are wholesome; but to begin it poor and *prospectively* rich! The man who has not experienced it cannot imagine the curse of it."

---

* My father was a St. Bernard and my mother was a collie, but I am a Presbyterian. This is what my mother told me, I do not know these nice distinctions myself. To me they are only fine large words meaning nothing. *A Dog's Tale*

Death was always a family member: it nearly claimed Samuel even before he was born and would hover close by his bed for his first seven years. Four of his six siblings died; his sister Margaret died when he was three and she was nine and his brother Benjamin died aged nine, three years later. Both died slowly and in distress from the yellow fever, carried—it was determined later—by non-native mosquitoes imported with the slaves from West Africa, and both died with the child Samuel in what we would now consider to be ghoulishly close attendance. Life's hold over death for these early European settlers was tenuous at best: if it had not been yellow fever that claimed his siblings it could have been the measles or the mumps, or cholera or malaria, and if one of these didn't succeed the recommended "cures"—either granny's potions or what Mark Twain later recalled as the "Indian doctor, grave and savage, remnant of his tribe, deeply read in the mysteries of nature and the secret properties of herbs"—might well have done so.

And the teenage Sam was death's prime witness outside the home too: he lent a tramp in Hannibal jail some matches and looked on in horror as the man accidentally burned himself to death; he saw an old-fashioned Wild West shoot-out one noon in Main Street; he watched as a slave took half an hour to die after being struck on the head with a piece of slag; he stood beside a dying young Californian emigrant as blood poured from his heart after a Bowie knife fight; from the bushes he saw a widow count to ten before blasting a drunken intruder with her shotgun; and most tragically of all, after securing his younger brother Henry a job on the paddle steamer *Pennsylvania*, he saw Henry perish from a doctor's mistaken overdose of morphine after his brother was badly hurt when the *Pennsylvania's* boiler exploded.

Missouri was a slave state, Hannibal a slave town and the Clemens house a slave house. Twain later remembered that his mother was sixty when slavery was abolished, and that in spite of being the kindest soul, with the biggest heart in all the world, she never saw anything wrong with it. For her and her generation "The Ennoblement of the Heathen" was not so much an excuse for slavery but part of the crusade for it, a God*-given chance to show the savages the higher ground. After all, if Abraham had slaves—and he did—and we have adopted his faith—and we have—surely we too should have slaves? From his childhood he remembered slavery to be of the mild domestic type, and that he never saw a slave mistreated, "and to have done so would have been most unpopular". If a slave got uppity he would be threatened with "selling down the river", which meant being sold to a "nigger trader" who would in turn sell

---

* It is said the ways of God are not like ours. Let us not contest this point. *Mark Twain's Notebook*

him into one of the brutal southern plantations. The Clemens family hired their slaves—one at a time—from a nearby farmer: a 15-year-old girl cost $12 a year, a strong middle-aged woman $40 a year, and the able bodied men $75-100 a year each.

Mark Twain also remembered, as the abolitionist voice grew louder, hearing the Bible Defense of Slavery preached with passion and conviction. From Genesis he heard that: "It was from the lips of this man [Noah] that the everlasting God´chose to announce the curse or malediction of servitude and slavery upon Ham and his race, as it is written." If anyone wavered at the certainty of *that* there was always Leviticus: "Both thy bondmen, and thy bondmaids, which thou shalt have, shall be of the heathen that are round about you; of them shall ye buy bondmen and bondmaids. Moreover of the children of the strangers that do sojourn among you, of them shall ye buy, and of their families that are with you, which they begat in your land; and they shall be your possession. And ye shall take them as an inheritance for your children after you, to inherit them for a possession; they shall be your bondmen forever."

The Presbyterianism of the dour and dank moors of Scotland, with its certainties of wrath and sin, punishment and damnation, condemnation and salvation, had flourished in the uncertainties of the lives and deaths of the Midwest pioneers. By the time the Clemens family had arrived in Hannibal it was the predominant denomination, and the Clemenses needed no encouragement to be in the front row pews. Sam's father was already Presbyterian by nature even before his calling; his mother less so, until after the death of Benjamin—when Sam was seven—she found explanations in homegrown mystical zealotry. Sam simply learned to loathe Sundays as a youth and any form of Puritanism, with its first cousins self-righteousness, hypocrisy, cant and humbug, as he matured. He came to be appalled by the Bible, with its "blood-drenched history; and some good morals; and a wealth of obscenity; and upwards of a thousand lies." From the vantage point of advanced years he would reflect that "Man is without any doubt the most intriguing fool there is. He hasn't a single written law, in his Bible or out of it, which has any but just one purpose and intention—to *limit* or *defeat* a law of God."

But perhaps the spirit, like nature, abhors a vacuum and Sam Clemens suspected, and later Mark Twain confirmed, that Providence answered the soul's questions from within. Although later he would light-heartedly say that "The proverb says that Providence protects children and idiots. This is really true. I know because I have tested it," he would return again and again to thank Providence for life's charms and would never blame Providence for its mishaps. He was an early practitioner of what the philosopher and Orientalist Alan Watts would later call the "Wisdom of Uncertainty". In his autobiography he tells the story of how one day his daughter Susy stopped praying. Her mother asked her why so. Susy replied: "Well mamma, the Indians believed they knew, but now we know they were wrong. By and by it can turn out that we are wrong. So now I only pray that there may be a God and a heaven—or something better." Twain carried this last sentence everywhere, and said that "its untaught grace and simplicity are a child's, but the wisdom and pathos of it are of all ages that have come and gone since the race of man has lived and longed and hoped and feared and doubted."

But we have jumped ahead of ourselves. When Sam's father died in 1847, the family had to move in as live-in help to wealthy neighbors; they were close to the bottom rung of the material ladder. His sister Pamela, who was by then twenty, gave the neighbors piano lessons. His mother became their housekeeper. His elder brother, Orion, by now twenty-two, had finished his printer apprenticeship in St. Louis and was remitting what he could, but by Sam's twelfth birthday it was clear that the family could no longer afford to keep him at school. He was to spend his twelfth and thirteenth years in whatever employ he could find: in a grocery store, until he was fired for stealing sugar, in a bookstore where he found "the customers bothered me so much I could not read with any comfort". He tried the town pharmacy but this didn't work out because "my prescriptions were unlucky, and we appeared to sell more stomach pumps than soda water." He had his first connection with newspapers, a paper round, then took on odd jobs in a blacksmith's workshop. But it was all still an education of sorts, and as he was later to remark: "I have never let schooling interfere with my education."

Then in June 1848, aged twelve, he followed in Orion's footsteps and became a printer's apprentice, in this case on the Hannibal *Courier*. When Orion returned to Hannibal three years later and bought the rival *Journal*, Sam switched print shops and continued his apprenticeship there, and soon found himself promoted to dogsbody. But Orion, like his father, was then and always would be a hopeless businessman, and when three years later the *Journal* folded the newly qualified Sam was jolted into action and at the age of seventeen left the dubious comforts of hometown Hannibal. His apprenticeship had served him well; printing work was easy to find as the new country expanded and newspapers and journals were springing up in every new town and expanding in every older city.

He soon found a job as a printer in St. Louis on the *Evening News* but once his travelling shoes were on they wanted to keep moving. He headed for New York in its most vibrant stage of growth, and worked for a pittance as a printer for the magazine publishers Grey & Green, and paid a pittance for rent in New York's squalid Irish quarter. When the pittances had lost their allure he headed for Philadelphia and found work as a printer and sometimes subeditor in Philadelphia on the *Inquirer* and the *Public Ledger*. On a visit to see Orion's family in their new home in Keokuk, Iowa, he started helping out on Orion's new newspaper venture there. He soon found himself back working as Orion's dogsbody, but was by now confident enough to sub-edit as well as print, and for the first time, slip in the occasional piece of reportage himself.

The frustration of working again for poor doomed Orion must have jolted Sam into taking stock, and jolted Providence into paying him another visit. By now just shy of twenty-one, he could reflect that he had spent the last eight years working in dirty, noisy, smelly print rooms for minimal wages, and after all that sweat and endeavor he had ended up back in Orion's dirty, noisy, smelly print room for no wages at all. All he could see ahead was more of the same. Providence agreed and sent him two gifts from her lockers. First, Sam happened to borrow a book about the Amazon and found it contained a chapter on the coca plant, "a vegetable product with miraculous powers... so nourishing and strength-giving that the native... would tramp up-hill and down all day on a pinch... and require no other sustenance." Sam's mind was set: he would take a boat to Brazil, buy some of this coca and sell it in Iowa, and maybe beyond. Providence then provided the means: he stumbled across a piece of paper blowing in the wind. He later remembered that "it was a fifty dollar bill... the largest assemblage of money I had ever seen in one spot." He headed for Cincinnati and then the Mississippi River paddle steamer to New Orleans, the first stop on the way to Brazil.

Unfortunately we shall never know how the Samuel Clemens Iowa-and-beyond cocaine concession would have fared as New Orleans was as far as he reached. Perhaps unsurprisingly there were no boats to Brazil, not even slow ones, but by the time he had reached New Orleans all thoughts of Brazil had probably deserted him anyway. He had become captivated by the romance and glamour of the Mississippi River and its paddleboat steamers, and within three days of arriving in New Orleans he had signed on as a two-year apprentice pilot, a privilege for which he had to pay his master and mentor, Horace Bixby, five hundred dollars over the training period.

Sam had grown up on the banks of the Mississippi but Hannibal was too early in the great river's journey to be of any use to the best of the river traffic. The real fun did not begin until St. Louis from where the Mississippi proper starts its twelve hundred-mile journey all the way down to New Orleans. Sam had the great privilege of being involved with the paddle steamers in their golden age, and in the days when a qualified pilot on a paddle steamer was a glamorous, responsible and well-paid profession.

It is easy to see how the paddle steamers and river life must have turned Sam's head. To the poor home boys and newly arrived slaves standing on the river's banks they must have been the very scene of wonder; even more worldly folk could only stand and shake their heads in awe. They would hear them first, whistles blowing behind the trees, then they would see the smoke billowing from the chimneystacks, and finally the floating wedding cake would heave into view. Soon they would see it had three storeys, each one's awning decorated with gingerbread, the stairwells finished off with ornate carvings, the paintwork glistening alongside polished brass and varnished mahogany. Flags would billow and pennants flutter from the myriad of masts and poles. Passengers would promenade along the topside verandas; crewmen would scurry and scuttle along the lower deck. At night they anchored or tied up alongside a levee or town. If our poor boy or new slave could peer into the upper portholes he would see maids and slaves dressing their charges in their finery, oil lamps reflecting in gold frame mirrors, flickering on the brocaded walls and velvet curtains. Downstairs in the salons there would be a gaming room for the gentlemen, a withdrawing room for the ladies and a ballroom for those inclined to two- or three-step to an orchestra, a parquet floor below and chandeliers above. Inside this floating palace they would glimpse a civilization from another planet, a civilization peopled by planters, gentlefolk, slavers, farmers, gamblers, whores, soldiers, snake oil salesmen, immigrants, trappers, hustlers, cowboys, molls and preachers. It was a microcosm of all that was best and worst in this new land of freedom, hope and opportunity.

From 1856 to 1861, between the ages of 21 and 26, Sam made over one hundred and twenty passages up and down the great river piloting as many as twenty different paddle steamers. At their peak in the final antebellum years there were nigh-on a thousand steamers, many of them remarkable feats of enterprise and engineering, reflecting perfectly the young America at the height of its uppity can-do think-bigism. Some were pre-Titanic or pre-Spruce Goose monsters of over 500 feet in length and over 500 tons in weight. The safety record was appalling: as many as one hundred and fifty of them sank, either from snagging one of the ever-shifting underwater banks or running over a previously wrecked sister, or flooding as they were frequently overloaded with their cargo flush with the deck, or collisions, or most horrifyingly explosions from the overworked steamers. They were anyway built to be profitable now not indestructible later, and few paddle steamers lasted more than five years before they sank or drowned or exploded.

The Mississippi River is wide but not deep, especially in the summer. Boats going downstream would ride the current mid-river, whereas those heading north would close the banks as near as they dared. The pilot's job was to know the river, every cable of her, and Sam said he learned it like learning a book off by heart. He would work closely with the leadsman, and the latter's job was to throw a leaded line off the bow, mark the depth and shout it back to the pilot. The larger paddle steamers, fully laden, would have about ten feet of hull below the water line. They marked the depths in fathoms: six feet is one fathom; twelve feet is two, or twain, fathoms. At two fathoms, close to running aground, the leadsman would shout to Sam "Mark Twain". The shout became the name and the name became the man.

"I supposed—and hoped—that I was going to follow the river the rest of my days," he later recalled, "and die at the wheel when my mission was ended." Alas for him, and otherwise for us, it was not to be. The new country was about to turn on itself. On 25 May 1861 the 25-year-old Sam was on the *Nebraska* as she approached the Unionist-blockaded Memphis. A jittery rifle shot from the barracks shattered the glass in the wheelhouse along with Sam's blissful career. The Unionists were press-ganging the overwhelmingly secessionist Mississippi boatmen, and Sam fled back to the safety of Hannibal.

But Hannibal was itself in a bind, unsure which side to support. Missouri was a slave state, yet was surrounded by abolitionist states. Most folks were slave owners yet did not favor withdrawal from the union and the isolation that would follow. As it happened most of Hannibal joined the Union but in the early days could equally well have gone the other way; and the *most* never became the *all*, especially in the rural areas around the town. Sam just wished the whole lot would go away, but came up against Leon Trotsky's famous dictum: "You may not be interested in war but war is interested in you."

Forced to make a decision, Sam joined up with his friends and formed the Marion Rangers; exactly whose side they were on remains unclear except all dozen of them proclaimed themselves to be anti-Union. They certainly weren't fighting to retain slavery, and later Sam would remember they were motivated more by cussedness than any form of conviction. A fellow volunteer recalls Sam arrived for duty on a four-foot mule called "Paintbrush", perched on which were a valise and an umbrella, a squirrel rifle, a homemade quilt and a frying pan. The motley crew made camp in another volunteer's farmhouse. The Rangers made the local telegraph operator their general, and Sam was deemed second lieutenant. The mind boggles.

Sam didn't have a great war; in fact he barely had a war worth the name at all. The only action the Rangers saw involved a sentry hearing noises off in the dead of night, and all hands rushing to blast away at the noise in the anxious darkness. The next morning they went to bury the enemy dead. The enemy dead was the brushwood that had been making a noise in the wind and a clipped horse who wasn't too happy to see them.

Two weeks later the Marion Rangers dissolved as surreptitiously as they had evolved. Mark Twain later wrote in jest that he resigned as he had been "incapacitated by fatigue through persistent retreating". More thoughtfully he added: "[The Civil War] seemed an epitome of war; that all war must be just that—the killing of strangers against whom you feel no personal animosity; strangers whom, in other circumstances, you would help if you found them in trouble, and who would help you if you needed it."

Cue Providence, just when Sam needed her. For once in his life the hapless Orion had got lucky. As a reward for campaigning for Lincoln he had been given the job of assistant chief to the chief assistant in the governorship of Nevada. Nevada was not yet a fully-fledged state but still a Territory, a Wild West Territory. Volunteers were not exactly lining up for Orion's job, but Sam saw Orion's posting as the ideal way out of the theoretical battlefield that so far had been his Civil War.

Their two thousand-mile wagon journey across the magnificent vastness of this unspoilt America would remain as one of Sam's liveliest memories. The further west they clattered the more Sam became enraptured by the whole reality that was the West. He loved the space—not just as space, of which there was plenty in Missouri, but as space in the wild Big Country setting by day, and the infinite Big Sky setting by night. He loved the characters—as much larger than life as the scenery was larger than landscape. He loved the opportunities; everyone was heading west to make their fortunes, and tales of fortunes made and just missed and about to be remade were the talk of the bars. He loved the irreligiosity. He had read as a cub pilot Thomas Paine's *The Age of Reason*—a direct rebuttal of the hell* and brimstone sermons of his Presbyterian youth—and he was open to Paine's call to liberation. Paine had

---

* The dying man couldn't make up his mind which place to go to—both have their advantages, heaven for climate, hell for company. *Notes & Journals*

called Christianity "a heathen mythology", and there in the Wild West Sam saw openness and tolerance. Why, he even heard even laughter on a Sunday, so deeply frowned upon in the mild west of Missouri.

The capital of Nevada was—and is—Carson City, and while Orion settled into his government job there Sam headed twenty miles north to the silver mines of Mount Davidson and the instant town of Virginia City. The West was in one of its Gold Rush moments. Virginia City, a city in name alone, a place of shacks and bars and brothels and shovel stores, was spreading as fast as the rumors about its hidden treasures. Sam was caught up in the fever, writing home that "[Mount Davidson] is fabulously rich in gold, sliver, copper, lead, iron, quicksilver, marble, granite, chalk, plaster of Paris, gypsum, thieves, murderers, desperadoes, ladies, children, lawyers, Christians, Indians, Chinamen,* Spaniards, gamblers, sharpers, coyotes, poets, preachers and jackass rabbits." When he wasn't digging he was bartering shares in other claims, but he never learned the old lesson that the people making money in a mining rush are the ones selling picks and shovels.

For eighteen months Sam tried to get rich quick. He lived for months on end in camps and shacks out in the wilderness, digging earth and hustling shares. He somehow managed to set fire to a forest he had claimed, worked as a common laborer in a saw-mill just for eating money, and saw shootouts over dubious claims. He wrote letters home and letters to Orion, and from time to time sent sketches of life in the outback to the Virginia City *Territorial Enterprise*. He wasn't paid, but he was published, and his pieces were popular, his spring shoots of journalism. Sam, in some desperation, decided to see if he could make his pastime pay. He asked Orion for newspaper contacts. Orion came up trumps: the very same *Territorial Enterprise* owed the Territory a favor. When Orion introduced the anonymous sketch writer as the favor's payback a deal was quickly done, and Sam took the first steps to becoming Mark Twain as a staff journalist on the *Territorial Enterprise* on $25 a week.

The 26-year-old cub reporter took to journalism with as much gusto as the keenest teenage cub reporter. At last the years of drift and kismet had been brought up short; at last regular dollars found their way into his pocket. Virginia City was as exciting and bustling and incredible as only a boomtown

---

* The Chinese are a harmless race when white men either let them alone or treat them no worse than dogs; in fact they are almost entirely harmless anyhow, for they seldom think of resenting the vilest insults or the cruelest injuries. They are quiet, peaceable, tractable, free from drunkenness, and they as industrious as the day is long. A disorderly Chinaman is rare, and a lazy one does not exist. *Roughing It*

can be, and a town full of black sheep has only one rule: no questions. The booming town needed a newspaper to match its kaleidoscope of readers and the *Territorial Enterprise* provided the perfect response: no answers. A cross between the *National Enquirer* and the *Kiss 'n' Sell*, it had no pretensions of being a newspaper of record, and it didn't let its lack of pretensions down. Sam readily took to the journalist's credos "never let the facts stand in the way of a good story" and "everything is true except the facts." From these loose interpretations of reality he soon dispensed with reality altogether and began inventing stories lock stock and barrel. There were no rules, only his exuberance at finding his true calling and the devil's eye for mischief and observation.

Four months after Sam had started on the *Territorial Enterprise* the editor needed someone to visit Carson City to report on the Territory's short legislative session. With some misgivings, and with a warning to keep his imagination in check, the newspaper sent Sam to report on proceedings. After sitting through the first interminable session of political waffle, and with ample time to consider all things to be considered, Sam sat down to file his report. The first sentence was: "I feel very much as if I had just awakened from a long sleep." At this stage one might assume he was referring to having to sit through that day's legislative assembly. He finished the piece with the byline "Mark Twain"—which puts rather a different complexion on his opening sentence. Both, for once, would appear to be true. As Sam started to call himself Mark Twain from this time, I hope it will be agreeable if this narrative does the same.

The state of journalistic bliss that was to be a single twenty-seven-year-old *Territorial Enterprise* staff reporter on $25 a week plus board and expenses lasted for a whole year. There were diversions, like visits to San Francisco and Sacramento. There was the constant prowling of Virginia City's bars looking for stories from upcountry, hard luck stories, good luck stories. Here he was attending the dance halls and cabarets and writing reviews; there he was eating and drinking at the many new eateries and drinking venues that the instant Virginia City was gathering around itself. Accuracy was an option, one to be used only when the story was extraordinary enough to stand it own ground. Integrity was a quality expected in doctors, not expected in lawyers, and not considered at all by gold rush journalists. Admiration for newspapermen was still high; gullible readers saw it as a gallivanting public service and demand for this first mass media was insatiable.

Insatiable it might have been, but in May 1864 a markedly hubristic Mark Twain fed it something shocking and indigestible. He invented a story that the proceeds from the Carson City Sanitary Ball were no longer going to their designated charity but were being diverted to a "Miscegenation Society somewhere in the East"—in other words to a society that would promote interracial marriages. If Twain had been looking for the rawest nerve in America he had found it: the Emancipation Proclamation was only two years old and more honored in the breach than the observance, memories—bad memories—of the Civil War were still fresh and bitter, many whites blamed blacks for the War in the first place, and race relations were now touchier than in the slavery days as poor whites now had to compete with free blacks for bottom rung work.

Nemesis was quick to strike Twain and this piece of mischief; even the editors of the *Territorial Enterprise* saw this as a prank too far and he was unceremoniously run out of town—and to save Orion any embarrassment he took the opportunity to run himself out of state. He headed west to his favorite city, San Francisco, and soon landed himself a reporter's job on the San Francisco *Morning Call*.

But this was an unavenging nemesis: San Francisco was hardly a hardship posting. The bohemian city on the bay of the mid-1860s was a direct precursor of the San Francisco of a century later. The countercultural arts, literary and music scenes flourished in the easygoing atmosphere. Poets held sway in the Park; dandies strolled up and down and down and up the hilly streets; all artists seemed to be performing artists too. Added to this was the frisson of earthquakes as the city shook and tremored dozens of times during Twain's first six months there.

The *Morning Call* job was, like the paper itself, a stiff, the very opposite of the freewheeling *Territorial Enterprise*. The San Francisco paper *was* interested in becoming a paper of record and instructed its new reporter just to stick to the (dread-word) facts. He later claimed to have quit the "fearful drudgery, soulless drudgery, [the job] almost destitute of interest", but actually—to use the vernacular euphemism—he was "let go". And let go he did, freelancing around the thriving San Francisco newspaper and magazine scene and becoming involved in alternative theater. It was during this highly creative time that he wrote *The Celebrated Jumping Frog of Calaveras County*, his first attempt at outright humor, a sort of shaggy dog story whose humor has not withstood the test of time. Yet the *Jumping Frog* became a national hit as it was reprinted across the country and was his first national exposure, and exposure as a humorist.

The unexpected nationwide success of *Jumping Frog* awakened in Mark Twain a quality hiding its light under a tumbleweed bushel: ambition. He was later to become socially ambitious (successfully) and financially ambitious (unsuccessfully) but here for the first time he showed professional ambition. The whole journalistic experience, the beginnings of his vocation, had come upon him almost as an afterthought and the success of the experience came upon him almost as an aftershock. But once ambition had got up and made its bed it took a firm hold of him, leading directly, and now in short order compared to the meandering that had come before, to the Holy Land and *The Innocents Abroad*.

His first venture abroad was to the Kingdom of Hawaii, then still more commonly known by Captain Cook's name for the archipelago, the Sandwich Islands. Once there Twain regretted Cook had not called it by the more apt Rainbow Islands—there being more rainbows than sandwiches. The California Steam Navigation Company had responded to requests from US sugar interests to lay on a service from San Francisco to Honolulu. Their new flagship *Ajax* could whisk passengers, and more importantly sugar and freight, there and back in a month. The new route was in itself a significant story and Twain managed to persuade the *Sacramento Union* to send him to this new, and still exotic, location for three months in exchange for all expenses and twenty-five articles at twenty-five dollars a piece. Thus was started his career as a seaborne travel writer; not just that, but following the success of *Jumping Frog*, a travel writer with a twist of sideways humor. From one of the islands the up-market *Union* readers, in a still easily shocked Sacramento, read that: "At noon I observed a bevy of nude naked young ladies bathing in the sea, and went and sat down on their clothes to keep them from being stolen. I begged them to come out, for the sea was rising and I was satisfied they were running some risk." The bevy—if they ever existed—out-patienced him; or maybe not.

They say it's an ill wind that blows nobody any good, and while he was in Hawaii a career-changing piece of good fortune washed up on the beach of one the Hawaii's outer islands. Six weeks before then the *Hornet*, a clipper en route from New York to San Francisco via Cape Horn had caught fire and sank near the equator. The crew of thirty-one boarded the three lifeboats, but two of these were subsequently lost in a storm. The third lifeboat, with the *Hornet*'s captain and fourteen crew, wandered aimlessly around the Pacific for forty-one days on ten days' rations before drifting onto a beach two hundred miles south of Honolulu.

Mark Twain burst into action; a schooner was due to leave for San Francisco the next morning. He interviewed the survivors in the Honolulu hospital and spent all night writing up the story, dispatching it on the schooner as she left port. A month later it was the lead story in the *Sacramento Union*; within another month it had national coverage, and a month after that was in newspapers all over the world. Mark Twain had landed himself a worldwide scoop.

He returned home with a full-length magazine article and the bare bones of a lecture on the Sandwich Islands and the *Hornet* saga. Lecturing was big box office and big business in America. Twain's ambition gander had been let out of its coop and he wanted to cash in while he and the story were hot. Against pretty well everyone's advice, and his own nervous system as the big night arrived, he hired the biggest hall in San Francisco, the 2,000-seat Academy of Music. No doubt he did the mathematics: 2,000 seats at a dollar a time is $2,000, $500 for the hall, $500 for the posters, $1,000 for me.

He took the whole endeavor very seriously; it has often been said the more comic the show, the more serious the prep. It has also been said that an amateur practices till he's got it right, whereas a professional practices till he can't get it wrong. The audience expected a lecture of one hour fifteen minutes, they did *not* expect a reading (Dickens excepted) and they *did* expect a performance. Twain honed and cut and polished and learnt his passages off by heart. He exaggerated his already exaggerated appearance, kept his auburn hair and moustache unkempt, and kept his matching clothes unpressed. He stretched his Missouri drawl to breaking point. He prepared the poster, now for sale on Mark Twain tee-shirts and drying cloths at the Mark Twain Museum, or indeed the Mark Twain Boyhood Home, the one just around the corner from the Mark Twain Dinette (best reached on the hop-on/hop-off Too-Too Twain) on the corner of Mark Twain Avenue and Sam Clements Drive, Hannibal, Missouri:

A SPLENDID ORCHESTRA
Is in town, but has not been engaged.
ALSO
A DEN OF FEROCIOUS WILD BEASTS
Will be on exhibition in the next Block
MAGNIFICENT FIREWORKS
Were in contemplation for this occasion.
But the idea has been abandoned
A GRAND TORCHLIGHT PROCESSION
May be expected; in fact, the public are privileged
To expect whatever they please.
Dress circle $1. Doors open at 7 o'clock.
The trouble to begin at 8 o'clock.

The evening was a massive success. He was a natural public speaker, funny and intimate, who fed on and off audience participation. He understood shock and tension and the relief that humor offers from them: after explaining native practices he proposed to demonstrate what he meant by cannibalism by eating a baby on stage, if someone would be kind enough to offer him one. He then milked the pause of anticipation and strung out the surprise that no baby was forthcoming.

He needed little encouragement to take this show on the road. For three months he filled theaters and dance-, church- and music-halls across California and Nevada, including a triumphant return to Virginia City where old embarrassments were conveniently forgotten. With each performance his act developed as he learnt what worked and what didn't. Now knowing the Sandwich Islands/*Hornet* script backwards he ad-libbed freely, safe that he could return to base at any time. At the start of the tour his lecture was interesting first and humorous second and as one evening led to another the humor would come first and the interest would be the prop for the humor. He had ventured, somewhat unintentionally, into stand-up comic territory. But as any stand-up will confirm, touring is exhausting on mind and body, and was even more so in the days before confirmed bookings, smooth roads, air conditioning and the occasional massage. After three months Mark Twain was a wreck, but could at least enjoy the novelty of being a rich wreck, recovering in the Occidental, San Francisco's glamorous hotel *du jour*.

As he re-gathered himself in the Occidental he took stock. He was already the most famous, and now the highest earning, journalist/lecturer on the West Coast. Back east he was hardly known at all, although the *Jumping Frog* and *Hornet* stories would ring some bells and open a few doors. The Sandwich Islands lectures had anyway run their course. What he needed was a new platform, a new travel adventure like the Sandwich Islands but bigger, better. A voyage that left from the East Coast would be perfect, and he could then repeat the Sandwich Islands/San Francisco formula but to a bigger, better paying and more challenging audience.

Meanwhile, a few blocks away from the Occidental, the editors of the *Daily Alta California* were having circulation-boosting thoughts too. The *Sacramento Union* had stolen a march on them by sending this Mark Twain character to the Sandwich Islands. Twain had lucked out with the *Hornet* story it was true, but why not repeat the trick, only make it bigger, better and maybe he'll luck out again, but this time luck out *Alta*-wise. Why not think big? They would send him around the world, first to New York, then across the Atlantic to the Great

Exhibition in Paris, then onward stopping everywhere interesting eastbound until Japan and then back to San Francisco on the China Mail Steamship. It would be expensive but the *Alta* would own the copyright—an oversight on Twain's part that would come back to haunt him with *The Innocents Abroad*.* In the meantime, with the *Alta California* deal in the offing, it seemed to him that once again Providence had stepped up to the crease, especially as the eastabout trip would give him time in New York to work on promoting his work there. A deal was struck to everyone's satisfaction.

In those days the best way to cross the country was not to cross it at all, but to take a steamer down to Panama, disembark and cross the twenty-mile isthmus on horse, re-embark on the Atlantic side and steam up to New York. So it was done, but it was a journey from hell. On the first night they encountered their first storm, a storm so bad that the crew readied the lifeboats while passengers prayed on their knees besides them. On arrival in Panama they disembarked straight into a cholera camp: thirty-five of the waiting westbound passengers and forty natives had already succumbed. The eastbound passengers picked up the disease too and within days of leaving Panama eight had died on board. On successive nights there were mechanical breakdowns and the steamer floundered. Nearly everyone was seasick. In desperation the ship put into Key West, Florida, to unload the dead and the dying. Half the healthy fled the wretched ship too. Five days later, and after two more breakdowns and a vicious Atlantic winter gale, on 12 January 1867 the thirty-one-year-old Mark Twain arrived back in New York. His Mark Twain was about to become our Mark Twain.

But it was not going to be as easy as he thought. It had been fourteen years since the newly qualified printer had scraped along the bottom of New York. The vibrant city had changed in every possible way for the bigger: business and immigration were booming, politicians and hucksters were snaffling, culture and fashion were blooming. The publishers had moved from Boston; the academics from Philadelphia. As Twain advised his *Alta California* readers: "Make your mark in New York, and you are a made man." It was still thus for Frank Sinatra one hundred years later.

A tour of the publishing houses with a portfolio of articles, including a revised version of *Jumping Frog*, drew blanks. One publisher told him: "Books—look at these shelves. Every one of them is loaded with books that are waiting for publication. Do I want any more? Excuse me, I don't. Good morning." (The foolhardy publisher may or may not have been the one who a

---

* If I'd knowed what a trouble it was to make a book I wouldn't a tackled it and ain't a going to no more. *Huckleberry Finn*

few years earlier had pronounced: "*Whales*, Mr. Melville?")

Yet if the larger imprints were closing their doors in his face, at least the newspapers and journals were opening theirs. The *Saturday Press,* the *Sunday Mercury,* the *Weekly Review, Harper's Monthly,* the *Evening Express* and the *New York Weekly* all ran his stories, either fresh or reworked sketches. In the meantime, in a particular cold New York winter, he was waiting to see the spring schedules for the transatlantic crossings and the resumption of the *Alta California* voyage.

On one of these bitter mornings, 3 February, he went to church. More precisely, the editor of the New York *Sun,* to whom he was trying to sell a story, took him to church, all the way across the icy East River to Brooklyn. One can only imagine Twain's horror when he discovered that this was not just any old church but a Presbyterian church, and not just any old Presbyterian church but a packed full Congregational church led by a charismatic preacher. The Plymouth Church of the Pilgrims of Brooklyn Heights even claimed direct congregational descent from the Plymouth brethren. That's about as high as a low church can get, he might have said to himself.

The service was led by the Reverend Henry Ward Beecher.* Beecher had only been on his feet for a few moments before Mark Twain became transfixed by his performance. Looking at him, listening to him as a fellow public speaker, Twain noted "his rich, resonant voice, and distinct enunciation", and observed how he "makes himself heard all over the church without very apparent effort... sparkling with felicitous similes and metaphors... using the language of the worldly... poetry pathos, humor, satire, and eloquent declamation were happily blended upon a ground work of earnest exposition... forsaking his notes he went marching up and down the stage, sawing his arms in the air, hurling sarcasms this way and that... halting now and then to stamp his feet three times in a row for emphasis..."

Afterwards the *Sun* editor arranged an introduction to the charismatic preacher and Twain heard of a project that must have made every journalistic hair on his head stand on end. Beecher was organizing a tour of the Holy Land, as much to raise funds for his own forthcoming "fifth gospel" as to educate his congregation. It was already heavily subscribed; neither Twain, nor the *Sun* editor, nor anybody else had heard of it before as the hundred or so pilgrims/passengers were nearly all from the Plymouth Church. Beecher showed them the prospectus:

* Mr. Beecher is a remarkably handsome man when he is in the full tide of sermonizing, and his face is lit up with animation, but he is as homely as a singed cat when he isn't doing anything. *Daily Alta California*

EXCURSION
To the
THE HOLY LAND, EGYPT, THE CRIMEA AND GREECE
AND
INTERMEDIATE POINTS OF INTEREST

A FIRST-CLASS STEAMER, TO BE UNDER OUR OWN COMMAND, AND CAPABLE OF ACCOMMODATING AT LEAST ONE HUNDRED AND FIFTY CABIN PASSENGERS, WILL BE SELECTED, IN WHICH WILL BE TAKEN A SELECT COMPANY, NUMBERING NOT MORE THAN THREE-FOURTHS OF THE SHIP'S CAPACITY. THERE IS GOOD REASON TO BELIEVE THAT THIS COMPANY CAN BE EASILY MADE UP IN THIS IMMEDIATE VICINITY, OF MUTUAL FRIENDS AND ACQUAINTANCES.
THE STEAMER WILL BE PROVIDED WITH EVERY NECESSARY COMFORT, INCLUDING LIBRARY AND MUSICAL INSTRUMENTS.
AN EXPERIENCED PHYSICIAN WILL BE ON BOARD.

Details of the itinerary were then listed below.

The "first-class steamer" had in fact been selected, the 1,500-ton, side-wheeled paddle steamer *Quaker City*. As the USS *Quaker City* she had fought with some distinction on the Unionist side in the Civil War, mostly on blockade duty in Chesapeake Bay. After the War she was decommissioned and sold at auction. No doubt the thought of being back on board a paddle steamer only added to Twain's sense of anticipation. The fare was $1,250 in cash, payable to the Plymouth Church, and passengers were advised to take $500 in gold for use en route.

Twain asked if there was space for one more, even if not "from the vicinity"? There could be, Beecher replied, he would check with Captain Duncan, who when not at sea served as the Plymouth Church's Sunday-school teacher. Without waiting for Captain Duncan's reply Twain rushed off a telegram to the *Alta California* editors suggesting excitedly that this Beecher excursion outranked their previous plan for him and pleading for the $2,000 subscription. The *Alta California* team had as much of an eye for a scoop and serial rights as Twain and readily agreed. Wasn't it typically ironic of Providence, he must have asked himself, that she comes skipping along to a Presbyterian church—of all places—to offer up The Big One on a silver collection plate?

But like all best laid plans of mice and men the plot started to fall apart almost immediately. Firstly, Twain fluffed the interview with the teetotal and sanctimonious Captain Duncan. The potential Excursionist showed up at the *Quaker City* booking office with an equally inebriated friend after a good and liquid lunch. Twain introduced himself as the Reverend Mark Twain, a Baptist minister from San Francisco and the Sandwich Islands. Before committing to the trip he wanted to be assured that he could preach alongside the Reverend Beecher, on account of how the organizing reverend was of a different denomination. Duncan had the presence of mind to tell the Reverend Twain that he didn't look like a Baptist preacher* and didn't smell like one either. The not-now so Reverend Twain observed back that "as a ceaseless, tireless, forty-year advocate of total abstinence the captain was a mighty good judge of second hand whisky". They never did get along; one of Twain's enduring pleasures on the *Quaker City* was winding up the already spring-taut Captain Duncan.

In spite of Captain Duncan's misgivings Twain's place on board was in fact safe, as behind the scenes the Excursion was in some trouble. The main attraction, Henry Ward Beecher himself, had decided to pull out, citing congregational pressure for him to stay behind. Later, once his view of the whole affair had been tempered with jaundice, Twain believed he never planned to make the Excursion at all but just to milk the money from it. Thirty other Plymouth passengers withdrew with him, and his celebrity replacement, General Sherman, withdrew two weeks later. From being a well-funded Brooklyn Heights closed shop for Presbyterian pilgrims the Excursion was now scrambling for passengers nationwide—it even found a local worthy from little Hannibal, Missouri. By the eventual date of departure, 9 June 1867, Mark Twain had been become the main celebrity, at least the only person whose name one or two of them might have heard of. More importantly it also enabled him to claim the stateroom, which soon became Refusenik HQ.

A clear division among the passengers soon opened up. In Twain's camp were the black sheep, mostly female and mostly journalists; he called them "the Sinners". Sideline sinners included the ship's doctor and purser, in fact anyone who hadn't paid or volunteered to make the *Quaker City* excursion. Just outside the Sinner camp—at least in the early days—was a sulky high society teenager, Charles Langdon, sent by his parents on a sort of early version of the gap year. The parents wanted him to snap out of whatever he had snapped into, but one thing led to another and two years later he was to become Mark Twain's brother-in-law.

In the other, very much larger camp were the white sheep that Twain soon

* Preachers are always pleasant company when they are off duty. *Daily Alta California*

labeled the "New Pilgrims". Beecher's original passenger list was dominated by Plymouth Presbyterian worthies peppered with sundry WASPs, a Unionist general or two and the odd East Coast showbiz type. When he pulled out he opened the doors to dilution of the planned worthiness, and their places were taken by lesser-spotted versions of the same breed. These newly determined middle-class passengers, mostly from the professions, were all uniformly grey in spirit if not in color, sanctimonious and pious to the point of taxidermy, and desperate for social respectability and spiritual—or more precisely religious—salvation. A well-worn Bible was always close at hand, and the tut-tuts always close to lips. The *Quaker City* God Squad* was guaranteed to bring out the Devil** in Twain, and of course to provide him with wonderful source material for *The Innocents Abroad*.

It is beyond the scope of this book to delve too deeply into the Excursion before it arrived in the Holy Land—far better to read a much better book, *The Innocents Abroad*, but within its scope to outline briefly the changes that came over Mark Twain as the trip progressed.

He started off brightly enough. After ten days of storms, queasiness and Bible study the *Quaker City* arrived in Fayal in the Azores, then as now a Portuguese colony, to be met by locals "with brass rings in their ears, and fraud in their hearts". Soon he was not the rose-tinted tourist of expectations, and noted: "The group on the pier was a rusty one—men and women, and boys and girls, all ragged and barefoot, uncombed and unclean, and by instinct, education, and profession beggars. They trooped after us, and never more while we tarried in Fayal did we get rid of them." He found that the "the community is eminently Portuguese—that is to say, it is slow, poor, shiftless, sleepy, and lazy," which could explain why "Oxen tread the wheat from the ear, after the fashion prevalent in the time of Methuselah. The good Catholic Portuguese crossed himself and prayed God to shield him from all blasphemous desire to know more than his father did before him."

Gibraltar was the next stop, which he found as ghastly then as it is now, but he led a few of the Sinners on a side trip to Tangier. This was much more enlivening—the Exotic for which he had been craving: "And lo! In Tangier we have found it. Here is not the slightest thing that ever we have seen save in pictures—and we always mistrusted the pictures before. We cannot anymore. The pictures used to seem exaggerations—they seemed too weird and fanciful

* The *Quaker City's* strange menagerie of ignorance, imbecility, bigotry and dotage. *Letter, 1867*

** Satan hasn't a single salaried helper; the Opposition employ a million. *Unattributed*

for reality. But behold, they were not wild enough—they were not fanciful enough—they have not told half the story. Tangier is a foreign land if ever there was one, and the true spirit of it can never be found in any book save *The Arabian Nights*. Here are no white men visible, yet swarms of humanity are all about us... There are stalwart Bedouins of the desert here, and stately Moors proud of a history that goes back to the night of time; and Jews whose fathers fled hither centuries upon centuries ago; and swarthy Riffians from the mountains—born cut-throats—and original, genuine Negroes as black as Moses; and howling dervishes and a hundred breeds of Arabs—all sorts and descriptions of people that are foreign and curious to look upon."

They sailed onto Marseille where he came across his first Ugly American. At first all was well. "We are getting foreignized rapidly and with facility. We have learned to go through the lingering routine of the *table d'hote* with patience, with serenity, with satisfaction. We take soup, then wait a few minutes for the fish; a few minutes more and the plates are changed, and the roast beef comes; another change and we take peas; change again and take lentils; change and take snail patties; change and take roast chicken and salad; then strawberry pie and ice cream; then green figs, pears, oranges, green almonds, etc.; finally coffee. Wine with every course, of course, being in France. With such a cargo on board, digestion is a slow process, and we must sit long in the cool chambers and smoke."

But the equilibrium was spoiled when "We were troubled a little at dinner today by the conduct of an American, who talked very loudly and coarsely and laughed boisterously where all others were so quiet and well behaved. He ordered wine with a royal flourish and said: 'I never dine without wine, sir', and looked around upon the company to bask in the admiration he expected to find in their faces. This fellow said: 'I am a free-born sovereign, sir, an American, sir, and I want everybody to know it!' He did not mention that he was a lineal descendant of Balaam's ass, but everybody knew that without his telling it."

Overall his impression of Europe so far was positive, but he had really only dug deeply in France. All that changed in Italy, and the tone of *The Innocents Abroad* changed too. Gone is the reverence for older cultures—the inferiority complex—and in came the assertion that the optimism and hope, the progress in the human condition found in America, were more worthwhile than the fateful acceptance of decay—the superiority complex.

It started to go sour in Genoa. A guide huckstered them to the Chapel of St. John the Baptist: "In this Chapel is a marble chest, in which, they told us, were the ashes of St. John; and around it was wound a chain, which, they said, had confined him when he was in prison. We did not desire to disbelieve these statements, and yet we could not feel certain that they were correct—partly because we could have broken that chain, and so could St. John, and partly because we had seen St. John's ashes before, in another church. We could not bring ourselves to think St. John had two sets of ashes... They also showed us a portrait of the Madonna which was painted by St. Luke, and it did not look half as old and smoky as some of the pictures by Rubens. We could not help admiring the Apostle's modesty in never once mentioning in his writings that he could paint."

After another visit to another relic-filled church he reflected: "But isn't this relic matter a little overdone? We find a piece of the true cross in every old church we go into, and some of the nails that held it together. Then there is the crown of thorns; they have part of one in Sainte Chapelle, in Paris, and part of one also in Notre Dame. And as for bones of St. Denis, I feel certain we have seen enough of them to duplicate him if necessary." By the time they reached Milan he had had enough: "The priests showed us two of St. Paul's fingers, and one of St. Peter's; a bone of Judas Iscariot, and also bones of all the other disciples; a handkerchief in which the Saviour had left the impression of his face. Among the most precious of the relics were a stone from the Holy Sepulcher, part of the crown of thorns, a fragment of the purple robe worn by the Saviour, a nail from the Cross, and a picture of the Virgin and Child painted by the veritable hand of St. Luke. This is the second of St. Luke's Virgins we have seen."

By now he was even becoming jaundiced about the high art. The next day in Milan, in "an ancient tumble-down ruin of a church, is the mournful wreck of the most celebrated painting in the world—*The Last Supper*, by Leonardo da Vinci." Twain lamented the sorry condition into which it had been allowed to deteriorate: "[It] is painted on the dilapidated wall of what was a little chapel attached to the main church in ancient times. It is battered and scarred in every direction, and stained and discolored by time, and Napoleon's horses kicked the legs off most the disciples when they (the horses, not the disciples,) were stabled there more than half a century ago." He saw that "The colors are dimmed with age; the countenances are scaled and marred, and nearly all expression is gone from them; the hair is a dead blur upon the wall, and there is no life in the eyes. Only the attitudes are certain. I am satisfied that the Last Supper was a very miracle of art once. But it was three hundred years ago."

On the way to Venice they crossed through "Interior Italy. We were in the heart and home of priest craft—of a happy, cheerful, contented ignorance, superstition, degradation, poverty, indolence, and everlasting unaspiring worthlessness."

They had read so much gushing travel literature about Venice that *La Serenissima* was bound to disappoint, and at the time of their visit it *was* in a particularly sorry state: "This Venice, which was a haughty, invincible, magnificent Republic for nearly fourteen hundred years; whose armies compelled the world's applause whenever and wherever they battled; whose navies well nigh held dominion of the seas, and whose merchant fleets whitened the remotest oceans with their sails and loaded these piers with the products of every clime, is fallen a prey to poverty, neglect and melancholy decay. Today her piers are deserted, her warehouses are empty, her merchant fleets are vanished, her armies and her navies are but memories. Her glory is departed, and with her crumbling grandeur of wharves and palaces about her she sits among her stagnant lagoons, forlorn and beggared, forgotten of the world."

By the time *The Innocents Abroad* had reached Rome, Mark Twain had had enough of his own wordy descriptions of dilapidated churches, enough of being disgusted by well fed priests and starving beggars,[*] enough of the acceptance of ignorance and the culture of superstition[**] enough of the defeatist fatalism. He could not help but deplore the indolence of Italy, and could not help but compare it with the energy of America. He decided to turn the tables on the slothful Italians, and wrote his famous 1,500-word "turnaround-piece", imagining he was an Italian travel writer in newly arrived America. This is the writer's favorite piece from his time in Italy—and from which:

> I saw there a country which has no overshadowing Mother Church, and yet the people survive. I saw a government, which never was protected by foreign soldiers at a cost greater than that required to carry on the government itself. I saw common men and common women who could read; I even saw small children of common country people reading from books; if I dared think you would believe it, I would say they could write, also…There are hundreds and thousands of schools, and any body may go and learn to be wise,

* We are all beggars, each in his own way. One beggar is too proud to beg for pennies, but will beg for an introduction into society; another will inveigle a lawyer into conversation and then sponge on him for free advice. The man who wouldn't do any of these things will beg for the Presidency. Each admires his own dignity and greatly guards it, but in his opinion the others haven't any. Mendicancy is a matter of taste and temperament, no doubt. *Mark Twain, a Biography*

** When the human race has once acquired a superstition nothing short of death is ever likely to remove it. *Autobiography of Mark Twain*

like a priest. In that singular country if a rich man dies a sinner, he is damned; he cannot buy salvation with money for masses... Hair does not grow upon the American women's heads; it is made for them by cunning workmen in the shops, and is curled and frizzled into scandalous and ungodly forms... In that country, books are so common that it is really no curiosity to see one. Newspapers also. They have a great machine which prints such things by thousands every hour.

... I saw common men, there—men who were neither priests nor princes who yet absolutely owned the land they tilled... Jews, there, are treated just like human beings, instead of dogs... they can practice medicine among Christians; they can even shake hands with Christians if they choose... they don't have to stay shut up in one corner of the towns... they never have had to run races naked through the public streets, against jackasses, to please the people in carnival time...

... Mendicant priests do not prowl with baskets begging for the church and eating up their substance... In America the people are absolutely wiser and know much more than their grandfathers did. *They* do not plow with a sharpened stick, nor yet with a three-cornered block of wood that merely scratches the top of the ground. We do that because our fathers did, three thousand years ago, I suppose... they cut their grain with a horrid machine that mows down whole fields in a day... If I dared, I would say that sometimes they use a blasphemous* plow that works by fire and vapor and tears up an acre of ground in a single hour—but—but—I see by your looks that you do not believe the things I am telling you. Alas, my character is ruined, and I am a branded speaker of untruths!

Having got that lot off his chest he approached Athens, or more precisely its port, Piraeus, in a much better state of mind—a better state of mind until he found that the *Quaker City* had been embargoed and all aboard confined to quarantine for eleven days. In theory, if they could leave the ship, they were leaving behind the decay of Catholic Europe and entering the heathen world of the Ottoman Empire—only later did they find that it too had its own version of decay. Newly independent Greece promised to be an exciting stepping-stone between the two religions and cultures—if they could get off the boat.

This doesn't sound much like Athens now: "So exquisitely clear and pure is this wonderful atmosphere that every column of the noble structure [the Parthenon] was discernible through the telescope, and even the smaller ruins

---

* Blasphemy? No, it is not blasphemy. If God is as vast as that, he is above blasphemy; if He is as little as that, He is beneath it. *Mark Twain, a Biography*

about it assumed some semblance of shape. This at a distance of five or six miles."

That night a full moon lit up the Acropolis in the clear night air and Mark Twain's thoughts turned to clandestine skullduggery. With three others he slipped ashore in one of the tenders on a covert operation to visit the Parthenon. After many scrapes with roused peasants and wild dogs they arrived at the locked entry to the Acropolis. "The garrison had turned out— four Greeks. We clamored at the gate, and they admitted us. [Bribery and corruption.]"

Once inside he found the moonlit figures haunting and ghostly: "Here and there, in lavish profusion, were gleaming white statues of men and women, propped against blocks of marble, some of them armless, some without legs, others headless—but all looking mournful in the moonlight, and startlingly human!... It startled us, every now and then, to see a stony white face stare suddenly up at us out of the grass with its dead eyes. The place seemed alive with ghosts. I half expected to see the Athenian heroes of twenty centuries ago glide out of the shadows and steal into the old temple they knew so well and regarded with such boundless pride."

As they walked around the perimeter they looked down on Athens sleeping below: "... a vision! And such a vision! Athens by moonlight! The prophet that thought the splendors of the New Jerusalem were revealed to him, surely saw this instead! Overhead the stately columns, majestic still in their ruin—under foot the dreaming city—in the distance the silver sea—not on the broad earth is there another picture half so beautiful!"

With his spirits raised by the spirits of Ancient Greece he headed next to Constantinople; the spirits were raised higher still as they approached the wondrous skyline of Istanbul at dawn. But he soon found that "Its attractiveness begins and ends with its picturesqueness. From the time one starts ashore till he gets back again, he execrates it."

It is fair to say that he hated the squalor, corruption, crookery and above all the freak-show beggary that was Constantinople. What had seemed exotic in Tangier seemed in Constantinople as plainly rabid as the famed and mangy dogs that "cleanse these terrible streets". All their dealings with the Turks were fraught: "It comes natural to them to lie and cheat in the first place, and then they go on and improve on nature until they arrive at perfection. In recommending his son to a merchant as a valuable salesman, a father does not say he is a nice, moral, upright boy, but he says, 'This boy is worth his weight in broad pieces—for behold, he will cheat whomsoever hath dealings with him... there abideth not so gifted a liar!'"

On leaving Turkey he reflected, with some gallows humor: "Mosques are plenty, churches are plenty, graveyards are plenty, but morals and whiskey are scarce. The Koran does not permit Mohammedans to drink. Their natural instincts do not permit them to be moral. They say the Sultan has eight hundred wives. This almost amounts to bigamy. It makes our cheeks burn with shame to see such a thing permitted here in Turkey. We do not mind it so much in Salt Lake, however."

If he thought that his first experience of the Ottoman Empire in its capital Constantinople was dispiriting, he would come to detest all it stood for in its colonies, part of which was the famed Holy Land to where they were now heading. But first they had the fun of a small diversion across the Black Sea to Yalta.

This was an unscheduled stop as behind the scenes the *Quaker City*'s owners were trying to sell her, and the Russian royal family had shown some interest in making her their royal yacht. Fortuitously for the owners the excursion was due to visit Sebastopol and Balaklava anyway, and so a quick stop for their majesties to inspect her needed only a slight delay. The passengers did not really expect much from the stop, and were amazed when Aleksandr Nikolaevich Romanov—Czar Alexander II—invited them to visit his summer palace, and then instructed his brother and son to show the passengers their palaces too. Twain, like many a natural born republican before him, was quite swept off his feet by the graciousness of well-behaved royalty. Unfortunately the graciousness did not do the poor czar much good: he was assassinated by revolutionaries fifteen years later. His grandson, Nicholas II, and his family didn't fare much better when the Revolution became official one October thirty-five years later.

It was in this happy, pre-revolutionary temper that Mark Twain and the Sinners, not to mention the erstwhile New Pilgrims along with Captain Duncan and his crew, approached the port of Smyrna and their entry into the Holy Land, the focal point of the great Excursion.

1: Ephesus

Mark Twain started his tour of the Holy Land in Ephesus, although there hadn't been anything particularly holy about it for nigh-on thirteen centuries. But after the experience of all the faux relic-ridden holy sites of Italy and the shock of seeing holiness in the raw in Istanbul, the old Greek and Roman site at least could claim properly documented and verified dispatches in the New Testament. Saints Paul and Timothy*, as well as John the Apostle, were certainly known to have been there. Mary Magdalene and the Virgin Mary have also been associated with Ephesus; in Mark Twain's time it was still widely held that the latter died there too.

The *Quaker City* was moored off the city of Smyrna, now called Izmir. Then and now this is the nearest anchorage to Ephesus, whose grand harbor—the harbor on which her fortune was made—had silted up over a thousand years before the Excursionists' visit. Mark Twain noted that Smyrna was a sensual riot: "Every where there is dirt, every where there are fleas, every where there are lean, broken-hearted dogs; every alley is thronged with people; wherever you look, your eye rests upon a wild masquerade of extravagant costumes; the workshops are all open to the streets, and the workmen visible; all manner of sounds assail the ear, and over them all rings out the muezzin's cry from some tall minaret, calling the faithful vagabonds to prayer; and superior to the call to prayer, the noises in the streets, the interest of the costumes—superior to every thing, and claiming the bulk of attention first, last, and all the time—is a combination of Mohammedan stenches, to which the smell of even a Chinese quarter would be as pleasant as the roasting odors of the fatted calf to the nostrils of the returning Prodigal."

~~~

* Martyrdom covers a multitude of sins. *Mark Twain's Notebook*

As I have mentioned the *Quaker City* and her manifest of Excursionists this is probably a good time to introduce the reader to *Vasco da Gama* and her crew of footstep footsloggers. The latter are the writer and his wife—shipmate, soulmate, photographer and bell-ringer; the former is our yacht—floating home, library, wine cellar and general HQ. We will be following in Mark Twain's wake as much as his footsteps, docking where he docked and from there excursioning where he excursioned. Right now she is lying alongside the same town quay that the *Quaker City* used and judging by the Brown Windsor soup around her hull and the bad eggs smell in the air lying in the same dirty water too.

We are more used to the charms of Asia Minor these days, and anyway the charms themselves have been somewhat depleted to meet the Western world half way. The main offence of Izmir today against the senses is its ugliness. Of course it has a wonderful excuse: earthquakes, twelve since Mark Twain's visit alone, including three which challenged the outer limits of Dr. Richter's earthquake-ometer. Buildings are short and square and squat, all right angles and cost benefits. Contractors skimp on the specs. Should the earth quake one can stand in the middle of the new main streets which are wide and open, wide enough to stay free from falling masonry above if not gaping holes below; there aren't any *old* main streets. The best that can be said for Smyrna then, and Izmir now, is that it has a train station which doubles up as the gateway to Ephesus.

For Ephesus-bound passengers the thirty-mile railway link today is as suburbanly efficient as one in, say, Oslo, Norway—the same Oslo, Norway to which British Airways keep sending my bags. Izmir's suburbs now stretch halfway to Ephesus, not so much spreading like larvae in a duck pond as expanding like amoebae in a Petri dish. The best diversion from the drabness outside is the ticket collector's uniform: a typically Turkish affair, which turns the humble cheerful clippie in to a five star general of no mean pomp and not inconsiderable circumstance.

For Mark Twain and the Excursionists the train journey was a great steam-driven adventure, more so for having unexpectedly been taken under the wing of a remarkable British railway engineer, architect and amateur archae-ologist, John Turtle Wood. By now in his mid-forties, Turtle Wood had been sent five years earlier to the Ottoman province of Aidan by an English civil engineering consortium, the Smyrna and Aidin Railway Company, to build a railway from Smyrna to Denizli. Turtle Wood's specialty was the architecture of railway stations, and while constructing the station at Selçuk, the town nearest Ephesus, he became fascinated by the undug ruins of the great Greek and Roman capital of Asia Minor nearby, a city which in its pomp had half a million citizens, was second only to Rome in its glory, but which had now lain neglected and deserted as a pagan pile for seven centuries by its Islamic Ottoman rulers.

By 1865, two years before the *Quaker City* visit, John Turtle Wood had negotiated for himself a reduced involvement with the railway company, made up for by an allowance from the British Museum—the latter in exchange for property rights should his digging prove fruitful. Property rights were freely available; one just had to pay for the digging via an elaborate system of reverse patronage, and pay again to take the artifacts home—usually to London. The Ottomans held no interest in non-Islamic images and found the Christian interest in Greek and Roman paganism quite baffling, if profitable. Just before Mark Twain's arrival Turtle Wood had unearthed evidence that the Temple of Artemis, one of the seven wonders of the ancient world, unseen for over five hundred years, was relatively close at hand. By now a monomaniac with a mission he was to devote the next four years to what must have seemed to the expenses clerks at the British Museum like the wildest of goose chases, but in December 1869, having upended twenty feet of earth over 550 square feet of ground, he did indeed find the first remains of the Temple of Artemis.

$$\approx$$

On a slightly less ambitious quest the writer cannot resist visiting the nearby Ephesus Train Museum, which boasts "the largest collection of steam engines in Europe", even though it is not actually—sorry for the sudden attack of pedantry—in Europe at all. I want to see if there are any exhibits relating to John Turtle Wood, or the Smyrna and Aidin Railway Company, or maybe by some minor miracle the group photograph taken that day which Mark Twain mentions, but which has yet to be found. The museum is as empty and deserted as Ephesus must have been in Turtle Wood's day, its only occupant being a weasly looking Belgian, owner of the equally deserted *LeWagon* restaurant, both restaurant and restaurateur hiding in a dark and damp corner of the museum site.

He doesn't speak much English, so we settle for schoolboy French. He had married the daughter of a Turkish guest worker in Antwerp and decided to come to Selçuk, her home town, to make his fortune as a restaurateur. One could not help feeling that both sets of parents must have been disappointed by the union. He has not heard of Turtle Wood or his railway company, or of Mark Twain or his visit, nor has any interest in either, nor anything come to think of it. The museum, he assures me, has no curator or records, just the twenty-five steam engines lying outside. He has no customers. How does he manage? A grant from Selçuk municipality. Does he want any more customers? Not really. And Belgium? Huh! I must be joking. Gone to the dogs, just like here.

～

Anyway, with some relief, back to Mark Twain, John Turtle Wood and more stirring times. I suppose you could say John Turtle Wood was Mark Twain's first Holy Land Ferguson. Let me explain.

In Paris the New Pilgrims came across the first of many guides they would use throughout their Mediterranean tour. Like every other breed, there were guides and there were guides. The one is Paris was of the less successful variety. This one presented his card and Mark Twain read the unlikely name of "A. Billfinger". The American was disappointed; he had hoped for a guide called "Henri de Montmorency, or Armand de la Chartreuse, or Alexis du Caulaincourt" or his final suggestion "Alphonse Henri Gustave de Hauteville."

"Let's call him Ferguson," said his fellow Sinner, Dan. And the name stuck and became the generic name for any guide from the useless to the brilliant for the rest of the *Quaker City* excursion.

(The Ferguson in Paris will sound familiar to anyone who, like the writer, habitually uses guides when in foreign parts. "As long as we had that fellow he was always hungry; he was always thirsty. He could not pass a restaurant; he looked with a lecherous eye upon every wineshop. Suggestions to stop, excuses to eat and to drink, were forever on his lips." He was always looking for ways to chisel them out of money: "On the shallowest pretences he would inveigle us into shirt stores, boot stores, tailor shops, glove shops—anywhere under the broad sweep of the heavens that there seemed a chance of our buying anything." Later the Sinners managed to shake Ferguson off and took in a show: "The music struck up, and then—I placed my hands before my face for very shame. But I looked through my fingers. They were dancing the renowned "*Can-can*.")

Along with the Excursionists, Turtle Wood loaded a coral of donkeys into the freight cars, donkeys so small that Mark Twain called them "scarcely perceptible". The mini-donkeys would be fitted with specially raised saddles to keep their passengers' feet in the air and would be needed to carry the group around "for we had much ground to go over". They then had a much more interesting train journey than has the modern traveler from Izmir to Ephesus, seeing "some of the most grotesque costumes, along the line of the railroad, that can be imagined. I am glad that no possible combination of words could describe them, for I might then be foolish enough to attempt it."

Decanting from train to donkey they set off to see Ephesus. Turtle Wood took them first to "a high, steep hill, toward the sea, [where there] is a gray ruin of ponderous blocks of marble, wherein, tradition says, St. Paul was impris-oned eighteen centuries ago." Tradition has since been found wanting: the ponderous blocks of marble are now known to have been laid three hundred years later. As a result of this new found lack of authenticity this hill site has now been abandoned again, and is in fact off-limits—a shame for the modern traveler because Turtle Wood had taken them to the place which offered the best views of the grand amphitheater and the surrounding ruins, and which would now still offer the best view of the greatly expanded site as a whole. No doubt a *téléphérique* operator is measuring up the angles right now.

Walking down the hill, grappling with the sub-sized and single-minded donkeys, their platform saddles not quite platform enough, the tourists had their feet dragged over what would later be unearthed and known as Harbor Street, the restored broad colonnaded avenue that connects the grand amphi-theater to what would have been the grand harbor. It is hard to imagine that as recently as 1867 Turtle Wood was the only archaeologist—in fact the only outsider of any description—working there, and he was more inter-ested in the Temple of Artemis, five miles off-site, than the Roman remains of the great city underneath him. It was to be a further thirty years before an Austrian delegation of archaeologists set to work uncovering the past glories of Ephesus. Indeed, a self-renewing new delegation of Austrian archaeolo-gists are uncovering the past glories of Ephesus now; the Austrians have the Ephesus dig and sift concession—and a very fine job they are making of it too.

But there's no doubt that Mark Twain was quite overcome with the histor-ical significance of the once-great, now hidden city:

> It is incredible to reflect that things as familiar all over the world to-day as household words, belong in the history and in the shadowy legends of this silent, mournful solitude. We speak of Apollo and of Diana—they were born here; of the metamorphosis of Syrinx into a reed—it was done here;

of the great god Pan—he dwelt in the caves of this hill of Coressus; of the Amazons—this was their best prized home; of Bacchus and Hercules—both fought the warlike women here; of the Cyclops—they laid the ponderous marble blocks of some of the ruins yonder; of Homer—this was one of his many birthplaces; of Cirmon of Athens; of Alcibiades, Lysander, Agesilaus— they visited here; so did Alexander the Great; so did Hannibal and Antiochus, Scipio, Lucullus and Sylla; Brutus, Cassius, Pompey, Cicero, and Augustus; Antony was a judge in this place, and left his seat in the open court, while the advocates were speaking, to run after Cleopatra, who passed the door; from this city these two sailed on pleasure excursions, in galleys with silver oars and perfumed sails, and with companies of beautiful girls to serve them, and actors and musicians to amuse them; in days that seem almost modern, so remote are they from the early history of this city, Paul the Apostle preached the new religion here, and so did John when many men still lived who had seen the Christ; here Mary Magdalene died, and here the Virgin Mary ended her days with John, albeit Rome has since judged it best to locate her grave elsewhere; six or seven hundred years ago—almost yesterday, as it were— troops of mail-clad Crusaders thronged the streets; and to come down to trifles, we speak of meandering streams, and find a new interest in a common word when we discover that the crooked river Meander, in yonder valley, gave it to our dictionary.

One hates to quibble, and Mark Twain had a journalist's rather than an historian's view of facts, but his history of Ephesus has rather improved with the telling. Apollo was born in Delos, and Mark Twain confused his sister Artemis with her Roman counterpart Diana; Pan and Syrinx dwelt on Mount Olympus; the Amazons lived mostly elsewhere in Anatolia; there is a statue of the Cyclops in Ephesus, but nothing more than that. But there's no gainsaying that Ephesus was *the* great Greek and Roman capital of Asia Minor, a mighty cultural and trading center, and certainly Lysander and Alexander the Great strode through there, and Anthony and Cleopatra wintered there, and as were all the other prominent Romans listed above and many more besides.

The Christian visitors Mark Twain mentioned are slightly more problematical. Paul was a Roman citizen and would certainly have been free to travel to Ephesus at his will, and his two visits are well documented by Luke in Acts and—more reliably—confirmed by contemporaneous Roman accounts. The John that Mark Twain mentioned was "John the Apostle"; in Mark Twain's time it was thought he was also the writer of John's Gospel, now reckoned to be a later John, "John the Evangelist". But John, as in "John the Apostle", was known to have led the church—a church at this stage meaning a gathering of worshipers rather than building—in Ephesus.

Of the two Marys there is no hard, or even soft, evidence to suggest that Mary Magdalene was in Ephesus, nor that the Virgin Mary died there. The first suggestion of the latter event as even a possibility was not floated until 431 AD at the First Council of Ephesus. Mark Twain's observation that "albeit Rome has since judged it best to locate her grave elsewhere" has been super-seded by yet more hopeful prodding: "Rome" has now moved it again, and this time made it official. In 1812 a German nun, one Anne Emmerich, dreamt that the Virgin Mary had died in Ephesus and on awakening the nun dictated her vision of the house and the cave nearby where she dreamt that Mary was buried. With determination equal to John Turtle Wood's, clerics from across the sects dedicated themselves to finding the site of the dream. In 1891 two Lazarist priests were able to declare that they had indeed found it, the exact spot. Confirmation from cardinals in Rome soon followed and Pope Leo XIII celebrated mass there in 1896. Pope Pius XII upgraded the site to a Holy Place in 1950, and since then there have been papal visits by Paul VI and John Paul II, and more recently, in 2006 by Pope Benedict XVI.

Non-believers in the fantastic can easily scoff, but as Mark Twain observed two weeks later in the Holy Land tour: "Wherever they ferret out a lost locality made holy by some Scriptural event, the [Catholic] Church straight-way build a massive—almost imperishable—church there, and preserve the memory of that locality for the gratification of future generations. If it had been left to Protestants to do this most worthy work, we would not even know where Jerusalem is today, and the man who could go and put his finger on Nazareth would be too wise for this world. The world owes the Catholics its good will even for the happy rascality."

⁓

Unfortunately, in spite of all this official, even papal, enthusiasm for the nun Anne's vision, in the last thirty years archaeologists have rather spoilt the party by declaring that the house in the dream dates from around 500 CE—soon after the very same First Council declared it to be here or hereabouts. Today it is a fully designated tourist destination, with car parks groaning under coaches and taxis, souvenir shops and drink stalls selling junk and stewed coffee (in Turkey!) and crowds from every conceivable corner of belief and non-belief swarming around the shrine.

Just after the ticket booth (six euros per adult) a scrubbed pine table and chair rest on the ground and a monk in a Capuchin hood (from whose appearance we derive the word *cappuccino*) sits in the folds of his habit. About where one would find a lapel he wears two small pin flags, the Union Jack and the Spanish. Like an air hostess, or even a flight attendant, I take it to mean he speaks English and Spanish. He looks around thirty, but I suspect he's a good ten years older than that. He is in demand. I eavesdrop but the questions are directional not theological. In a break I ask him if he'd like something to drink from the stall and from where he comes, how come he's here.

No thanks to the drink, then "Burlingame, California."

"And what do you make of this Tower of Babel?"

He smiles, patiently. "Benedictines find peace in the evening, and the morning. But it's a rush here all day, that's for sure. We are tired when they've all gone."

"I thought you were Capuchin. The brown hood."

"It's any dark color now, the habit, outside of the big occasions," he replies. "It will all come and go, all this activity."

"And the Virgin Mary, is this meant to be taken literally or symbolically?"

"You must take it one way or another."

"True, and you, how do you see it?"

"I'm easy with miracles.* I see us all as miracles," he replies.

"Good answer," I grant. "How come you are here, Burlingame is not exactly a bus ride up the hill?"

"There are four of us in Izmir. We stay in the Latin Convent. Today's my day." He smiles at some other world he keeps to himself.

By now others are jostling around me wanting to ask him more intelligent questions and I wander off into one of the crowds. They are speaking Mandarin, of which I can only remember a few *wheh*s and *nwah*s from time spent in the back streets of Kowloon. They have brought their own guide, and I wonder how he is explaining the concept of a virgin birth. There is no equivalent Chinese myth, even Confucius being blessed with straightforward ancestry. I'm sure the guide told them that the Virgin Mary has good company in this department, with none less than the Buddha, the Lord Krishna and even the mighty Mongolian Genghis Khan all having later followers claim virgin births for them.

It is often said that we have been confused because St. Matthew ambiguously translated the Hebrew *almah* into the Greek *parthenos* and we have come

---

* There is nothing more awe-inspiring than a miracle, except the credulity that can take it at par. *Mark Twain's Notebook*

to build a cult around the "virgin" rather than the "young woman" meaning of the Greek word. That's true but actually it is more interesting than that. The conception—as it were—of a virgin birth of a son (always a son) goes back to the earliest known myths. The Christian version of the virgin birth myth was introduced by St. Luke, a highly Hellenized Syrian from the Greek town of Antioch, some eighty years after the event. Luke constructed Jesus' virgin birth directly from that of Dionysus by his mother Semele, Zeus' adulterous lover. A constant theme is that a prophet, or god, or messiah, or a Greek- or Latin- style demi-god had to be given a leg-up by being born without leg-over.

Common to Christian scriptures from Adam* in Genesis is the belief that the female form is both inherently unclean and the ultimate temptation. This is a purely Hebrew invention. All other warrior gods married—and then some: Mars to Venus, Zeus to Hera (parents of the ultimate goddess Aphrodite); Arjuna (another virgin birth) had no fewer than forty wives but the Hebrew god Yahweh forbade all goddesses. In the Old Testament the Canaanite term for goddess is "abomination" and through ignorance the subjugation of women down the ages in the West has been as a result of this baseless biblical postulation.

Even if the Holy Place up on the hill isn't wholly authentic, there's no denying the deep sense of time and place to be found back in the amphitheater standing exactly where St. Paul and his disciples stood in the famous riot scene in Acts 19 onwards. The city's silversmiths, led by Demetrius, accused Paul of destroying their trade in religious knick-knacks by his outbursts against false gods in general and Artemis in particular. The assembly degenerated into a riot and St. Paul wisely decided there and then to finish his three-year stay in the city; exit stage left pursued by a mob.

Standing on that spot in the amphitheater today one also has a feeling of standing on a crucial point of Christian history, the point where thirty years after Jesus' death the new religion, as propagated by its brilliant advocate Paul, had gained enough critical mass to be unstoppable. The silversmiths' riot against Paul's effectiveness in Ephesus was a metaphor for the Jewish rabbis' and Roman pontiffs' concerns at the success of this new egalitarian, inclusive religion which threatened their respective authorities throughout the Empire.

They found Paul was particularly dangerous because he was a high-born Hellenistic Jew *and* a Roman citizen, the former by family tradition and the

* It all began with Adam. He was the first man to tell a joke—or a lie. Adam was not alone in the Garden of Eden, however, and does not deserve all the credit; much is due to Eve, the first woman, and Satan, the first consultant. *Notebook 1867*

latter by virtue of having been born in Tarsus, a Roman city, now in south-eastern Turkey, which had been granted special status due to its efficiency in paying its tributes to Rome. This unusual combination gave him access to the highest reaches of Jewish power in Jerusalem and the freedom to travel anywhere in the Empire he chose—and with the full protection of its law. He was also a born troublemaker and leader, a charismatic orator and collector of followers, with that particularly Jewish trait for not sitting on a fence when more challenging options are available either side of it. If he were alive now he would not just be an illegal settler in the West Bank but their architect, ringleader, advocate and spokesman too. He *believed*—and belief becomes a self-fulfilling prophecy even in a person with less developed consciousness; with Paul's level of presence prophecies found themselves self-fulfilling one after another.

The story of his enthusiastic persecution of the early followers of Jesus, and his conversion by the spirit of Jesus on the way to Damascus in about 33 CE, when he was around 23 years old, are well known. By the time he reached Ephesus for the second time, the time of the silversmiths' riot twenty years after his conversion, his message had changed to a marked degree, and it is largely this message that we call Christianity today.

At the time of Paul's conversion the followers of Jesus, the apostles, were preaching, as Jesus had done, to fellow Jews. Paul chose instead to use his privileges as a Roman citizen and his knowledge of the Greco-Roman cultures to preach to the polytheistic Gentiles, whom he considered to be not just a larger audience but also more in need of his new Messiah-based creed. Whereas the original apostles in Jerusalem were continuing to preach Jesus' essential message that "the Kingdom of God is among you"—a Buddhist, indeed a Perennial Philosophy message open to re-interpretation with each uninitiated telling—Paul concentrated not so much on the message of Jesus' life but on His death and resurrection—and how furthermore these were divinely ordained, thereby fulfilling God's covenant with Abraham and so then expiating all the sins of mankind. Paul's religion has been well called Cross-tianity.

Even without Paul's powers of persuasion and perseverance, his message was the right one at the right time. Whereas Jesus' Jewishness meant that His message as delivered by the apostles around Jerusalem was easily bogged down in internecine debate and persecution, Paul's version of His message to the polytheistic and superstitious Gentiles of the eastern Empire was a message of egalitarianism, forgiveness, hope and redemption. For those inclined to monotheism it was far simpler to adopt Paul's new creed of a saving Messiah than to learn the complexities of Judaism with its Covenant Law, its inbuilt racial doctrine and its semi-esoteric rites of diet and circumcision. Paul's message cut through all these carefully planted obstructions: baptism was as meaningful as circumcision, faith in salvation through the Christ as Messiah was equal to any amount of knowledge of arcane Mosaic laws. If all this was problematical to observant Jews it was easily accepted by Gentiles with no knowledge of Jewish tenets. It was Paul who first proposed that Jesus was the Son of God; again an idea hard for Jews to accept, but perfectly reasonable to a Greco-Roman audience used to the mythological interbreeding of gods and humans. The result of all this is that the Christianity we know today is decidedly Pauline and at some distance from the original Jewish teachings of Jesus: the Jesus of history is a very different person from the Christ of faith, and the less importance one attaches to the former the easier it becomes to love the latter. As Cardinal Bousson famously put it: "Saint Paul put the Christ in Jesus Christ," or as Mark Twain concluded—albeit from a completely unrelated non-Pauline angle: "If Christ were here now, there is one thing he would not be—a Christian."

This Thursday afternoon in the grand amphitheater of Ephesus in mid-April there are Christians a-plenty and as one ruminates on matters Ancient & Modern, one only has to wait an hour for another pilgrim tour to pass through. The writer is a great fan of hiring guides, hiring Fergusons as I must learn to say but in the case of Ephesus—and other concentrated sites—there is a better way of having one's Ferguson and eating him. The technique is to park oneself at a stop on the tour route and wait. Pretty soon another group will appear and one can just listen in on a squatter's rights basis. When the one you are listening to has finished one can just amble over to the next stop to await the Ferguson that follows.

The format for guided tours is the same in many ways as it was for Mark Twain and the New Pilgrims. A local guide—now a Turkish polyglot rather than John Turtle Wood—explains the historical context of the site. All the New Pilgrims in the amphitheater that day would have known the biblical context off by heart, but today it is explained for them by a second guide, their tour leader—as often as not the preacher from the organizing sect.

I think I have a glimpse of St. Paul preaching at Ephesus earlier this afternoon. A tour group—yet another tour group—arrives for what I suppose will be the usual five-minutes-and-move-on shtick about the amphitheater in any one of a number of languages. And so it is, for the usual five minutes. Then one of the tourists, a large man in his mid-fifties, clean-cut and open necked, with "Cummins, J." on his lapel, stands up, and faces the others his arms held aloft. In his right hand is a black Bible; he never opens it—he doesn't have to. "Brothers. Sisters. Fellow believers in the Savior." His voice is strong and clear, mid-Western, deep but not loud. "You know why we are here. This is the very spot. The true word of St. Paul had so shaken the unbelievers that there was an uproar—some say a riot. Acts 19, verse 23, right to the end."

He then recites Acts 19, verse 23 right to the end. It is a mighty impressive performance, all the better for being slightly underplayed, no thumping and gnawing and gnashing of teeth, but a sincere man doing what he thinks—and for him *knows*—is right. He then takes the group from the stalls to the stage, and sets one man aside to be Demetrius and tells him to read the first few verses—the ones accusing Paul—and two other men to be St. Paul's companions (St. Paul having fled) who stood as accused in Paul's stead. The other members of the group are told to be Ephesian artisans siding with Demetrius, and told to cry "Great is Diana of the Ephesians" at the preacher Cummins, J.'s prompting. The preacher is to be the Roman adjudicator, who in Acts calms the crowd and dismisses the case as the court is secular; a truly Roman approach to this troublesome new sect of quarrelsome Judaism.

By now a considerable crowd of other tour groups have stopped tour grouping and stand either on stage with the Ephesian mob, or on the stone seats nearby. Without any element of self-consciousness Cummins, J. then conducts the throng in Acts 19, verse 23, right to the end. First he quiets the crowd. Then he gives "Demetrious" his own as yet unopened Bible and tells him to read the accusatory verses; which "Demetrious" does. Then the crowd, by now a small mob, chants "Great is Diana of the Ephesians" and he keeps the howling running for a good minute or two. Next he stands up, quiets the crowd again and recites—no need to read—the final verses.

But the real *coup de théâtre* comes at the end. As the hubbub is dying down he raises his arms and looks to the sky. I have no idea what he is going to say or do, but I follow his arms up high and see two large birds, almost certainly vultures. Without a pause he says: "But they that wait upon the Lord shall renew their strength; they mount up with wings of eagles; they shall run, and not be weary and they shall walk and not faint. Isaiah forty; thirty-one." The writer isn't one of the Lord's flock, but has to say that if St. Paul was as good as Cummins, J.—and I'm sure he was even better—and if he stayed in Ephesus for three years—and we know that he did—it's no wonder that Demetrius and the Jews and the Romans were pleased to see him run out of town, and equally dismayed to see so many converts he had left behind. Today St. Ferguson of Ephesus may have converted one or two more.

Less than one hundred and fifty years ago Mark Twain, the New Pilgrims and the Sinners headed back to the train station, the New Pilgrims' pockets filled, as was their wont, with fragments stolen from the site just visited. Settling down on the train they were "rudely disrupted by an Order—from Constantinople no less—to disgorge the contents of their pockets forthwith. Outrage followed; and abuse of their Mohammedan hosts followed the outrage. What typical hatred of Christians and Christianity! Do they think we are common thieves? Do they not recognize esteemed and genteel collectors? A New Pilgrim grabbed the Order and saw it bore the stamp of the British Embassy in Constantinople. It was a disgrace, if typical and predictable, to be insulted by the Ottomans; but to be treated as criminals by a representative of the Queen caused horror and mayhem." Mark Twain tried to calm them, pointing out "the same precautions would have been taken against *any* travelers, because the English Company who have acquired the right to excavate Ephesus, and have paid a great sum for that right, need to be protected, and deserve to be." Pockets were emptied with reluctance and weariness and the hubbub receded.

Later, back in his stateroom on the *Quaker City*, Mark Twain opened his journal with the words: "This has been a most stirring day." Same for me, my friend, a *most* stirring day. The Holy Land tour is *on*!

2. Beirut

M ark Twain arrived in Beirut—and the Holy Land proper—on Tuesday 10 September, 1867. The Excursionists arrived "in the wildest spirit of expectancy, for the chief feature, the grand goal of the expedition, was near at hand—we were approaching the Holy Land! Such a burrowing into the hold for trunks that had lain buried for weeks, yes for months; such a riotous system of packing and unpacking; such a making up of bundles, and setting apart of umbrellas, green spectacles and thick veils; such a critical inspection of saddles and bridles that had never yet touched horses; such a cleaning and loading of revolvers and examining of bowie-knives; such a half-soling of the seats of pantaloons with serviceable buckskin; then such a poring over ancient maps; such a reading up of Bibles and Palestine travels; such a marking out of routes; and morning, noon and night such a general raising of the very mischief, was never seen in the ship before!"

If one could transport Mark Twain forward in time to any of the cities he had visited on his way to Beirut—to Gibraltar, Marseille, Genoa, Naples, Athens or Istanbul, he would be able to tell us immediately where he was. Beirut, on the other hand, would be completely unrecognizable. What was once a sleepy coastal town, barely one-up from a fishing village and even then one of the least significant ones in the Holy Land, is now a fully blown commercial experience. Nearly two million humans endeavor tirelessly, swaggering from deal to deal; patience is a pre-war memory, the relentless sound of endless car horns is punctuated only by high revving earthmovers, short-tempered cement mixers and the bepp-bopp-bipp-bupp of PIN numbers on a spending spree. Beirut is not for the faint of heart, nor for the light of wallet, nor for one of Life's amblers or ramblers.

What distinguishes Beirut from other ports on the Levant are its wonderful surroundings, the dramatic setting in which the city nestles. From the bar on the 27th floor of the Four Seasons Hotel you can see Mark Twain's point: that Beirut must have been "a beautiful city" with an "upland that sloped gently down to the sea; and also at the mountains of Lebanon that environ it." Now only the undulations remain, each one covered in countless concrete blocks going nowhere in particular. All ways inland out of the city require a steep climb up the slopes of Mount Lebanon, the name not of a particular mountain but of the dramatic range that runs north to south down the country's spine—a range that was providing sanctuary for the fleeing Christians of Greater Syria in Mark Twain's time and now entertains skiers in the winter and viniculture in the summer.

The harbor where Mark Twain "bathed in the transparent blue water that rolled its billows about the ship" is now the Levant's major deep-water container port, and outside its striding breakwaters a dozen huge behemoths await their turn to unload their cargoes of cement and oil, consumer trinkets and designer stopgaps. The behemoths leave Beirut noticeably higher on their boot lines: Lebanon's exports are of mind and body, not bore holes and night shifts.

At first sight Beirut was not the most obvious staging port for the Holy Land tour. In 1867, fifty-three years before the League of Nations granted the French[*] a mandate to create what would later become Syria and Lebanon, Beirut was a minor harbor along the Levantine coast. Tripoli, just to the north, was the Ottoman rulers' favored port, and with Raymond de Saint-Gilles' vast crusader castle overlooking it and the incomparable Crac des Chevaliers nearby, one with far greater Christian significance. Just south of Beirut are Sidon and Tyre, with their Phoenician histories and biblical references. The most obvious Holy Land tour staging port would have been Acre, with its large natural harbor and recollections going back to the sixteenth century BC, and with much better proximity to the major New Testament sites which the Excursionists planned to visit.

So why did the New Pilgrims choose Beirut? The answer lies in Evangelical Protestantism. By the early 1860s the American Board of Commissioners for Foreign Missions (ABCFM) had established a Protestant mission in Greater Syria headed by Dr. Daniel Bliss. Bliss was a remarkable man, who not only developed the church just outside Beirut, but also a boarding school, a hospital and then a teaching hospital which went on to become the world-renowned American University of Beirut (AUB). (Bliss' great-great-great-great-great-great grandson, Peter Dorman, is President of the AUB and a living archive on all matters Bliss.) During his frequent fundraising trips to New York Dr. Bliss

---

[*] The French are the connecting link between man and the monkey. Whatever is trivial to another man is important to a Frenchman. It is this that makes the French the most artificially polite society. *Notes & Journals*

met Henry Ward Beecher, the Plymouth Church of the Pilgrims preacher behind the Holy Land tour and himself an active member of the ABCFM. As Beecher was organizing the Excursionists' itinerary at a time when he himself was planning to be the tour leader, it was only natural that he would want to meet his foreign mission partner, Dr. Bliss, here in Beirut.

The one hundred and twenty Excursionists had decided *en passage* that when they reached the Holy Land they would divide up into a dozen, more manageable, groups—groups reflecting their fitness and ambition. The toughest group would form a proper caravanserai and take an arduous three- or four-week route into the heart of the Holy Land; the averagely able would try to survive a night or two at camp at a time before rejoining the *Quaker City*, while the most sedate group would content themselves with day tours from the mother ship, and they would all meet up a month or so later in Joppa, now Jaffa, a suburb of Tel Aviv in Israel. Mark Twain, being one of the youngest on the tour, as well of course as being a working journalist sent specifically to cover the tour, elected to join the tough guys' tour. The main problem, as they foresaw it, would be logistical. As Mark Twain wrote: "We knew very well that Palestine was a country which did not do a large passenger business, and every man we came across who knew any thing about it gave us to under-stand that not half of our party would be able to get dragomen and animals. At Constantinople every body fell to telegraphing the American Consuls at Alexandria and Beirout to give notice that we wanted dragomen and trans-portation. We were desperate—would take horses, jackasses, cameleopards, kangaroos—any thing."

On arrival in Beirut Mark Twain made a special effort to visit the US consul in the Levant, Jeremiah Augustus Johnson. He wrote that: "We have never been much trouble to a Consul before, but we have been a fearful nuisance to our Consul at Beirout. I mention this because I cannot help admiring his patience, his industry, and his accommodating spirit. I mention it also, because I think some of our ship's company did not give him as full credit for his excel-lent services as he deserved."

In the spirit of following in Mark Twain's footsteps I think it would be amusing to contact the current US incumbent in Beirut, to invite her to enjoy a light lunch together and see what records, if any, remain about Jeremiah Augustus

Johnson or even his notes about his meeting with Mark Twain. But, as an early indicator of the troubled times in which we live, my early efforts are discouraged, and later efforts rebuffed. One starts by calling the American Embassy switchboard, explaining what one wants to do, being put through to the Public Diplomacy Department, explaining it all again, being referred to the Press Desk, explaining it all over again, being asked to apply in writing explaining it all again and to "allow at least five working days for State to reply". The request goes to Washington? "We don't vet here." You need to vet me? I'm British. "Sir, we need to vet the request, so yes."

After a week there is no reply from State, so trying not to think about the cell phone bill for the next half hour I call again. Yes, there has been some internal "traffic": "there is no record of correspondence to or from Mark Twain during that period." Fine—I know that already and had not asked if there had been, but what about my offer of lunch with the ambassador? "Due to security assessments... non-essential activities... in principle, not treating with third party nationals... no, sir, I know you are British... there's no need to take that attitude... what do you mean by guff?"

Luckily there is no such nonsense with the British Embassy, and I have a most enjoyable and informative lunch with Piers Cazalet, the Deputy Head of Mission. He has some sympathy for the American diplomats, who know that working in a fortress on a hill in a far-flung suburb is not the ideal way to pursue diplomacy; in fact they know it's totally counterproductive, as they would put it, "hearts and minds-wise".

"They are not even allowed out of their compound without a bodyguard, so there would have been three at lunch anyway," he tells me.

"After all the kerfuffle I was so curious about the American Embassy so I took a taxi out there. It's a kind of scaled down version of one of the crusader castles one finds hereabouts," I suggest.

"But don't forget they had the worst terrorist attack on an embassy ever here in Beirut," he replies. "In 1983 a Hezbollah suicide bomber killed sixty diplomats and marines. It was one of Hezbollah's first acts. So there is a fortress mentality."

"Exactly as Hezbollah intended. And what of Hezbollah now?"

"Stronger than ever," Piers replies, "they have fifteen seats in parliament and a vetoing balance in the cabinet—but actually their support is far greater than that."

"How so?"

"Constituency boundaries, in some Shia—so Hezbollah—seats there are maybe 100,000 voters, in some Christian ones only 10,000. It's a very fluid mix."

"High octane fluid."

"Just so. Also, don't forget Israel can never defeat Hezbollah like it has defeated the Arabs. It can only hope to hold onto its gains and limit its losses."

When the French Mandate ended and Lebanon was penciled-in as a country in the mid-1920s the population was largely Maronite—an eastern Christian sect which nominally, sometimes highly nominally, offers allegiance to Rome—and Druze—a sort of esoteric Shia spin-off who believe that the schizophrenic Caliph al-Hakim was God after all and that he never died but was taken straight to heaven. By the time of independence from France, in 1943, a significant Sunni presence had evolved and the founding constitution of that year reflected the religious and political divide: the president was to be a Maronite Christian, the prime minister a Sunni Muslim, and the speaker a Druze, or Shia Muslim.

The Maronites are an interesting religious and political sect, and worth a quick visit. Originally they were followers of St. Maron, a particularly extreme ascetic sixth-century Byzantine monk. When he died he must have cast a spell over his future followers, as no sooner had he succumbed than the first of many Lebanese civil wars broke out among them on how to deal with his remains.

The Maronites were later declared heretics by the Byzantine Church over their stance supporting the esoteric doctrine of Monothelitism, proclaiming that Jesus Christ had two natures (divine and human) yet only one—combined—will. Persecuted for this schism they fled to the range of Mount Lebanon where, left alone, they prospered. When the crusades arrived four hundred years later the Maronites deemed it politic to ally themselves with Rome, with whom they have been allied, somewhat loosely, ever since. When the French inherited greater Syria from the defeated Ottomans in 1920, they soon found themselves in league with their co-religionists, and at the Maronites' request formed the "State of Greater Lebanon" so that they, the Maronites, could have their own Christian country.

Still today the Maronite ties to France remain magnetic. Like Mark Twain, we arrived in Beirut by boat, in our case on *Vasco da Gama*. I am writing this where we are moored, in the delightfully oasis of the Automobile et Touring Club du Liban in Jounieh, some twelve miles north of the mayhem that is Beirut. We could be in a five star sports resort in Antibes. Everyone, except the Filipino chauffeurs and nannies, speaks French, and only French. They all have French names, many have French cars. This week the 2010 football World Cup is playing in South Africa, and French flags fly from radio aerials and rear windows. The tennis courts resound to claims of *quarante quinze*. The bar rejoices to shouts of *trois bières*. Even the swimming pool squeals to *Maman! Maman!*

On enquiring about a taxi to a nearby Shia area, Gillian was told not to go because of the "dirty Arabs—dangerous Muslim area." Of course they are just as much Arab as any local Muslim, yet armed partly with a much better education than the Muslim Arabs and partly with an adopted *hauteur*, they have invented themselves a faux-Phoenician historical identity and a faux-French cultural identity. As we shall see, their militia, a kind of faux-Foreign Legion doubling up as faux-Crusaders, played a particularly vicious role as Israel's proxy in the 1980s civil war. One forsakes to be judgmental about other people's beliefs, but with the best will in the world it is hard to see anything very much actually Christian—as originally intended by Jesus or Paul or anyone else—in the Maronite sect.

Since 1943 the population mix has blended, whereas the constitution has remained fixed, and one can feel the politico-religious tectonic plates looking for relief again, just as they did before the civil war broke out in 1975. The Christians now represent only about 25 per cent of the population, an accelerating reduction caused by the much-vaunted "brain drain" and lower population growth, and also a feeling among them that the Christian game in the Middle East is up, that this last pocket of resistance is a *fin de race*. They see that elsewhere in Asia Minor the Christian population has all but vanished in the last century as Islam has become less tolerant politically and religiously. There need no longer be a Turkish genocide, as against the Armenians, or a Turkish massacre, as against the Greeks, or a Syrian slaughter of the Christian Arabs, or an Israeli cleansing of Palestinian Christians to discourage the Maronites from staying; the Christian feet are doing the voting for the Muslim fundamentalists, who conveniently forget that Byzantine Christianity was prevalent in Asia Minor for many centuries before Islam arrived, that Islam shares so much with Christianity that for many centuries in remote areas the two congregations prayed alongside each other.

I ask Piers if it is more than a gross oversimplification to say that socially and economically one can grade Lebanon as having prosperous and educated Christians at the top table, followed by worthy Sunnis as a buffer to the Shia rabble making up the numbers. "A very gross oversimplification," he agrees, "but some sort of snapshot. But there are other complications."

"Such as?" I ask.

"Politics is religious. Religion* is political. There are eighteen official religions, twelve of them Christian. Most of them have political ties too, so there are no political parties as we know them but loose alliances based around religious sects, or around personalities or extended families. Proportional representation stirs it up. No one party has ever won more than 12.5 per cent of the vote, and no coalition can rely on more than a third of the MPs. Likewise the law. In theory the Napoleonic Code is supreme but in practice localized religious law is what is recognized."

"And militias?"

"For now back in their basements, but Hezbollah has never disarmed, in fact their logo is a Koran and a Kalashnikov. The Phalange are still well armed."

Well armed and trigger ready, I would not be surprised. Inspired by a visit to the Waffen SS in 1936, in the 1980s civil war the Maronite militia took on an anti-Islamic Crusader identity, complete with Holy Cross or Madonna motifs on their uniforms and armaments. They gave themselves crusader names too: the Wood of the Cross, the Knights of the Holy Virgin, the Phalanx (hence Phalange) of St. Maron. They distinguished themselves in the Sabra, Chatila, Tel el-Za'atar and Ein Helweh refugee camp massacres, where they were allowed—some say encouraged—to run rampant by Israel's General Sharon and where as many as two thousand Palestinian refugees were slaughtered. Leaving aside the vile irony of the Israelis teaming up with the fascists, and however much one may blanch at the Hezbollah flag adorned with the Koran and a Kalashnikov, today's Shia militia are merely following the Maronite lead: the Phalange flag has a cross and sword in flames motif and the wholesome motto: "It is the Duty of every Lebanese to kill at least one Palestinian."

After lunch, and impressed as always by the quality and *nous* of our diplomats, I research the religious mix to which Piers referred. It's likely that the official estimate of twelve Christian sects** is an under-estimate. Apart from the ruling Maronites, there are Greek Catholics and Greek Orthodox, and Syriac Catholics and Syriac Orthodox—Jacobite and non-Jacobite, Armenian Catholics, Armenian Orthodox and Armenian Apolistic. Then we find the Assyrian Church of the East, the Nestorians, the Ancient Church of the East, the Assyrian Catholics and Assyrian Pentecostals, the Chaldean Catholics and the Melkites. More familiarly there are Latin Catholics, and some Protestants,

---

* Man is kind enough when he is not excited by religion. *A Horse's Tale*

** What God lacks is convictions—stability of character. He ought to be a Presbyterian or a Catholic or something,—not try to be everything. *Mark Twain's Notebook*

called Evangelics here, Lutherans and Baptists. Amongst the Muslims there are the usual Sunni and Shia sects, plus the spin-offs: the Druze, the Alawites, the Sufis and the Alevis. No-one knows the Muslim Shia/Sunni mix in Lebanon as there is no mechanism to gauge it, but most estimates suggest 55 per cent Shia to 45 per cent Sunni, this shift complicated by "second hand" Palestinian Sunni refugees from Jordan and the considerably higher Shia birth rate.

We'll come across the Sunni and Shia split down the road apiece, so it's worth taking a paragraph to remind ourselves as to why they too are at each other's throats.

When Mohammed died his followers needed a successor, a caliph, to carry on the good work. The Shia hold that Mohammed pronounced his son-in-law and cousin Ali to be that man, and thereafter Ali's direct male descendents to follow in his footsteps. The Sunnis can find no evidence of this divine appointment and prefer to follow the lead of the first four caliphs and descend from there. Taking sides is not recommended, neither is an air of disbelief or *laissez-faire*. Shia are big in Iran and Yemen, smoldering in Turkey and, as we've seen, increasingly virulent in Lebanon, but persecuted by the Sunnis elsewhere, notably in Iraq, pre- and post- the Bush/Blair invasion, as well as by the Taliban in Afghanistan where persecution tends to mean Turkish-style elimination. An added twist is that the majority of Lebanon-based Palestinian refugees are Sunni, but their cause has been taken up, to great effect, by Iran-backed Shia group Hezbollah.

As an aside to matters religious, the South Africa World Cup continues during my stay in Beirut. The Lebanese are enthusiastic followers of the event, and flags of the competing countries hang from balconies and car aerials and rear windows. We are moored in the faux-French Maronite Christian area and the flags are mixed—mostly French, but then a lot of Brazilian and Argentinian ones, some American, and then from elsewhere in Europe a cross section of Italian, German and, heaven help us, English. But driving to the airport, through the Muslim areas, the flags are predominantly German. In an airport hotel lounge with a big flat TV I have the humiliation of watching Germany beat England 4-1; I am the only Brit and find myself surrounded by German-supporting Lebanese Sunni Muslims going wild with excitement every time Germany scores, in other words fairly frequently. After the fourth goal, when my neighbor finishes kissing the German crest on his German kit shirt, I ask him: "Why?" "Germany good." "Mmm, maybe, but why?" "Germany Israel boosh!" "Ah." "Yeah, Germany Jew-man boosh!"

In Mark Twain's time there were none of these complications as what few local tribesmen he came across, and these overwhelming Bedouin, were Sunni Muslim. In Jerusalem he found a Christian community, but in a state of multi-sect civil war between the Latin Catholics, Eastern Orthodox and the various Armenian and Syrian sects and sub-sects. In Jerusalem he found Jews too, living without obvious persecution; in fact tolerance of other patriarchal Abrahamic religions was a hallmark of the Ottoman Empire; tolerance tolerated for a price, another hallmark of the Ottoman Empire.

Mark Twain spent only a day and a half sightseeing in Beirut before leaving for Baalbek. While he and been busy communing with the American consul and admiring the "bright, new houses nestled among a wilderness of green shrubbery", the business end of his group had been organizing their caravanserai. And what a splendid and proper caravanserai it was! Led by a Maltese dragoman, Abraham, assisted by his deputy dragoman, Mohammed from Alexandria, it contained no fewer than twelve horses for the eight Americans and the dragomen, nineteen porters, bearers and waiters, all on foot, and twenty six pack-mules and camels* laden with all the paraphernalia of a deep desert camping expedition. Abraham was to stay as Ferguson-in-chief throughout the Holy Land tour but never really drew the Excursionists' admiration.

If Mark Twain was impressed by the size of the caravanserai he was less enthused by its shape. The horses in particular were "the hardest lot I ever did come across. One brute had an eye out; another had his tail sawed off close, like a rabbit, and was proud of it; another had a bony ridge running from his neck to his tail, and had a neck on him like a bowsprit; they all limped, and had sore backs, and likewise raw places and old scales scattered about their persons like brass nails in a hair trunk; their gaits were marvelous to contemplate, and replete with variety under way the procession looked like a fleet in a storm. It was fearful."

In compensation the *Daily Alta California* would not have quibbled about

---

* Camels are not beautiful. They have immense, flat, forked cushions of feet, that make a track in the dust like a pie with a slice cut out of it. They are not particular about their diet. They would eat a tombstone if they could bite it. A thistle grows about here which has needles on it that would pierce through leather, I think; if one touches you, you can find relief in nothing but profanity. The camels eat these. marktwainquotes.com

the expenses: five dollars in gold a day each, all in. Mark Twain packed "a blanket and a shawl to sleep in, pipes and tobacco, two or three woollen shirts, a portfolio, a guide-book, and a Bible. I also took along a towel and a cake of soap, to inspire respect in the Arabs, who would take me for a king in disguise."

They spent the first night en route to Baalbek at Temnin-al-Faouqa, then as now on a "breezy summit of a shapely mountain overlooking the sea, and the handsome valley where dwelt some of those enterprising Phoenicians of ancient times we read so much about." Temnin-al-Faouqa is now another sprawling eyesore; the breezy summit and shapely mountain remain but the handsome valley has gone the way of the Phoenicians—in fact there's so much smog one cannot even see the sea let alone the Phoenicians, faux or real.

The caravanserai was equipped for three weeks camping, and if the going was to be rough and thirsty across the bone dry scrub and desert in the day, the group could always look forward to the evening's Bed & Breakfast, when the twenty beasts of burden desaddled their cargo and the nineteen bearers set up camp. Mark Twain had been used to camping out in his mineral prospecting days in Nevada and California, and simple and rough camping it was too. When he first heard of camping caravanserai-style he was plainly suspicious: "They said we would lie as well as at a hotel. I had read something like that before, and did not shame my judgment by believing a word of it." But that first night at Temnin-al-Faouqa had him dumbfounded and, as he himself said, speechless: "Five stately circus tents were up—tents that were brilliant, within, with blue, and gold, and crimson, and all manner of splendid adornment! I was speechless. Then they brought eight little iron bedsteads, and set them up in the tents; they put a soft mattress and pillows and good blankets and two snow-white sheets on each bed. Next, they rigged a table about the center-pole, and on it placed pewter pitchers, basins, soap, and the whitest of towels—one set for each man. Then came the finishing touch—they spread carpets on the floor!"

Soon night fell and the tents became candlelit, with "candles set in bright, new, brazen candlesticks". When the dinner gong sounded they all repaired to the dining tent, "high enough for a family of giraffes to live in, and very handsome and clean and bright-colored within".

Dinner arrived, served on starched white tablecloths and laid next to starched white napkins. The nineteen porters had become waiters, and "those stately fellows in baggy trousers and turbaned fezzes brought in a dinner which consisted of roast mutton, roast chicken, roast goose, potatoes, bread, tea, pudding, apples, and delicious grapes; the viands were better cooked than any we had eaten for weeks, and the table made a finer appearance, with its large German silver candlesticks and other finery, than any table we had sat down to for a good while."

Breakfast was no less splendid. The porters had taken down the side flaps of the dining tent, leaving only the roof as shade and allowing the dawn breeze in from "the open panorama" to cool them. While the Excursionists had slept, the Arabs had been preparing a breakfast of "hot mutton chops, fried chicken, omelettes, fried potatoes and coffee—all excellent. As I called for a second cup of coffee, I glanced over my shoulder, and behold our white village was gone—the splendid tents had vanished like magic! It was wonderful how quickly those Arabs had 'folded their tents'; and it was wonderful, also, how quickly they had gathered the thousand odds and ends of the camp together and disappeared with them."

Five dollars—but not in gold—is still what it costs to travel from Beirut to Baalbek, but nowadays all it buys you is a seat of fear in the back of a minibus. No horses, no servants, no pack-mules, no circus tents, no fine white linen, no dragoman; you are in a one minibus caravanserai, and it's always in a hurry and it's always playing with the dice of oncoming death. I have survived two rides in a Lebanese minibus before and know that for the next two hours life is going to lie on a thin thread.

At Beirut bus station we head for the Baalbek line. Amidst the choked air and carefree decibels three minibuses are being hawked full. I have noticed how Lebanese minibuses wear their battle scars without shame—indeed with pride. I try to choose the least scratched and dented of the three waiting to leave. The drivers are all in their mid-thirties, prematurely graying, two are smoking—as they will be throughout —when not simultaneously talking in to their cellphones all the way to Baalbek. I choose the least battered minibus, a Korean-made SsangYong Istana in a mild shade of purple with scratched silver hubcaps and sporting four aerials idiot dancing on the roof shouting from the rooftops. So far it's also the only one not blaring out trebled-up Lebanese pop music. One of the smoking drivers is standing at the driver's door.

"Are you the driver?" I ask.

"Driver, yes," he replies. "You go Baalbek?"

"Yes, Baalbek. You drive slow or fast?"

He pauses, angling for the reply I have in mind. "Slow. Drive slow."

"Safe? Not maniac."

"Yes, safe, safe. Everyday safe. Slow."

By now four or five others have joined our conversation. One of them speaks French. He translates into Arabic my wish to be alive at lunchtime, and not to be frightened witless in the meantime. The driver laughs and claps, flicks his cigarette out into the yard and ushers us round to the passenger seats alongside him. I thank him but take the middle seats in the middle rows, surrounding Gillian and myself—for my ears only—with eight Arab airbags. I think I'm turning into Mark Twain and must pull myself together.

⁓

Back in 1867, after their first memorable breakfast, the caravanserai broke camp at Temnin-al-Faouqa and rejoined the Beirut to Aleppo track, an old feeder route into the Silk Road souk town of Aleppo. Mark Twain noted with some surprise that "all the Syrian world seemed to be under way also. The road was filled with mule trains and long processions of camels." Oh boy! If only he could see it now...

⁓

The writer has driven, and been driven, all over the world, but there is nowhere more frightening than Lebanon. One accepts that in India, to use a familiar example, driving is haphazard by nature, somewhat anarchic, and seemingly fatalistic, but consolation comes because the chaos and drama are all played out in slow motion. Accidents happen, but slowly: few cars are capable of even cantering and even if in theory one or two may be capable of a gallop the steeplechase roads soon put a stop to speedy ambition. Not so in Lebanon, where a combination of out-sized, over-powered cars—typically the most throbbingly penile SUVs that America makes (a Hummer is about right) or the most bellicose sports saloons that Germany makes (AMG tagged Mercs or M tagged BMWs pass muster, Audis are a bit feeble)—driven by vengeful people with pumped-up identities on smooth yet unmarked eight-lane highways combine to create a kind of mad Dantean circus of powerful egos in powerful cars clashing with clashing egos in clashing cars.

The only hope, and thank heavens for it, is the gridlocked traffic. In Beirut the gridlock is permanent by day, and if your luck holds for much of the night. On the open road, the road to Baalbek for example, traffic blocks come in fits and starts, either at road-works or an accident; one hopes for lots of the former and none of the latter on a "be careful what you wish for" basis. Passengering in the traffic jams is still stressful, as instead of just creeping gently along the drivers will accelerate flat out for ten yards then stomp on the brakes to stop in half a yard, all followed by the obligatory blast on the horn. One feels like a shake puppet in a Punch & Judy routine as one involuntarily follows the body language of the cars.

There is only one experience in Lebanon worse than being a passenger and that is being a pedestrian. There are no pavements, no traffic lights let alone pedestrian lights, no foot soldier quarter is given, no infantry slack is cut. Courtesy is concept that fails to translate, like there being no real German word for humor—or English word for *Schadenfreude*. If you are on foot you become a sub-species, an easy target for the pit-bull terrier four-wheel drives itching for a fight. Yet it is not cars but horns which provide the worst foot-borne experience of all: no taxi driver can pass a pedestrian, even one going nowhere or the other way, without blowing his horn to catch their attention. If you ignore it they just blow again; if you still ignore it they just lean on the horn until you wave them "no". Beirut is easily the most tiresome place in the world.

The SsangYong Istana minibus, fully laden, swerves erratically as it climbs up to Temnin-al-Faouqa and then over the brow of the summit above Beirut. Somehow we have avoided hitting anything, and nothing seems to have hit us. Over the summit the view changes completely: there lies the famed Bekaa Valley. From above it looks distant and dusty, yet lightly populated and farmed. The minibus plunges down the other side, hurtling along on the edge of control on a much better road financed by "The Government & Citizens of Saudi Arabia: Towards Our Islamic Reconstruction". Thanks for nothing, government and citizens of Saudi Arabia. As we level out the floor of the valley disappoints. Either side of the road is covered in old plastic: bottles in all shapes and sizes, bags in all colors and logos, crumbling polystyrene packaging and dirty yellowed sheeting. The farms are fallow, the petrol stations closed, the villages lifeless. The only signs of life are signs of learning, as for some reason this area of desolation has become home to any number of private universities signposted off the main road: the Lebanese Canadian University, the Arab University of Beirut, the Bekaa Valley Campus—the latter flying clean new Swedish and European Union flags. It is such an incongruous area to which to entice private students that one's thoughts immediately turn to what kind of front they all are: espionage, money-laundering, people trafficking, identity swapping, opium refining—we are just south of the poppy and marijuana growing areas—or perhaps Dr. No dens?

After five miles an ayatollah poster hangs from a lamppost, then another, then crossed yellow and green Koran and Kalashnikov flags, and then we are in Chtaura and the start of Hezbollah country.

Farming in most of the Bekaa has always been marginal and as first the Christians and then the Sunnis moved to an easier life on the coast and the towns, Shia farmers from the east moved in. After the 1980s civil war the area was under Syrian control and poorer than ever. Hezbollah, the Party of God, was already active in South Lebanon as a reaction to the Israeli-proxy Phalange militia, the SLA—the South Lebanon Army. With the cease-fire holding and their fellow Shias in the north in destitution Hezbollah and their sponsors, the Iranian Revolutionary Guard, approached the Syrians for permission to establish a formal local headquarters at Baalbek. The Syrians, seeing this as an opportunity to unburden themselves of responsibility for the Bekaa farmers and associate themselves with an organization sworn to "Destroy the Zionist Entity", readily agreed; now, of course, they regret having what has become a *de facto* Iranian province across an open and porous border. We have already come across one of Mark Twain's tenets, Providence, now it's time to cue the other: the Law of Unintended Consequences. We are going to come across it so often it deserves an acronym to save my typing fingers: TLUC, tee-luck.

From Chtaura the road and the countryside improve, in fact it is transformed. The Party of God is only too pleased to tell you, albeit still in French, that there is so much more to it than "Annihilating Israel from Palestine and the Face of the Earth". The Iranian money has build the best road in Lebanon from Zahle to Baalbek, has installed irrigation ditches and health clinics, organized farmers' markets, set up a transport co-operative, opened its own TV and radio station and built dozens of new mosques. Quite the little Sweden, Kalashnikovs notwithstanding.

By this stage of his Holy Land tour Mark Twain had seen enough of the local politics to find them indigestible. "If ever an oppressed race existed," he wrote at camp that night, "it is this one we see fettered around us under the inhuman tyranny of the Ottoman Empire. I wish Europe would let Russia annihilate Turkey a little—not much, but enough to make it difficult to find the place again without a divining-rod or a diving-bell." I presume one of the dragomen had just explained the wonderful world of Ottoman taxation. The ruler of a province would estimate the amount of taxes he thought his region should bring. He would then auction off parcels of land, cash up front, to individual tax collectors. These parcels would still be too big for the top rung of collectors, so they in turn would auction off the collecting rights to a lower level, and so on, sometimes down to village level. In this sort of franchised reverse pyramid collecting system the peasant farmer was routinely routed. When it came to the tax collection "the peasant [has] to bring his little trifle of grain to the village, at his own cost. It must be weighed, the various taxes set apart, and the remainder returned to the producer. But the collector delays this duty day after day, while the producer's family are perishing for bread; at last the poor wretch, who can not but understand the game, says, 'Take a quarter—take half—take two-thirds if you will, and let me go!' It is a most outrageous state of things."

But back to now – and these good new roads mean even more daunting passengering and I'm pleased to jump out of the minibus at Karaq, thirty miles before Baalbek. It's here we are going to change from public to private transport; waiting for us should be Francis, nephew of—and recommended by—the manager of the Palmyra Hotel in Baalbek, of whom and of which more later. He is to be our guide around Baalbek and then he will drive us to Damascus. Francis speaks better French* than English and Gillian speaks better French than me (by a factor of *une mille* it has to be said) and so it is she who three days ago spent long enough haggling with him on the phone to feel we have been swindled more or less equally. At the end of the phone call we had a little Lebanese moment. Francis said "Je suis catholique, est-ce un problème?"; of course Gillian said "Pas du tout."

* In Paris they just simply opened their eyes and stared when we spoke to them in French! We never did succeed in making those idiots understand their own language. *The Innocents Abroad*

Armed with our new Ferguson, Francis, we re-join the Excursionists on their first visit to a Holy Land site: Noah's Tomb*—the "Noah of Deluge notoriety" as Mark Twain puts it, the tomb of "the honored old navigator". Of course it is no such thing and never has been.

Unfortunately today the word "myth" has come to mean something that is untrue. The "Mythbusters", claiming to unearth misconceptions, is a popular TV series; the phrase "urban myth" has come to mean a story that is widely held to be true but is actually untrue; myths are ripe for "debunking". A myth, as it was understood from the beginnings of knowledge until the Age of Reason, meant a story that helped explain the inexplicable. When we hear that the sea parted to help a fleeing race, the myth behind it was not concerned with what actually happened, let alone when or how, but what an event meant. A myth by its very nature could not be, did not claim to be, "true", as a fact is true; a myth only started where fact/truths could not be explained. In fact, as Jung discovered in his search for the soul, myths have always used deliberately ficti-tious motifs and like all good fiction have asked those "what-if?" questions that take us beyond what we like to think of as "ourselves" and gives us a glimpse of the Self in all.

The flood myth is one of civilization's original myths, and always has as its motif divine retribution for mankind's waywardness. The earliest dating is in the Sumerian book of Genesis in the eighteenth century BC. It became a central myth of the Babylonians. The polytheistic Egyptians, Hindus and Greeks all evolved versions of the deluge myth as did the Levantine tribes of Asia Minor. From those shores, somewhere around 1000 BC, it found its way into the Old Testament** Genesis, but modernized to have occurred in only around 4000 BC. Islam too has adopted the myth, with the Genesis dating, and there is even an Irish flood myth featuring Noah's granddaughter as an early Irish settler.

Like all myths it has a basis in reality, something that happened once and could happen again. In this case it was the great flood caused by the combining

---

* Nobody but a farmer could have designed such a thing, for such a purpose. *Mark Twain's Notebook*

** The two Testaments are interesting, each in its own way. The Old one gives us a picture of these people's Deity as he was before he got religion, the other one gives us a picture of him as he appeared afterward. *Letters from the Earth*

of the Black Sea and the Mediterranean, a truly terrifying, catastrophic event in which a great wall of water swept over cultivated plains destroying everything and everyone in its path. And like all great myths it explained the inexplicable in concepts easy to understand. Interestingly enough, literal readers of the Bible are still searching Mount Ararat for remnants of the ark, and a long search they will have too; such is the ironic power of myth; such is the ironic mind so much more evolved than the literal mind.

It's quite likely that most, if not all, of the New Pilgrims in Mark Twain's group favored the literal version and believed that the "honored old navigator" really was buried there, but Mark Twain could barely keep the smile off his face. He noted that "the proof that this is the genuine spot where Noah was buried can only be doubted by uncommonly incredulous people. The evidence is pretty straight. Shem, the son of Noah, was present at the burial, and showed the place to his descendants, who transmitted the knowledge to their descendants, and the lineal descendants of these introduced themselves to us to-day. It was pleasant to make the acquaintance of members of so respectable a family. It was a thing to be proud of. It was the next thing to being acquainted with Noah himself. Noah's memorable voyage will always possess a living interest for me, henceforward."

〜

Nowadays old Noah's Tomb has become a Hezbollah madrassah, empty of students when we visit but with all doors and windows open in the heat of mid-afternoon. I learn later that the conversion from tomb to madrassah is a new enterprise, only completed last winter. The long low building in which the tomb was said to have rested has been converted into a classroom with three dozen low lying desks at which the children kneel and learn the Koran by rote—not unlike the way the Jewish Orthodox children have to learn the Torah. All wisdom is contained within the Koran or the first five chapters of the Old Testament, depending on where you are, and no other education is needed. Behind the desks, along the back wall, giant posters with gilded Koranic quotes rest on trestle tables, themselves holding racks of Koranic tracts; from the ceilings new green-shaded bar-room-style lights on long leads hang down over the tiny desks; the barefoot floor is spotless and disinfected.

Alongside the madrassah a small mosque has been added, again in the last few months, its walls decorated not with Koranic posters but pin-ups of various ayatollahs. Over the windows the Hezbollah flags flutter in the breeze, the yellow and green motifs of Korans and Kalashnikovs shading the room. A heavier Hezbollah *kilim* or rug hangs loosely from the connecting lentil.

Outside is deserted too. The new Muslim cemetery has been replanted with oleander and fig trees, its paths weeded, its wrought iron railings repainted black. In the grounds lie its first three martyrs. Each grave has a photograph in a glass case above the tombstone. The Hezbollah flag flies over the glass case. Francis leads us over and translates. Engraved signs at the foot of the grave in Arabic tell each martyr's story: all three young men were born in Karaq but died elsewhere. One presumes recent interment. Two of them are in army fatigues, the third in a shiny suit; the first two were killed in action in 2006. The third, Abdul Al-Fahadi, 1990-2007, was a suicide bomber. One looks closely at his photograph again, but the eyes were dead even when he was alive. Gillian and I look back at the madrassah in despair; Francis looks back in dread.

It is hard to see why Baalbek was included in the Mark Twain's Holy Land tour; it is surely magnificent, quite magnificent, but its magnificence stems from it being the Roman Empire's most sacred site of pagan worship, and the largest temple complex in the whole Roman Empire. The Temples to Jupiter and Bacchus are still standing, just about, and the one to Venus still has its substructure in place. The Temple to Mercury, built on an adjacent hill, has all but disappeared. Later local gods were incorporated into the worship there.

Mark Twain noted that Baalbek was "a noble ruin whose history is a sealed book. It has stood there for thousands of years, the wonder and admiration of travelers; but who built it, or when it was built, are questions that may never be answered." In 1867 this was so, but thirty years later Kaiser Wilhelm II visited the site and, like everyone before and since, was overwhelmed by the scale of the endeavor. He bought permission from the Ottoman Sultanate to excavate the site, a task since taken over by teams from France as a part of the spoils of the First World War.

Although the site has been used for worship since 9000 BC it was not until Alexander the Great passed through in the mid-330s BC that work started on building along the classical Greco-Roman lines we see today. The period of greatest change came two hundred years later when Pompey ordered the building of the temples there today. Julius Caesar visited Baalbek in 50 BC and established it as a formal Roman colony. The temples took 120 years to build, and were only finished when Nero was emperor, in around 60 AD.

What was thought in Mark Twain's time to be the Temple of the Sun is now known as the Grand Court, and what he called the Temple of Jupiter is now known to be the Temple of Bacchus. Nevertheless the scale remains the same: 'These temples are built upon massive substructions that might support a world, almost; the materials used are blocks of stone as large as an omnibus and these substructions are traversed by tunnels of masonry through which a train of cars might pass. With such foundations as these, it is little wonder that Baalbec has lasted so long. The Temple of the Sun (actually Jupiter) is nearly three hundred feet long and one hundred and sixty feet wide. It had fifty-four columns around it, but only six are standing now—and six more shapely columns do not exist. The columns and the entablature together are ninety feet high—a prodigious altitude for shafts of stone to reach, truly—and yet one only thinks of their beauty and symmetry when looking at them; the pillars look slender and delicate, the entablature, with its elaborate sculpture, looks like rich stucco-work.'

We know these to be the tallest columns ever made. Mark Twain noticed "the great fragments of pillars among which you are standing, and find that they are eight feet through; and with them lie beautiful capitals apparently as large as a small cottage; and also single slabs of stone, superbly sculptured, that are four or five feet thick. You wonder where these monstrous things came from, and it takes some little time to satisfy yourself that the airy and graceful fabric that towers above your head is made up of their mates. It seems too preposterous."

The temples were ordered to cease pagan worship by the Christian emperor Constantine the Great in 324 AD, but the worshipers of Jupiter, Bacchus, Venus and Mercury refused to obey and it wasn't until two hundred years later when Justinian ordered some columns to be moved to Constantinople to help build the Hagia Sofia that pagan worship died. Since then the site has been abused into different forms from Byzantine basilica to Muslim citadel, suffered half a dozen earthquakes—and had its foundations shaken by Israeli bombs in 2006. Today it hosts a yearly mid-summer jazz festival, and in the long autumn of its days still enjoys the look of awe and wonder on the faces of all those who visit it.

The comfort of the snug berth on *Vasco da Gama* is now a hard day's bus ride behind me, and mindful that Mark Twain was living it up in his caravanserai camp just across the road, I think a night at the Palmyra Hotel in Baalbek might be just the ticket. No ordinary hotel, the Palmyra, more a living testament to the glory days of travel before anything as common as tourism, when to travel* hopefully was better than to arrive. From the bright sunlight of the world outside one enters through worn out spring doors into virtual darkness. The eyes take a moment to recalibrate and then you notice how cool it is, then how quiet—clearly no air conditioning. From a passage off to the right a pale stooping figures appears, shuffles up slowly and bids you "welcome". This you learn later is Simon (as in See-mon), as much part of the hotel as the pictures of famous guests down the ages. With an impish smile he gestures you to sit and wanders off to find the drink you ordered. You wonder if there is any ice, then become still enough for it not to matter. Ten minutes later Simon shuffles back in, balancing a tray on an upturned hand like he has done a thousand times before. On the tray is an open bottle of Coke, a glass with a slice of lemon and a folded linen napkin. In his other hand is a bucket of ice.

The rooms are old and shabby, but clean and comfortable. It's the kind of place that Mark Twain would loathe, resting on its laurels, unthinkingly Old World, not too bothered about the New. I feel rather at home here. I lie on the bed, the springs yield and fail to bounce back. The hot shower is a warm trickle; the loo needs several good pushes to flush but then gargles a reluctant gurgle before succumbing to gravity. The reading lamp is an old 40 watter, and there's no TV. Out of curiosity I run my finger across the top of the doorframe, seeing about the dust. There isn't any, which I find curiously disappointing.

The next morning Simon shows me the gallery of famous guests. His eyes smile at the memories. Pride of place goes to Kaiser Wilhelm II, who had the hotel rebuilt in the late nineteenth century; there's also a large poster of him in the hall. Simon wasn't born then, but it must have been close. In the First World War this was the German HQ, but only Kaiser Bill is represented.

Then we see a young Charles de Gaulle, trademark cap at a jaunty angle. "Was he well behaved?" I ask.

"Always in a hurry," Simon replies, "not so friendly, not like him."

He was pointing at Mustafa Kamal, better known as Ataturk. "I was very

---

*   Travel is fatal to prejudice, bigotry, and narrow-mindedness, and many of our people need it sorely on these accounts. Broad, wholesome, charitable views of men and things cannot be acquired by vegetating in one little corner of the earth all one's lifetime. *Innocents Abroad*

young, but I served him. He asked about working here. A gentleman."

There are several photographs of Jean Cocteau, as well as letters and sketches.

"It seems like he came here many times?" I ask

"Mais oui. Many times, for long times too. Everybody loved him. He was very jolly."

"And her?" I point to Agatha Christie.

"Ah yes, she stayed for a month, I think about one month."

"Writing?"

"I can't say, but yes, I suppose. We had many British here in the Second World War, the officers stayed here as their base. But no photographs."

"He looks familiar," I say.

Simon laughs, "Yes, James Bond." We are looking at Ian Fleming.

But after Fleming the gallery only serves to chart the hotel's decline. There are Miles Davis and Charlie Parker, although Simon "did not understand what they said" and after that the B-lists and C-lists and on downward to... Demis Roussos. Then there is a power cut and the gallery and the whole hotel are dark once more.

Later at the bar I ask Simon: "How are things now, for you, for the hotel?"

"With the Muslims?"

"Yes"

"I am old. It is better. There is money now. There is peace. They have respect. I am Catholic, but some of the Christians we have here... these Muslims are better Christians than the Christians."

"And the hotel?"

"It is too old. Maybe we die together."

Before leaving Baalbek Mark Twain wanted to see the quarry from which the enormous stones came; I was equally intrigued. He wrote that he "cannot conceive how those immense blocks of stone were ever hauled from the quarries, or how they were ever raised to the dizzy heights they occupy in the temples. And yet these sculptured blocks are trifles in size compared with the rough-hewn blocks that form the wide veranda or platform which surrounds the Great Temple. One stretch of that platform, two hundred feet long, is composed of blocks of stone as large, and some of them larger, than a street-car." Quite so, but even more so: "I thought those were large rocks, but they sank into insignificance compared with those which formed another section of the platform. These were three in number, and I thought that each of them was about as long as three street cars placed end to end, though of course they are a third wider and a third higher than a street car. Perhaps two railway freight cars of the largest pattern, placed end to end, might better represent their size."

One can walk down to the quarry and now see the self-styled "World's Largest Stone"—and there's no reason to doubt that it is. The site has been tidied up and made into a petty tourist attraction. Mark Twain observed: "In a great pit lay the mate of the largest stone in the ruins. It lay there just as the giants of that old forgotten time had left it when they were called hence—just as they had left it, to remain for thousands of years, an eloquent rebuke unto such as are prone to think slightingly of the men who lived before them. This enormous block lies there, squared and ready for the builders' hands—a solid mass fourteen feet by seventeen, and but a few inches less than seventy feet long!"

Being an enthusiast of technical explanations Mark Twain would have loved to know how they did it, how they not only pulled these 1,200-ton monster blocks up the hill to the temples site, but just as miraculously how they then maneuvered them so exactly into place. Unfortunately I cannot help him as the museum built under the temples since his visit is so poorly lit and inadequately diagrammed as to be useless. But if one man can push his own weight uphill, and that man was an undernourished slave weighing one hundred pounds, there must have been over two and a half million slaves to move that 1,200 ton rock—er, no that can't be right. Must have had pulleys and ropes and all sorts too. I can sense him badgering me, but one hundred and fifty years later.

The first serious fall-out among the Excursionists occurred as the caravan-serai left Baalbek. It was a Friday morning. Damascus was some sixty hot and ragged miles away. The dragomen Abraham and Mohammed told them it would take three days. The New Pilgrims counted on their fingers: Friday, Saturday, Sunday—and declared that would be impossible as it would mean travelling on the Sabbath; they would all have to complete the journey in two days to retain their saintliness.

Mark Twain led the protests: "We were all perfectly willing to keep the Sabbath day, but there are times when to keep the letter of a sacred law whose spirit is righteous, becomes a sin, and this was a case in point. We pleaded for the tired, ill-treated horses, and tried to show that their faithful service deserved kindness in return, and their hard lot compassion. But when did ever self-righteousness know the sentiment of pity? What were a few long hours added to the hardships of some over-taxed brutes when weighed against the peril of those human souls?"

Mark Twain's own religiosity had long since turned a corner. Ten years previously, in his Mississippi steamboat days, he had read Thomas Paine's *Age of Reason*. In the days before acceptance of Darwin's General Theory settled the creation question and Israeli and other archaeologists confirmed the Israelites-in-exile-in-Egypt to be the second part of the classical hero myth, skeptics like Mark Twain had to turn to free thinkers like Paine for confirmation of the wisdom of their uncertainties. We have already seen how the free thinker Paine had liberated Mark Twain from the fear and guilt built into his childhood. In an inspiring rebuttal of the certainties of the hell and damnation Presbyterian sermons of Mark Twain's childhood Paine wrote that: "Putting aside everything that might excite laughter by its absurdity, or detestation by its profaneness, and confining ourselves merely to an examination of the parts, it is impossible to conceive a story more derogatory to the Almighty, more inconsistent with his wisdom, more contradictory to his power, that the [Old Testament] story is."

But back on the road to Damascus Mark Twain held his peace; he could hardly do otherwise. Mile after mile they trudged through the scrub under the scorching sun to complete their journey in two days. One can imagine Twain composing to himself: "It was not the most promising party to travel with and hope to gain a higher veneration for religion through the example of its devotees.* We said the Saviour who pitied dumb beasts and taught that the ox must be rescued from the mire even on the Sabbath day, would not have counseled a forced march like this. Nothing could move the pilgrims. They must press on. Men might die, horses might die, but they must enter upon holy soil next week, with no Sabbath-breaking stain upon them. Thus they were willing to commit a sin against the spirit of religious law, in order that they might preserve the letter of it."

As Twain was to explain in later life the New Pilgrims' observance of the Sabbath was anyway dependent on which of the three versions of the commandment was mentioned in the Old Testament. In Exodus the fourth commandment instructs all believers and their slaves to refrain from any

---

* I cannot see how a man of any large degree of humorous perception can ever be religious— except he purposely shut the eyes of his mind and keep the, shut by force. *Notes & Journals*

work on the day. (A chapter later God instructs Moses about how to buy and sell slaves—having bored their ears through with an awl—before offering guidance on how to sell one's daughters.) In the Deuteronomy myth the Sabbath becomes not a day of rest after six days of creation but as an anniversary of God leading the chosen ones out of Egypt.

Mark Twain was yet to know the interpretation of the Sabbath in Judges or the matter might have been settled. Here the observance of the Sabbath touches on humanity, not to say productivity, for masters and slaves alike: "Six days thou shalt do thy work, and on the seventh day thou shalt rest: that thine ox and thine ass may rest, and the son of thy handmaid, and the stranger, may be refreshed." In the meantime he could only reflect, along with Thomas Paine: "These Books are spurious, Moses is not the author of them; and still further they were not written in the time of Moses, that they were a much later attempted history of the life of Moses, and of the times in which he is said to have lived, written by some very ignorant pretenders long after his death." It might sound harsh on ignorance but for the modernist technocrat Mark Twain: "back then everyone was ignorant, ignorance was their dollars and cents, why nobody knew anything about anything."

The next day, the Saturday, provided no rest as the New Pilgrims continued their march; instead, "The next day was an outrage upon men and horses both. It was another thirteen-hour stretch. It was over the barrenest chalk-hills and through the baldest canons that even Syria can show. The heat quivered in the air every where. In the canyons we almost smothered in the baking atmosphere. On high ground, the reflection from the chalk-hills was blinding. It was cruel to urge the crippled horses, but it had to be done in order to make Damascus Saturday night. We saw ancient tombs and temples of fanciful architecture carved out of the solid rock high up in the face of precipices above our heads, but we had neither time nor strength to climb up there and examine them."

Mark Twain would have loved to have known that Biblical scholars now attribute the Sabbath concept to have originated in Babylon. The Babylonian and Old Testament creation* myths both have the gods/God resting after creation, although the Babylonian myth does not specify a specific time of rest. The Babylonians created the days of the week from astrology; they attributed special powers to the sun and moon and the five planets. So we have Sat(urn)day, Sunday, Mo(o)nday, etc., and in most Latin languages the days still refer directly to the Babylonian roots. The Babylonians then devised them

---

* Man was made at the end of the week's work when God was tired. *Mark Twain's Notebook*

into moon-cycle months, but found certain days to be consistently unlucky: the 7th, 14th, 19th, 21st and 28th. Over time the 19th was dropped and the seven-day bad luck cycle established. The Babylonian idea of a day of rest was not so much to replenish, let alone worship, but based on the knowledge that any work attempted was bound to be in vain—so they might as well rest and be thankful.

By the time they were nearing Damascus, late on the Saturday afternoon, with their sanctity intact, Twain was still fuming: "They lecture our shortcomings unsparingly, and every night they call us together and read to us chapters from the Testament that are full of gentleness, of charity, and of tender mercy; and then all the next day they stick to their saddles clear up to the summits of these rugged mountains, and clear down again. Apply the Testament's gentleness, and charity, and tender mercy to a toiling, worn and weary horse?— Nonsense—these are for God's human creatures, not His dumb ones. What the pilgrims choose to do, respect for their almost sacred character demands that I should allow to pass."

At least the caravanserai did not have to deal with any borders or visas. Today the overland traveler in the Holy Land is kept guessing as to which border post is open and which not, which old exit stamp in your passport will cause trouble and which not, and which type of passport needs a visa before arrival and which not. Syria has the most awkward visa system of all as the government cannot quite make up its mind if it wants outsiders there or not—at total variance with the Syrian people, I must immediately add, who could not be more welcoming. We tried to buy visas at the Syrian Embassy in London before leaving, but were told it would take a minimum of six working days— no exceptions. In addition to the wait one needs to complete an enormous form with questions about one's parents, provide two color photographs, a letter from one's employer and a referee in Syria. As I had to fly to Scotland for a family affair before leaving for Syria, it was impossible.

I had heard that one can just buy a visa on arrival, although the *Lonely Planet* Thorn Tree forum was ambivalent. US citizens could only enter with a Washington DC-issued visa, whereas French and Scandinavian EU passport holders could breeze straight through. The Brits seem to be caught in the middle; at the whim of the officer on the day. But over the years I've learnt a trick or two about borders, and felt pretty sure we could bluff it on the day. I have found it pays to look quite smart when travelling—I always put on a white shirt, and if not in the tropics wear a tie too. Gillian digs out her diplomatic frock. There's always a special channel for VIPs, normally a Diplomatic Channel, or Business Channel, or sometimes it is actually called a VIP Channel. Head up, shoulders back, done this a thousand times before, a very good morning to you too, sir, it a pleasure to be back in your beautiful country, and so on—and in you go. They are normally quite pleased to have something to do, and somebody on their side with whom to do it. And so it was on the Syrian border post at Menaa, on the Beirut to Damascus trunk road. And, by the way, you can just buy a visa there and then as simply as buying a train ticket. When I'm back in London I'll pin a notice on the Syrian Embassy's visa section door.

But I must backtrack the story as we now have to backtrack the trail. When the Excursionists left Baalbek they chose the most direct route to Damascus, and if there had been a border they would have crossed it at Sirghaya, a village now just inside Syria, where in fact they camped on the Friday night. I ask Francis about the border; he thinks it has been closed since the last Israeli bombing, four years ago, but he isn't sure. The road is bad and his Mercedes is old, he jokes, nearly as old as the ruins; if it is closed he'll take us through the Menaa crossing and then to Damascus. The next day after breakfast we are loading up his old blue bashed-up Merc and heading off to one or both of the borders.

The road up to Sirghaya is paved but caked with crud. As soon as we leave the valley the Hezbollah area ceases, but then so does everything else. There is no farming, no sign of movement, nothing at all. Mark Twain noted that along this road they journeyed "thirteen hours through terrible hills, barren and unsightly, and wild rocky scenery, and deserts in the roasting sun", but it doesn't seem that bad to me sitting in the relative comfort of a bouncy old Merc with hot air blasting in through the open windows, the warble of echoed Arabic music playing on the tinny speaker, and marveling at the enormous dust cloud seen in the splintered door mirror. We are in a road movie, but when we reach Sirghaya we are in a spaghetti western. The hilltop border post on the edge of town is deserted, its door flapping in the breeze, and the town beyond is empty apart from a few children scampering in the shade and a few fully *abaya*-ed old women shouting after them. Francis' taxi causes a stir, and all eyes are now on the yellow-caked old Merc just driven in from the south.

"Syria!" says Francis, somewhat surprised.

"Syria," I agree, "where is everybody?"

"Gone".

"Gone. But gone where?"

"Israeli bomb," he replies, gesturing an explosion with his cheeks and hands. But I don't think so. There's no record of bombing near Sirghaya in accounts of the 2006 war. One thing is for sure, we are indeed in Syria, but without an entry stamp we can't get an exit stamp. We need to backtrack towards Baalbek, then head east to Menaa and do it properly. Leaning through the car windows half a dozen smiling, well cared for Syrian children hustle baksheesh, alternating between looks of hunger when we look a them and happiness when we don't. Francis is enjoying it too and gives one of the girls a thousand Lebanese lire note—less than a pound, a euro or a dollar and they all shriek in delight. I do the same, more shrieks, more delight. Francis pulls away slowly, smiles and shrieks all round, and we head north through the dust back into *terra recognita*.

Before reaching Damascus, by now early on the Saturday evening, a thoroughly out of sorts Twain and the caravanserai stopped at Mohammed's Lookout Perch. This in on the final hill as one approaches Damascus from the north. The legend is, and legend it is, that when the Prophet Mohammed... well, best let Mark Twain tell the tale: "when Mahomet was a simple camel-driver he reached this point and looked down upon Damascus for the first time, and then made a certain renowned remark. He said man could enter only one paradise; he preferred to go to the one above. So he sat down there and feasted his eyes upon the earthly paradise of Damascus, and then went away without entering its gates. They have erected a tower on the hill to mark the spot where he stood."

They have, but unfortunately they have now also sealed it off and made it into a no-go area with razor wire and guards. Francis thought it was because the Israelis had tried to vandalize it "many years ago"; it was needed for protection "from Islam's enemies, against the Muslims' most sacred site." Of course the prophet had never actually ventured this far north, and an even better view of Damascus is on the higher hill just behind it. We drive up to enjoy the vista and not to enjoy a particularly stagnant Turkish coffee.

What is so striking about the view—and it is a spectacular scene laid out across the valley below—is how little Damascus has grown from Mark Twain's time. Unlike his three most recently visited cities, Athens, Istanbul or Beirut, the size of Damascus has expanded rather than exploded. One can clearly see the Old City east of the center, that walled-in part of Damascus that was the entire city until the early twentieth century, and see how the New City has blossomed around it. Blossomed comes to mind because it is remarkably green, much greener from on high than from in its midst. Even the exhausted and thoroughly jaundiced Twain couldn't help agreeing that from above "Damascus is beautiful from the mountain. It is beautiful even to foreigners accustomed to luxuriant vegetation, and I can easily under-stand how unspeakably beautiful it must be to eyes that are only used to the God-forsaken barrenness and desolation of Syria. I should think a Syrian would go wild with ecstasy when such a picture bursts upon him for the first time. And when you think of the leagues of blighted, blasted, sandy, rocky, sun-burnt, ugly, dreary, infamous country you have ridden over to get here, you think it is the most beautiful, beautiful picture that ever human eyes rested upon in all the broad universe!"

Later, having spent two days there, he added a typical Twain "snapper": "If I were to go to Damascus again, I would camp on Mahomet's hill about a week, and then go away. There is no need to go inside the walls. The Prophet was wise without knowing it when he decided not to go down into the paradise of Damascus."

But that Saturday night, 14 September 1867, with the untapped Sabbath intact, they left Mohammed's Perch and entered the city through the Bab-as-Salaam, the Gate of Welcome. They were now not only in the walled city but in the Christian Quarter, each quarter having its own locked gates at night. It was exotic enough to cheer Mark Twain up a bit: "There are no street lamps there, and the law compels all who go abroad at night to carry lanterns, just as was the case in old days, when heroes and heroines of the *Arabian Nights* walked the streets of Damascus, or flew away toward Baghdad on enchanted carpets. At last we got to where lanterns could be seen flitting about here and there, and knew we were in the midst of the curious old city."

They had arrived—exhausted, depleted, out of sorts, saddle sore, the New Pilgrims feeling saintly, Mark Twain feeling pain and Paine, but in spite of it all firmly in Damascus.

3: Damascus

If you were to read the *Lonely Planet* guide to Syria and Lebanon, you will find the Damascus chapter opens with this Mark Twain quote:

> "... no recorded event has occurred in the world but Damascus was in existence to receive the news of it. Go back as far as you will into the vague past, there was always a Damascus... She has looked upon the dry bones of a thousand empires, and will see the tombs of a thousand more before she dies."

The full paragraph sees Twain in full flow and is worth repeating:

> Damascus dates back anterior to the days of Abraham, and is the oldest city in the world. It was founded by Uz, the grandson of Noah. "The early history of Damascus is shrouded in the mists of a hoary antiquity." Leave the matters written of in the first eleven chapters of the Old Testament out, and no recorded event has occurred in the world but Damascus was in existence to receive the news of it. Go back as far as you will into the vague past, there was always a Damascus. In the writings of every century for more than four thousand years, its name has been mentioned and its praises sung. To Damascus, years are only moments, decades are only flitting trifles of time. She measures time, not by days and months and years, but by the empires she has seen rise, and prosper and crumble to ruin. She is a type of immortality. She saw the foundations of Baalbec, and Thebes, and Ephesus laid; she saw these villages grow into mighty cities, and amaze the world with their grandeur—and she has lived to see them desolate, deserted, and given over to the owls and the bats. She saw the Israelitish empire exalted, and she saw it annihilated. She saw Greece rise, and flourish two thousand years, and die. In her old age she saw Rome built; she saw it overshadow the world with its power; she saw it perish. The few hundreds of years of Genoese and Venetian might and splendor were, to grave old Damascus, only a trifling scintillation hardly worth remembering. Damascus has seen all that has ever occurred on

earth, and still she lives. She has looked upon the dry bones of a thousand empires, and will see the tombs of a thousand more before she dies. Though another claims the name, old Damascus is by right the Eternal City.

There is no way of knowing exactly where the eight Excursionists stayed in Damascus but trying to track it down is a fine way to explore the nooks and crannies that make up the timeless Old City. We have a few clues. It must have been in the Christian Quarter and near one of the northern gates. Then there are Mark Twain's own clues: "In a little narrow street, crowded with our pack-mules and with a swarm of uncouth Arabs, we alighted, and through a kind of a hole in the wall entered the hotel"—that one not too helpful as every house starts with a "hole in the wall". Then he says: "We stood in a great flagged court, with flowers and citron trees about us, and a huge tank in the center that was receiving the waters of many pipes. We crossed the court and entered the rooms prepared to receive us"—that narrows it down to three hotels extant in the Christian Quarter, then we have: "In a large marble-paved recess between the two rooms was a tank of clear, cool water"—we are down to just two now, then we learn: "Our rooms were large, comfortably furnished, and even had their floors clothed with soft, cheerful-tinted carpets. There were great looking-glasses and marble-top tables." Found it! At least an identical one: the Hotel Dar Al-Yasmin. Luckily they have a double room for a couple of weeks, and I retrieve our bags and books from Seif & Shety's Internet Café in a "cramped and crooked lane" nearby and set up shop in the Dar Al-Yasmin, Old City, Damascus.

The exhausted Excursionists bathed and dined and then lay on the divans and smoked narghiles.

I was wondering how long it would take Mark Twain to get stuck into the narghiles, the long piped hubble-bubble, or hookah smoked throughout Greater Syria then and now; in fact now more than ever. I pick one up myself after dinner that night too.

The ceremony attached to smoking a narghile is as important as the smoking itself. First, they bring you a menu. The tobacco has three grades of strength and is then subdivided into flavors. The flavors are all fruit-based and there are as many flavors as there are fruits, but the most common are apple, grape, date and pear. Mango is fashionable just now. I chose grape. (I suspect Mark Twain would have chosen apple—just a hunch.) Next the contraption arrives and is set down beside the table and the bowl of tobacco, a chillum the size of a small coffee cup, is placed on top of the water bottle.

Next a heavy-duty perforated aluminum foil is stretched over the bowl. Now a stoker-wallah comes by swinging a low-slung brazier full of hot charcoal, swinging it to keep the charcoal well breezed and glowing hot. He then puts three bits of the charcoal on top of the foil and puffs up a mighty fug. Lastly he takes off his own mouthpiece, inserts a new one and hands you the pipe.

You draw on the pipe. Nothing happens. Late at night in full party mode I occasionally borrow a Marlboro Lite; one just has to look at one of those and it's up and running. The narghile is no Marlboro Lite and needs some serious suction to produce even a haze of smoke. There is enough in the bowl to last an hour, and as the tobacco wears down and your technique improves you are soon puffing away like a good old steam engine. The water is hubbling and bubbling, the tobacco is cool, the fruit is just on the tongue and the feeling of being an eastern potentate is there for the taking.

I am in the company of a practiced and expert smoker. "What I do know is all about smoking. I began to smoke immoderately when I was eight years old—that is, I began with one hundred cigars a month, and by the time I was twenty I had increased my allowance to two hundred a month. Now I'm thirty, I have increased it to three hundred a month."

Twain didn't believe in spending good money on good cigars: "With cigars I judge by the price only; if it costs above five cents, I know it to be either foreign or unsmokable." He wasn't too fussy about the make either: "I do not know what the brand of the cigar was. It was probably not choice, or the previous smoker would not have thrown it away so soon." He did, however, like to smoke modestly: "I have made it a rule never to smoke more than one cigar at a time. I never smoke when asleep and never refrain when awake."

But for now, this evening in Damascus, he wrote, "After the dreadful ride of the day, I know now what I have sometimes known before—that it is worth while to get tired out, because one so enjoys resting afterward."

The next morning, the famous Sabbath that had been the Excursionists' target, Mark Twain went on strike. In his notebook he wrote: "4 AM Damascus. Taken very sick." In his *Daily Alta California* article he wrote: "I lay prostrate with a violent attack of cholera, or cholera morbus, and therefore had a good chance and a good excuse to lie there on that wide divan and take an honest rest. I had nothing to do but listen to the pattering of the fountains and take medicine and throw it up again. It was dangerous recreation, but it was pleasanter than traveling in Syria. I enjoyed myself very well. Syrian travel has its interesting features, like travel in any other part of the world, and yet to break your leg or have the cholera adds a welcome variety to it."

∼

I suspect he had nothing of the sort, and certainly not cholera, or he'd hardly have been able to jump out of bed the next morning. Methinks that the prospect of a day of church-going with the New Pilgrims in the rabidly religious hothouse that was Damascus was the last thing on his mind. I reckon he said to himself: "Sam, my boy, you've ridden yourself and your beasts half to death to get here by the Sabbath, and if these religious maniacs want to scour the Christian quarter for their new mission and pray* there all Sunday morning and debate there all Sunday afternoon then they are on their own. It's the long divan, a smooth narghile and some running water for me today."

Mark Twain makes no mention of the New Pilgrims' churchgoing that Sunday—he was after all supposed to be *hors de combat*—but it's impossible not to believe they did not visit the Presbyterian church that had opened just two streets away the year before. It's almost as impossible to believe that there actually *was* a new Presbyterian church that had opened a year before considering the horrific Christian massacres that had occurred right there only five years before it opened. Mark Twain touched on the massacre when he wrote: "five thousand Christians were massacred in Damascus in 1860 by the Turks. They say those narrow streets ran blood for several days, and that men, women and children were butchered indiscriminately and left to rot by hundreds all through the Christian quarter; they say, further, that the stench was dreadful. All the Christians who could get away fled from the city, and the Mohammedans would not defile their hands by burying the 'infidel dogs'. The thirst for blood extended to the high lands of Hermon and Anti-Lebanon, and in a short time twenty-five thousand more Christians were massacred and their possessions laid waste. How they hate a Christian in Damascus!—and pretty much all over Turkeydom as well."

Whole books, whole shelves, have been written about the Christian massacres in Greater Syria. In a paragraph we can see the bare bones of how

* There is more than one way of praying and I like the butcher's because the petitioner is so apt to be in earnest. *Letter, 1879*

resentment spread from slow burn to fast flash: the Ottoman Empire was in advanced decline and treated its Syrian subjects as tax fodder and serfs, albeit fellow Muslim serfs; the European powers were snapping around the Greater Syrian edges, France favoring the trading Maronite Christians, Britain as France's enemy favoring the Maronites' enemy, the Druze; the Christians were better educated and more worldly than the Koran-restricted Muslims; the Christians therefore held Ottoman administration positions, causing further resentment; an attempt to divide what would become Lebanon into Christian and Druze areas backfired as both sides felt cheated; low level bloodshed started; at British and French prompting the Ottomans introduced religious reforms, further provoking the Muslims; when the Ottomans overlaid a new army surplus tax on the Syrians the Christians refused to pay on the grounds of non-conscription but still collected the Muslims' tax; the Syrian Muslim army began to mutiny against the Christian quislings; the Ottoman Muslim army looked on, detached; false rumors that France and Britain were about to invade Turkey inflamed the Muslim mob; some Turkish troops were withdrawn to defend the homeland, leaving Syrian Muslim soldiers somewhat in control; meanwhile in Beirut Maronite mavericks had shot dead three Druze at prayer; the Druze retaliating ferociously: the massacres had begun; news of the massacres and the Turkish soldiers' detachment spread to Damascus; a bloodstained Druze mob arrived in Damascus; the Turkish mayor arrested angry young Muslims for incitement; the mob became even more highly charged, forcibly released the arrested youths and went on the rampage. Thus the Damascus massacre had started. The only good news is that it did not spread to the neighboring Jewish quarter, largely because the Jews had paid their taxes and were seen to be self-contained—and as far as the Muslims were concerned had merely condemned a prophet and not murdered the Saviour.

Among the casualties in those four days and nights of horror was the American consul, Abdu Costi. We do not know if the Excursionists met his successor, Mikhayil Mishaqa, who later wrote extensively about the massacres and as consul reported to Jeremiah Augustus Johnson, whom Mark Twain at least had met in Beirut. But if the Excursionists had it might explain why they seemed to rush out of Damascus without seeing the timeless souk and the Omayyad Mosque, then as now two of the best reasons for visiting the Old City.

In a letter to Johnson, Mishaqa wrote that the Jews had also been spared because the Christians did the Jew-hating for the Muslims. Later he wrote: "It is hard to dissociate the divine from the material and the daily in a region largely considered as the birthplace of the three major monotheistic religions,[*] and where [people's exclusive claim to] 'God' himself is the problem." No problem today though. All is sweetness and light, religious tolerance compulsory between the faiths and even among each faith's sects. I am keen to visit this Presbyterian church started in 1866, and arrange to meet the vicar, the Reverend Butros Zaour. A big, hearty man with a generous smile and open gestures makes me comfortable, then makes himself comfortable too.

"First," he announces in perfect mid-West accented American English, "I have to set you right about your terminology. I am not the vicar, I am the pastor. And we are not Presbyterian—although we are, you know—but here we're Evangelical."

"Points taken," I reply, "but how so?"

"Awhile back, when President Bashar's father was in charge, the government insisted on religious tolerance and equality, Christians and Muslims— the Jews had gone by then. But they said to the Christians: hey, you guys got too many sects. Not just us Protestants, but all the Greek sects, the RCs and Maronites, the Armenians, local Syrians, everybody. Gotta get yourselves organized. We're gonna recognize four patriarchies here. That's it. Go sort. Greek Orthodox, Syrian Orthodox, Latin Catholic and Evangelicals."

"So," I suggest, trying to be helpful, "in Western terms the Evangelicals here are the non-Catholic, non-Orthodox refuseniks."

"Kinda style. We are under the Protestant umbrella. Right here we started off as Presbyterian, still are, but now in Damascus we have Anglicans, Alliance missionaries, Nazarenes, and Baptists, some Lutherans and Armenian Protestants. The latter are Congregational, a little awkward as they don't do hierarchies."

"Like the Plymouth Church of the Pilgrims, the ones along with Mark Twain, they were Congregationalists."

"Well, we have to say to the Congregationalists, you have to fit in. If the Maronites can fit in, anybody can fit in! It's OK, they come along after our Sunday service and have a quiet service themselves."

"I love the way everybody just rubs along together here," I say. "There'll be an electric wail of the muezzin one minute, then the ding-dong of church bells the next. Same in the streets and cafés, everyone is Damascene first and then their faith after that. But I want to ask you: after the terrible massacres of 1860, dreadful affair, all the churches sacked too, how come five years

---

[*]   The easy confidence with which I know another man's religion is folly, teaches me to suspect my own is also. *Conway's Sacred Anthology*

later a completely new mission arrived, a Presbyterian* mission that built this church—presumably on the very spot where other Christians had been slaughtered?"

"It's the way of the Lord," he replies. I must look blank. "You look blank. Our life in the church is not logical like maybe yours. The Lord calls and we follow. The Lord moves in mysterious ways with few straight lines. And don't forget the early missionaries came to convert the Jews, not the Muslims. Many thought that Islam was just a heretical branch of Christianity, another splinter group if you will—to add to all the others. After all, a Martian would find Christians and Muslims almost identical—why, we all used to pray together not so long ago. It was the Jews who needed their souls saving; the Jews more than the Muslims. The Muslim theology is not at its root a million miles away from ours, and the Jews, come to that, it's the societies that are so different."

"I don't mean to be rude, but wasn't it just one lot of nomadic and illiterate tribesmen needing explanations for the inexplicable versus another, just with different superstitions?"

"That's too simple, and too cynical. Old Testament maybe, up to a point. You can read it anyway you like, and that's the Judean way. For sure there was mass illiteracy and superstition, but our side, if I can put it like that, were largely settled and not nomadic, and by the time of the New Testament with a large body of work to draw from." the pastor replies.

"Fair enough. It's easy to be glib if you haven't been called. But the massacres here must have been ghastly. Let me read you this from Mark Twain, visiting here five years after the massacre, and only a year after your church opened. He wrote, 'In Damascus they so hate the very sight of a foreign Christian that they want no intercourse whatever with him. It is the most fanatical Mohammedan purgatory out of Arabia. Where you see one green turban of a Hadji elsewhere (the honored sign that my lord has made the pilgrimage to Mecca) I think you will see a dozen in Damascus... The Damascenes are the ugliest, wickedest looking villains we have seen. All the veiled women we had seen yet, nearly, left their eyes exposed, but numbers of these in Damascus completely hid the face under a close-drawn black veil that made the woman look like a mummy. If ever we caught an eye exposed it was quickly hidden from our contaminating Christian vision; the beggars actually passed us by without demanding bucksheesh; the merchants in the bazaars did not hold up their goods and cry out eagerly, "Hey, John!" or "Look this,

---

* It has taken a weary long time to persuade American Presbyterians to give up infant damnation and try to bear it the best they can. *Is Shakespeare Dead?*

Howajji!" On the contrary, they only scowled at us and said never a word.'"

"Sounds about right," the pastor replies. "Only hundred and fifty years ago, wasn't it? Everything here changed here with the 1970 coup. The al-Assads are Alawites, a minority Muslim sect that even the Muslims think are a bit wacky. In Pakistan they are still persecuted, mosque-bombed and suchlike. In Saudi, forget it—it's lamppost time. That's an unhappy place, Pakistan, by the way. The al-Assads knew that the only way to protect a minority is to declare majorities illegal—and unwholesome. It's worked. They've done wonderfully for all minorities. When the Muslim crazies got uppity in the 'seventies al-Assad Senior whacked them, good and hard. If he hadn't Syria would not be the great place it is today. Now I'll tell you, when your Mark Twain was here, in our early missionary* days, the Presbyterians were wary of the Alawites."

"The British Foreign Secretary of the time said that Druze and Alawites were Pagans, capital P," I say.

"Well, the Alawites thought that all women were created from the sins of the Devil and had no souls. That's all gone. Today just look at Syria's First Lady, an Alawite by marriage. She stands for everything that is gracious and right about modern Syria. Classy. She is the future." He pours our second coffee, Turkish, and out of the blue says: "I hate to say this about a fellow Christian, but George W. Bush was an idiot—a complete idiot."**

"Well, as Mark Twain said, politician and idiot are synonymous terms. You mean all the Axis of Evil guff?"

"He's an embarrassment. The Catholics here say ignoramus."

"And Obama?"

"The Syrians like him. But it's all about Israel. Is-rae-el as they say here. Bush junior just let them run riot. We'll see."

The pastor isn't the first person to have spoken well of the al-Assad dynasty's current dictator, Dr. Bashar al-Assad. What is slightly unnerving about the dynastic dictatorship's scion is that the poor boy just doesn't really look the part. Even when he's trying to look mean on the ubiquitous full size posters, with his aquamarine eyes and skimpy moustache President Bashar al-Assad looks like a friendly 45-year-old optician working for LensCrafters in a suburban shopping mall—which is exactly what he would have been if dynastic politics had not brought him up short. His father, Hafez al-Assad, a proper old-fashioned Ba'ath Party henchman, seized power in a *coup d'état*

---

* The first thing a missionary teaches a savage is indecency. *Mark Twain's Notebook*

** We are all erring creatures, and mainly idiots, but God made us so and it is dangerous to criticize. *Letter 1902*

in 1970 (the tenth coup since independence from France in 1946) and ran Syria as a Soviet bloc fiefdom, and a particularly unpleasant one at that. His eldest son, Basil, ran the secret police and was shaping up to be a proper Baby Doc while his youngest son Bashar was playing the young Michael Corleone in London, quietly studying ophthalmics and even marrying his Kay, a very bright London-born financier called Emma.

Then young Bashar's dreams of suburban anonymity were shattered in 1994 when the airbags in 31-year-old Basil's Mercedes 500SL failed to explode as he was rushing to the airport. Bashar was called home and sent to the military academy and fast-tracked to the top. When his father died in 2001, the 34-year-old Bashar was voted president by 97.62 per cent of the population—his father's old secret police are still looking for the 2.38 per cent of troublemakers. The word most commonly associated with Bashar is "disappointing", in the sense that westernized Syrians and others in the wider non-Arab world had hoped that with his European education, vocational calling and British wife there might be a Damascus Spring. They are still waiting. Also waiting are the youthful Syrians, stuck in a rut by the ruling classes, denying them the opportunity to improve themselves and their country.

Like all dictatorships, the Syrian one is at heart brutal and stupid, and Canute-like shuts down the newspapers and magazines that it can while being unable to stem the ever-flowing tide of information from cyberspace. When it tries to get cute with new technology, it finds itself locking up teenage girls who blog about Mahatma Gandhi. Another teenager was "questioned"—for six months—because he was moderating an online youth forum. Meanwhile serious journalists have fled and operate openly available—and highly critical— blogs and sites from beyond the borders. This regime can only lock up its techlit teenagers instead of fast-tracking them to greater know-how and success.

The writer has been in a few dictatorships: the Shah's Iran, Zia's Pakistan, Saddam's Iraq—and al-Assad Junior's regime is hardly Saddamesque, more lesser spotted inconvenience if politics or journalism are not your bent. In Syria one is reminded of another semi-dictatorship, that of King Mohammed VI of Morocco. another hard father to soft son act. As a legal front for the repression it hides behind a fifty-year-old State of Emergency which even al-Assad's civilian supporters are urging him to revoke; as an economic fact the government through its own efforts and its nationalized industries employs well over half of the workforce, giving itself an inbuilt quelling of dissent.

The area's biggest millstone, religious fundamentalism, has been neutralized by an intolerance of it of which the mullahs themselves would be proud. Arab societies, from Bedouin tribesmen to the pillars of academe, are traditional societies, and don't respond well to quick change. We might preach to the Arabs about the joys of democracy, and say it's done us well for over two thousand years. But it's a disingenuous argument: the Greek democracy was only for the propertied few, and universal suffrage in Western Europe is much less than a hundred years old—in France's case it didn't happen until after the Second World War. What the Greeks really gave us was dialectics, which in turn led to our whole system of reasoning by questioning and re-questioning—and from that came democracy and much more besides.

Far less impressive is al Assad's record on terrorism. Finding himself out of the Arab loop as Egypt then Jordan recognized Israel, the PLO fell apart into splinter groups and the Palestinians held elections, he has taken to keeping a toe in the Palestinian water by second-hand terrorism. Allowing his country to be used as a conduit for Iranian arms for Hezbollah to fire at Israel from southern Lebanon while keeping his own troops well away from Israeli wrath is cowardly and proves nothing.

Bashar can look around him and draw his own conclusions. To the north he sees Turkey, a democracy slipping backwards towards Islamism as fast breeding Anatolian peasants outvote secular Istanbul liberals. To the west he sees Lebanon, a democracy whose constitution is based entirely around confessional voting, whose own logic has brought it into the hands of Hezbollah and the longing for another vengeful war. To the south he sees Israel, another democracy, where multiparty proportional representation means political stagnation under the religious-right fundamentalists' veto. To the east he sees Jordan, not a democracy, but a reasonably liberal Arab monarchy of recent provenance where society progresses as it does in the Arabic way at an Arabic speed. One can see Bashar looking east, seeing what works, sprucing up his ten-year-old son Hafez and timing the changes conservatively. (Hafez was named after his grandfather; let's hope that's all they have in common.)

Meanwhile he can only hope that his subjects, high in youth and unemployment, low on opportunity and expectation and now with access to news of the Arab Spring changes elsewhere in the Middle East, don't push for that change in Syria faster than his regime is prepared to give it. Perhaps only then will we find out who really is in charge, the old guard who would have no compunction about maintaining their stranglehold on privilege and opportunity by spraying the rioters with live rounds or the more liberal Bashar circle who—it is popularly believed—would blanch at the prospect.

Having hoisted the New Pilgrims by their own petard and taken Sunday as a day off, Twain rejoined the Holy Land tour on the Monday. They found themselves a Ferguson and went to Via Recta, the "street which is called Straight", mentioned by Luke in Acts 9:10-19: "And there was a certain disciple at Damascus, named Ananias; and to him said the Lord in a vision, Ananias. And he said, Behold, I am here, Lord. And the Lord said unto him, Arise, and go into the street which is called Straight, and enquire in the house of Judas for one called Saul, of Tarsus: for, behold, he prayeth, And hath seen in a vision a man named Ananias coming in, and putting his hand on him, that he might receive his sight."

I must say there is a certain tingle to be walking down "the street which is called Straight", as though the Bible has connected the then and the now. There clearly was such a street here two thousand years ago, and for two thousand years before that. Biblical scholars accept Acts 1-12 as being broadly factual, St. Paul's obviously metaphorical blinding aside. Twain noted that, "The street called Straight is straighter than a corkscrew, but not as straight as a rainbow." Sure enough halfway along there is a chicane as the street kinks around a Roman arch.

They headed east along the street called Straight until turning left into Sharia Hanania just before the reconstructed Romanesque Bab Sharqi. "We called at the reputed house of Ananias. There is small question that a part of the original house is there still; it is an old room twelve or fifteen feet under ground, and its masonry is evidently ancient. If Ananias did not live there in St. Paul's time, somebody else did."

Nowadays, of all the Biblical sites of Damascus the St. Ananias Church is the most interesting. Its provenance is unprovable, but probable, and to some extent irrelevant. A plaque tells us that "Oriental tradition, according the Greek [Orthodox] menology, confirmed by the [Jesuit] Bollandists, tells us that Ananias was one the 72 disciples chosen by Jesus and that following the stoning to death of the deacon St. Stephan, Ananias returned to his home city, Damascus, where later he became the city's first bishop. The governor Licinius later had him stoned to death outside the Damascus city walls for being the head of the local Christians."

Archaeologists see the sequence of events thus: Ananias' house being used as a place of veneration by the early Christians, and the Christians then being ousted by the Romans who in 200 AD built a temple on the site; sometime during the Byzantine period and before the Muslim invasion, so sometime around 400 AD, the house was made into a church, the Church of the Holy Cross; and when the Muslims converted the Byzantine St. John's Basilica into the magnificent Omayyad Mosque, they rebuilt the damaged Church of the Holy Cross in compensation.

It wasn't at all uncommon for Christians and Muslims to pray together up to two hundred years ago. Eastern Orthodox Christians, and therefore the earliest Christians, prayed by prostrating themselves as Muslims do, albeit while crossing themselves as they did so; the kneeling while praying posture is a later invention of the Western Catholic Christian tradition. The site had well documented dual use as a church and mosque until 1820 when the Ottomans allowed the Franciscans to rebuild the now crumbling structure and restore it as a dedicated church. After it was desecrated in the 1860 massacre it was rebuilt again as it is now, and just in time for Mark Twain's visit in 1867.

I'm not sure to what other sites their Ferguson took them, or how he explained them, but today they have either vanished like "the place where the disciples let Paul down over the Damascus wall at dead of night—for he preached Christ so fearlessly in Damascus that the people sought to kill him, just as they would to-day" or are a kitsch sham such as "a tomb which purported to be that of St. George who killed the dragon" or a plain tall story such as "the honored old tradition that the immense garden which Damascus stands in was the Garden of Eden, and that the rivers Pharpar and Abana are the 'two rivers' that watered Adam's Paradise." Twain was having none of it: "It may be so, but it is not paradise now. It is so crooked and cramped and dirty that one cannot realize that he is in the splendid city he saw from the hill-top. The gardens are hidden by high mud-walls, and the paradise is become a very sink of pollution and uncomeliness... Damascus has plenty of clear, pure water in it, though, and this is enough, of itself, to make an Arab think it beautiful and blessed. Water is scarce in blistered Syria. We run railways by our large cities in America; in Syria they curve the roads so as to make them run by the meager little puddles they call 'fountains', and which are not found oftener on a journey than every four hours. With her forest of foliage and her abundance of water, Damascus must be a wonder of wonders to the Bedouin from the deserts. Damascus is simply an oasis—that is what it is."

Damascus is now is a wonderful combination of the old, the very old and the downright ancient. Today we are just adding another layer of activity on to all the other layers already there: writing as they wrote since writing was invented just across the valley, waking to the sounds of a holy man, washing in the ever running water, worshipping in a temple of whichever god is revered, walking the ever crooked streets—even the one called Straight, eating at a roadside stall, haggling in the souk, sleeping in the afternoon heat, promenading in the evening cool, bathing in the baths and sleeping high and open to catch the breeze.

While the rest of the world may be Dunkin' Donuts or Enjoyin' Pepsi, Damascus is still homogeneously Syrian; the increasingly standardized rest of the world has yet to seep through. The perception of its politics has kept the mass of visitors at bay and anyway the father and son dictatorships have not wanted the outside world with its fancy ideas encroaching too deeply into their domain. Tourism is still not actively encouraged as it is elsewhere, which means that those who do jump through the visa hoops and find a way around the transportation glitches will find a country where hosts and guests are still delighted to see each other. One day, when the rest of the world discovers Syria too, the inevitable overexposure to less sympathetic guests may well dent the famous Syrian hospitality, but for now it's a delightful pocket of resistance, a throwback to the days when traveling meant meeting the unexpected and living largely on your wits.

~~~~~

After only a day and a half in Damascus the caravanserai left at noon on Monday 16 September, heading up and over the Golan Heights and down to the New Testament Holy Land. They headed south back into the searing heat, heat so hot that "the sun-flames shot down like the shafts of fire that stream out before a blow-pipe barren scrub". On their and our right, to the west, lie the barely populated foothills of Mount Hermon, with its soaring ten thousand-foot peak known locally as El Sheikh, the Old Man, because the peak is always covered in snow.

Next we come across one of Christianity's most important sites, the spot at which St. Paul was converted on the road to Damascus, yet here on the ground it is one of the least proclaimed. Mark Twain only says, "Three or four hours out from Damascus we passed the spot where Saul was so abruptly converted" before adding longingly, "and from this place we looked back over the scorching desert, and had our last glimpse of beautiful Damascus, decked in its robes of shining green." One can be sure that if there had been anything there more than "a spot" he would have written it up.

Nevertheless it is in search of this spot that I now repair. Time to summon up a Ferguson and a very fine one he proves to be too. In fact he's so good we soon decide he should be promoted to the friendlier Fergy. As usual the British Embassy comes up trumps, this time in form of Samir, a Druze widower and a part-time driver for the British Council.

Part of the problem in finding St. Paul's spot, unless one knows Arabic, is that the transliteration from Arabic to English contains versions of the frequently-confused "K" and "Q" sounds and the "B" and "V" sound, as well as the optional prefix "Tal" and/or "El". Modern maps and Google Earth are as dumbfounded as the rest of us. Lonely Planet gives the spot as being in Darayya, which is actually several miles away. In case anyone is interested in finding it I shall give it the spelling in the only English sign for it: "Kawkab". Samir asks for "Tal Kawkab". (In ten years driving foreigners around Samir has never been asked to go there before.) It is signposted in the town of Al Kiswah, some nine miles south-west of Damascus, and is half a mile to the east of that. Al Kiswah is on the main road from Damascus to Quneitra, now in the United Nations-controlled Golan Heights, to where the Excursionists were heading then, and to where Samir is taking us now.

Following the sign from Al Kiswah one crests a small hill and sees ahead a forceful-looking church, about forty years old, clean to the point of pristine, not too hideous in the scheme of things, encircled by twelve asymmetrical arches—as Gillian presumes, one for each disciple. The stonework is gleaming white, the cross on the cupola is Syrian Orthodox, yet the writing on the gate is in Arabic and Greek. Samir translates: "Welcome to the Abbey of St. Paul the Messenger." The site is surrounded by newly painted bright green railings, and at the entrance one looks through them on to a fifty-yard drive leading up to steps below the entrance. It is deserted and seems to be locked. I press the buzzer on the off-chance. After a minute, as we are on the verge of heading off to Quneitra, a wizened old retainer with a lived-in face sandwiched between a cowboy check shirt and John Deere baseball cap shuffles out of the gate house a few feet away. He is so old I'm tempted to ask if he had witnessed the conversion himself. With a cheery and toothless smile and crumpled dimples he waves us in.

The gardens either side of the drive are immaculately kept and well watered; white and pink roses, origanum shrubs, fig, sycamore and olive trees. The drive itself is swept clean, no small feat in this sandswept landscape. There is not a soul in sight; it is becoming more and more mysterious. Skip up the steps and into the tiny chapel and one sees a small semi-circular room, unable to seat more than thirty-five, with no obvious Christian overtones on the walls. On plain wooden benches are Gideon's Bibles* in Greek, all virtually as new although, presumably, forty years old too. The floor is expensively inlaid with geometric—almost Islamic— motifs in marble, incongruous to the plainness of the rest of the space. Half a dozen plastic flowers sit in half a dozen plastic vases; touchingly there is real wobbly water in the vases. There is a visitors' book: the last entry, a Mr. & Mrs. Kellerman from Utrecht in Holland had a "beautiful experience"; I add my own "please keep it as a mission to find".

As we are leaving I tell Samir that I can't believe there aren't tour buses lined up outside, engines pouring out even hotter air for the a/c, rows of shops selling replica replicas and hosts of touts touting general tourist tat. This is after all, in terms of Christian significance, pretty much the Holy of Holies, the point from where you could draw a straight line to the Christianity of today as it has evolved from Christ's message to the Jews to Paul's message to the Gentiles. Samir replies that while we've been busy with notebook and camera he has spent the last half hour in the gatehouse taking tea with the old retainer and a young Orthodox novice. The novice had told Samir all about the conversion and the church. We head back to the gatehouse.

Samir translates: the road outside is the old road from Jerusalem to Damascus, the route on which Saul was travelling—and we saw a survey map later showing this to be the old trunk road; we know from the Bible that the conversion was near Damascus, and this is the first view of Damascus on the old road—again true as a look outside the gatehouse confirms; lastly, before laying foundations for the new church archaeologists found evidence of a first-century church and second-century liturgy; these are on display in the National Museum in Damascus. Two last questions: why is there Syrian

* When one reads Bibles, one is less surprised at what the Deity knows than at what He doesn't know. *Mark Twain's Notebook*

Orthodox symbolism on a Greek Orthodox Church?* "Now here co-opera-
tion"; and who pays for all this, and why? "The government asks the different
churches." And they can't say no? The three Syrians look at each other like
I'm mad. Well, well, witness to three miracles in one day. We thank them and
leave, and I for one am converted on the road to Damascus from outright
skepticism about the conversion to open-mindedness.

The New Pilgrims pressed on from there and three or four hours later
would have passed through what is now the massive inconvenience of no-man's-
land, the United Nations Disengagement Observer Force (UNDOF) area that
separates Syria from Israel. It is the intention of this book to retrace Mark
Twain's tour of the Holy Land as faithfully as possible, but the simplicity of
travel in the Ottoman Empire has given way to the political realities of actual
and disputed borders today—as we have already found at Sirghaya on the
Lebanese/Syrian border. Quneitra on the Syria/Israel UNDOF border is the
ultimate dead end. We can see two hundred yards away, past the large Israeli
flags, the road on which we will be traveling in a couple of weeks—knowing
it will take us all that time to reach there, looking down at where we are
looking up to now, almost in hailing distance.

Quneitra now is a horrible place. Destroyed by Israel in 1973 after the
Yom Kippur War** to provide Israel with a buffer zone, it is now merely
a selection of flattened buildings as though an even more than usually
gigantic giant had walked across it playing hop, skip and jump as he went.
In the cracks in the giant's pavement are burned out and rusted armored
cars and de-tracked tanks. To go there one needs special permission from
the Ministry of the Interior in Damascus—not the work of a moment. They
had never heard of Mark Twain, which is fair enough, and view all histo-
rians as open to Zionist bias, again fair enough. And having been there I
can see their underlying thought: why on earth would anyone want to visit
a shelled out monument to Syrian defeat, and one under the humiliation
of United Nations protection, unless to add to that humiliation by gloat-
reporting?

* I've been to the circus three or four times—lots of times. Church ain't a circumstance to a
circus. *Tom Sawyer: A Play*
** A wanton waste of projectiles. *The Art of War, 1881*

I thought it best not to mention to the Minister's assistant that Quneitra sounded so grim when Mark Twain camped there that the Israeli-flattened scene of devastation might well be an improvement. Mark Twain's view was that:

> [Quneitra] is a hive of huts one story high and as square as a dry-goods box; it is mud-plastered all over, flat roof and all, and generally whitewashed after a fashion. The same roof often extends over half the town, covering many of the streets, which are generally about a yard wide.

> When you [arrive] you first meet a melancholy dog, that looks up at you and silently begs that you won't run over him, but he does not offer to get out of the way; next you meet a young boy without any clothes on, and he holds out his hand and says "Bucksheesh!"—he don't really expect a cent, but then he learned to say that before he learned to say mother, and now he can not break himself of it; next you meet a woman with a black veil drawn closely over her face, and her bust exposed; finally, you come to several sore-eyed children and children in all stages of mutilation and decay; and sitting humbly in the dust, and all fringed with filthy rags, is a poor devil whose arms and legs are gnarled and twisted like grape-vines.

> These are all the people you are likely to see. The balance of the population are asleep within doors, or abroad tending goats in the plains and on the hill-sides. The village is built on some consumptive little water-course, and about it is a little fresh-looking vegetation. Beyond this charmed circle, for miles on every side, stretches a weary desert of sand and gravel, which produces a gray bunchy shrub like sage-brush. A Syrian village is the sorriest sight in the world, and its surroundings are eminently in keeping with it.

The New Pilgrims toyed with the idea that Quneitra might be the burial place of "Nimrod, the Mighty Hunter of Scriptural notoriety. Like Homer, he is said to be buried in many other places, but this is the only true and genuine place his ashes inhabit... When the original tribes were dispersed Nimrod and a large party settled where the great city of Babylon afterwards stood. Nimrod built that city. He also began to build the famous Tower of Babel. He ran it up eight stories high, however, and two of them still stand, at this day—a colossal mass of brickwork, rent down the center by earthquakes, and seared and vitrified by the lightnings of an angry God. But the vast ruin will still stand for ages, to shame the puny labors of these modern generations of men. Its huge compartments are tenanted by owls and lions, and old Nimrod lies neglected in this wretched village, far from the scene of his grand enterprise."

One senses that even Mark Twain's most devout fellow travelers thought this an unlikely tale, and indeed it is. Biblical scholars now see Nimrod as a figure who changed from composite to concrete as the tradition changed from Babylonian oral to the written form of Genesis.

As an aside, Mark Twain was a Freemason and Nimrod is mentioned in Freemasonry. In the Craft in the Old Constitutions we can find: "At ye making of ye toure of Babell there was a Masonrie first much esteemed of, and the King of Babilon called Nimrod was a Mason himself and loved well Masons." One presumes the Masonic reference to Nimrod while he was camping at Quneitra must have rung a bell or two with him. As a further aside, and I know we are in danger of falling off the book, he was a reluctant Freemason, suspended for non-payment of dues two months before the Holy Land Excursion started and kicked out altogether a month after camping out that night in Quneitra. No great loss either way, he may well have concluded.

The most remarkable site at Quneitra now is a brand new hotel right by the UNDOF barracks and watchtower on the barricaded road into Israel. A bit like the dancing poodle being remarkable for being able to dance at all, the remarkable thing about the Faradeis (Paradise) Hotel is not that it has been built so attractively but that it has been built at all. It stands proudly in a lush garden, no mean feat in itself, a two story building in the Mamaluk style with yellow and black layers. The hotel may well have been built on free land and with a sizable subsidy, but still it took a fair amount of determination and, as they would say a few hundred yards away, chutzpah.

Samir, Gillian and I have a soothing yoghurt shake and a bracing Turkish coffee. We wander over to the balcony and see Israel two hundred yards away behind the razor wire rolled loosely on the land. Behind us all is brush and scrub and collapsed buildings; ahead of us is lush farmed fields in harvest, wind farms twirling enthusiastically, military lookouts looking out from the Golan peaks and a busy main road with new vehicles speeding along purposively; above us the occasional sound of sonic booms as supersonic Israeli warplanes patrol the airspace above—and to make a point as there's no need to waste resources flying supersonically except to demoralize their opponents.

Soon we are joined by a jowly and brusque Arabic man who introduces himself and hands me his business card: "Welcome, my name is Walid al-Muallim, owner of the Faradeis Hotel. I have another one in Damascus, and one in Tartous. How do you find it?"

"It's remarkable. In style and opulence, and that it's here at all."

He wastes no time in coming to the point. "Look at that," he gestures towards the lush green Golan hills opposite, "the Israelis have stolen our land, our Golan Heights."

Now I always find this retrospective victimhood annoying. "You," I want to say but don't, "you started the war. War is war, soldiers fighting to the death. There's no point in moaning about the unpleasantness of it all from the luxury of peace, you shouldn't start the damn things in the first place." But instead I ask:

"Why?"

"Why what?" al-Muallim replies.

"Why did the Israelis take the land, the Golan Heights?"

"Israelis always take land. Take land, steal, take land. We must have our land returned or there is no peace."

I don't know why I'm getting into an argument about this, but find myself saying "We have a saying: To the victor the spoils. Syria was the aggressor against Israel. Twice. Had been harassing Israel from the Golan Heights for years before that too. Israel didn't wake up one morning and say to itself: 'I rather like the look of those Golan Heights, think I'll steal them.' You fired first, they fired second, you lost, they won. That's war. If you don't like it don't start it."

Al-Muallim now becomes rather angry. "That is your interpretation. You read the Zionist papers and believe the Zionist lies."

There's not a lot of point in continuing and we both drift off, me to Samir's car and he to his glass enclosed air-conditioned office with its masochistic panoramic views of Israel's wartime and peacetime achievements and corresponding myopic view of Syria's failures and humiliation.

Quite often after an impromptu argument one rehearses in one's head what one would like to have said. "Now look here, al-Muallid," I would like to have said, "much as I love Syria you need to have face a few facts. In 1967, in the Cold War days, Syria was Russia's client state in the Middle East, as was Israel America's. With Soviet prompting Syria joined a war pact with Egypt to attack Israel, or as your Air Force Chief-of-Staff and future dictator Hafez al-Assad put it, "to explode the Zionist presence in the Arab homeland". A reluctant Jordan was roped in to completely surround Israel. For reasons still unclear the Russians gave Egypt and Syria false intelligence that Israel was about to attack them, and this led directly to a massive build-up of force along the Arab side of Israel's borders.

"While Israel quickly and pre-emptively put the Egyptians to flight on the southern flank, in the north Syrian warplanes bombed civilian targets in northern Israel while Syrian emplacements on the Golan Heights shelled targets around the Sea of Galilee. The Israelis fought back as ferociously as one would expect and repelled the Syrian attack while leaving the Golan Heights neutralized.

"Then the great powers intervened again. The US noted that while Egypt had been humiliated, and Jordan appeared to have lost (the West Bank) disproportionately, Syria appeared to have escaped fairly lightly. It would not do to give the impression that a Soviet ally was to be treated leniently—it might encourage others to seek Russian protection. Thus encouraged by the US, Israel pressed on, well into Syrian territory and on the road to Damascus. The Syrians, hoping to attract Russian intervention, exaggerated the Israel advance. On hearing this the already demoralized Syrian forces deserted en masse; perhaps fighting for an unwanted minority dictatorship gave less weight to the endeavor than fighting for one's very future and one's homeland."

By the time I'd finished this imaginary one-way conversation with al-Muallid we were nearly back in Damascus. Although Quneitra's die were cast during the Six Day War, the actual devastation to the place that we saw today was as a result of the Yom Kippur War six years later. This time the Israelis were caught napping, the war was "a damn close run thing" as old Thunderboots would say and the Israeli response in victory was "never again".

This time on 6 October 1973, during Yom Kippur, the holiest day of the Jewish year, Egypt and Syria tried again. Again there was Soviet backing.

From the Syrian point of view the 1973 conflict was as much about restoring their honor and that of their dictator as about recapturing the Golan Heights. Samir drew parallels with the Bush family's adventures in Iraq, but then he would. Before the Six Day War, the Syrians had used the vantage of the Golan Heights to shell Israeli fishermen at random on the Sea of Galilee and to pick off Israeli farmers in the Hula Basin. The Israel victory had put an end to that harassment, but with no formal end of hostilities the Syrian dictator felt humiliated.

While the Egyptians attacked in the south, the Syrians launched a Soviet-style massive frontal assault across the Golan Heights, and this time had considerable Soviet air defense systems to stop Israel's air force counter-attacking. The Israeli defensive strategy was to hold the line with a minimal deployment and air cover until reserves could be brought to the front. The Syria offensive strategy was to complete the ground offensive by massively superior force before the reservists could arrive and to minimize the Israeli air force prowess with the Soviet ground-to-air missiles.

Over the next three days there were tremendous losses on both sides. On the fourth day the reservists arrived, the Syrian command was stalled by indecision, and once the tide had turned, demoralization set in again and the final Israeli victory was quick and decisive. This time the Syrians were driven back beyond Quneitra, and a year later UNDOF established a buffer zone, a zone they still buffer today, the one in which Mark Twain camped, the one in which the querulous al-Muallid has built his extraordinary hotel and the one in which Gillian, Samir and I have come to a dead end.

4: The Detour

Samir, Gillian and I are standing behind a red and white striped barrier. Across it lies a disorganized red, white and black Syrian flag. Two border guards are loafing about playing backgammon quietly in the shade. Our passports are lying idle beside them while we are taking photographs and ruing our blocked route. I say goodbyes to the Excursionists up ahead. The caravanserai, with its swaying cargo of two Middle Eastern dragomen, nineteen Arab porters, twenty-six pack-mules and camels, twelve horses, seven American Protestant biblical enthusiasts and one American journalist in rather a foul mood, drifts serenely into the near distance. From the dragomen Abraham in the lead to Mohammed in the rear, the caravanserai stretches over and past the one hundred-yard no-man's-land that now separates Syria from Israel. As Mohammed passes the first UNDOF watchtower on the Israeli side we turn our thoughts on how to meet up with them again. It's time for The Detour.

Firstly, the easy part. From Damascus Samir takes us to the Syria/Lebanon border: one (sorrowful) hour. From the border we catch a shared taxi to Beirut: two (terrifying) hours. After the usual barrage of bargaining abuse we then take a regular taxi from the transport depot to the Automobile et Touring Club du Liban in Jounieh: one (gridlocked and bad-tempered) hour. We open up *Vasco da Gama*; she seems pleased enough to see us, we give her a shower and a refill, take one of each ourselves, and wander over to the clubhouse to watch the World Cup semi-finals: Holland 3 Paraguay 2.

Secondly, the paperwork part. The next morning we gird up our loins for the wearisome bureaucracy of sailing out of Lebanon and into Israel. Out of Lebanon one does not breezily depart; into Israel one does not breezily arrive. The process involves subterfuge with the former and patience with the latter. It also involves the start of the passage planning as all concerned need to know where we will be and when we will be there.

When the *Quaker City* and the bulk of the Excursionists left Beirut for

Joppa, now Jaffa, they stopped off at all the evocative biblical ports now forbidding yachts entry: Sidon and Tyre, currently in Hezbollah-controlled Lebanon, and Acre, now in Israel. After Acre they anchored off Haifa, in 1867 a small fishing village but with an increasing Jewish population—Haifa was one of the early centers of political Zionism. Haifa is also our destination, the most northerly of Israel's ports of entry. For the *Quaker City* coastal hopping to Haifa meant a passage of sixty nautical miles, about seventy regular miles. For *Vasco da Gama*, having to skirt around international waters and warzone reporting points, the same journey becomes ninety nautical miles. We average five knots, five nautical miles per hour, so have to plan on an eighteen-hour voyage, which means an overnight passage.

As we leave Jounieh marina, just north of Beirut, the following evening the harbormaster finishes his instructions with the explanation, "... because we are at war with Israel". And so they consider themselves to be; for the time war without bullets and bombs, but at war in every other way they can think of—and boy, can they think of them. As a result the Lebanese authorities will not issue exit papers for Israel-bound vessels. The standard procedure is to check out to Larnaca in Cyprus, make a passage west for thirteen miles (one mile into international waters) and then make a 100° turn to port to fashion a southerly course to Israeli waters while staying over twelve miles off the Lebanese coast. This adds quite a dogleg onto the journey, and we chose a variation on the theme, checking out to Port Said, Egypt. The advantage of this latter subterfuge is that the course to Port Said is southwesterly, and one can justifiably chose a waypoint twelve miles offshore in the south-western corner of Lebanese waters to transit from Lebanese to international waters.

So with that *ruse de guerre* in place it's time to deal with the Israelis. There is an entry procedure—one suspects deliberately Delphic to deter the daydreamers—that involves emailing the Israeli Defense Force (IDF) with one's intentions and requesting the form "Yacht IMOT" in return. The IDF are as efficient as burdensome and back whizzes the IMOT straight away. One fills it in online. The questions are the usual suspects: Who? How many whos? Whence? Where before whence? Why? Any other whys? When? Arriving when and departing when? What? What yacht, what flag, what size, what weapons? Our IMOT will be circulated to Israel Navy stations on shore and at sea and all the answers we give tested against those on the IMOT—and so I trundle off to find a printer so that the IDF and we are reading the same answers.

Thirdly, the enjoyable part. Well, the sea passage is usually an enjoyable part but we are apprehensive about the warzone aspect of this one. We leave Beirut at four in the afternoon, planning to arrive in Haifa at ten the next morning and thereby avoid the worst of the Levant midday heat. One-off night passages have their own rhythms, rhythms impossible to predict as the body cannot swiftly adapt to regular night watches as both bodies become tired at the same time: bed time. Couples sail all over the oceans and soon by necessity settle into a watch system but every voyage starts with a few nights of unsettled watches as bodies adapt to their new sleeping rhythms. Everyone has their favorite on/off watch rota, and ours is no watches from sunrise to sunset and then three hours on/three hours off throughout the night. Some crews prefer to swap the first watch every other night to alternate the grave-yard watch just before dawn, when it is not just the darkest hour, but also the tiredest, hungriest and loneliest; others prefer set watches to assist the body clock. Either way you do get to see the sun rise, as the sunrise does get to see you. It's important that the captain does not become too tired—and must never be dog-tired—as tiredness causes wrong decisions and wishful thinking. Seamanship is a mixture of common sense egged on by experience, instinct to deal with troubles arising and intuition to foresee the troubles before they arise. Or as the old sea saw says, "Good judgment comes from experience; experience comes from bad judgment." Tiredness prevents intuition keeping trouble at bay and dulls the instinct when trouble then does arise—and when the common sense asks the tired brain for mental deductions the cogs in the brain trip over themselves. At least that's what happened to this captain once in the North Sea.

Apologies, one digresses. Now, Lebanese waters are tightly controlled by an entity called Operational Control, or Oscar Charlie in VHF radio-speak. On our passage we report our position just west of the Beirut lighthouse as requested and are then told to exit Lebanese waters twelve miles due west of there, the standard entry and exit route for commercial shipping. Luckily they sympathize with my plea for an old and slow sailing boat being unable to hold the westerly course in the westerly wind and permit us to exit by their south-west corner as in the passage plan.

By now it is dusk and we settle down for a long night of interference from the Lebanon Navy. A month before, arriving from Syria—a country not too ill disposed towards Lebanon—we felt like we had been part of a Lebanon Navy war exercise. Now we are dreading how much worse it is going to be as we head towards their sworn enemy to the south. But of the Lebanon Navy there is not a squeak nor sight and we sail into an empty void, passing the old

Phoenician and biblical ports of Sidon and Tyre—now in Hezbollah's hands—
which no one is allowed to visit by sea. At times we have to remind ourselves
we are in the busy Mediterranean at all; in vain the eyes scan the horizon for
signs of ships' lights; the radar on six miles range sees nothing, nor on twelve
miles; the chart plotter sees no Automatic Identification System (AIS) trian-
gles, the large ship movement indicators that that tell yachts when and where
the former are about to run down the latter. We reason that no cruising boats
are out because of the 8.00 p.m. curfew in Lebanese waters, no fishing boats
are out because of the curfew and the dead sea, and no patrol boats are out
because... well, that is the mystery, unsolved until we see what Israel's Navy
has to offer, then understood with some sympathy.

It is four a.m. and I'm on deck alone with this notebook, a pen, a torch
and an empty coffee mug—oh, and half a Snickers, soon to be dispatched.
I cannot claim we are sorry to be leaving Lebanon. It strikes us as a most
unhappy and inharmonious country, and one heading inexorably to war. Most
countries at war long for peace but in Lebanon the mood is snappy and ugly,
the love of hatred deep and internecine; if they can't find a war soon with
someone else they'll have another one with themselves.

In some countries—and Turkey comes to mind—any political unpleasantness one encounters ashore can easily be dispelled by casting off and sailing
in its beautiful waters—a case of burying your head in the sea. Not so in
Lebanon where the mess ashore is a mirror to the mess afloat. There are no
fishing boats as there are no fish—and no seabirds. The sea is, however, full
of plastic bags of every denomination, many of them semi-submersible and
looking to get themselves tangled up in your propeller or clog up your engine
intake, and countless empty plastic bottles bobble decoratively on the surface.
Every movement between ports is met with an outrageous bill for "agent's
fees" and is anyway subject to monitoring by Big Brother, Oscar Charlie. Any
unreported movement will soon be followed by a visit from a Lebanese Navy
patrol boat, endless questions and the inevitable on-the-spot "fine". Anchoring
is forbidden anywhere; and anyway there's that 8.00 p.m. curfew on all yachts.
The harbormaster at Beirut Marina told me, "We don't need or want visiting
sailing yachts here," a sentiment to describe, Jounieh apart, the unfortunate
country of Lebanon as a whole.

As the graveyard watch welcomes in the first glimmer of grey, and as
the Distance to Waypoint—the exit point from Lebanese waters and into
international waters—counts down to below five miles, and the Time to
Waypoint suggests we have an hour to run, I notice a radar blip coming

from the starboard quarter. On the radar screen we have all kinds of Clever Clogs—and I'm afraid I have no idea of how of any of this works but I do know how to work it—and one of the Clogs tells me the blip is heading straight for us, while another Clog declares the blip is travelling at twelve knots. The blip is now large enough to warrant an AIS signal, but none was forthcoming; a sure sign of someone's warship.

An hour later the Waypoint Alarm sounds, then just two cables into international waters the VHF radio comes to life. "This is United Nations warship *Varn*. Vessel at 33 degrees 09.78 minutes north and 034 degrees 52.49 minutes east, identify yourself." The voice is a tired female nasal monotone, with no early hint of a nationality.

Gillian looks at the readout and says, "That's us," quickly followed by, "your turn."

And so it is. I reply: "Warship *Varn*, this is the sailing vessel *Vasco da Gama*, *Vasco da Gama*. We are the vessel at 33 degrees 09.78 minutes north and 034 degrees 52.49 minutes east. Channel 11."

Then from *Varn*: "Sailing vessel responding, spell your vessel's name." I do.

Then: "OK, that's *Vasco da Gama*." A Canadian, tired, female nasal monotone, I'm beginning to think. "What are your intentions?"

"My intentions, madam, are entirely honorable, and furthermore they are now in international waters. But for the record we are out of Beirut for Haifa, ETA Israeli waters 0830 Zulu. Passage plan filed with Israeli Navy."

"It not my intention to impair or impede your passage, but under United Nations Resolution 283 you are required to provide additional security information. What is your crew?"

"We are two souls on board, myself the captain and my wife the admiral."

"I'm sorry, captain, I didn't copy that," the tired, female, Canadian nasal monotone replies. "Please say again."

I say again, and a lot more besides. Fifteen minutes later we say our goodbyes. Dawn is now well established and we are on deck enjoying fresh coffee. Thirty minutes later: "Vessel at 33 degrees 05.86 minutes north and 034 degrees 48.15 minutes east, this is Israeli Navy. Identify yourself." Although international waters is generally accepted to mean twelve miles offshore, Israel has upped her boundary to fifteen miles. Of course it's not worth arguing the toss, as their ability to mess you around is almost unlimited.

Before she has another chance to delegate, I say to Gillian, "your turn" and she repeats much the same information, again on channel 11, being careful to read from the IMOT crib sheet. They tell her we have been under observation since leaving Jounieh. One hour later the same details are requested again, my turn this time, all bang on the IMOT button.

By nine in the morning, post-porridge and pre-elevenses, we are well within sight of the new industrial port of Haifa and close enough to lament the building of skyscrapers on Mount Carmel. We are just saying "thank heavens, that's the Israel Navy over and done with", when a patrol boat zooms up alongside and in a great wallow of bow wash slows down to our five knots. We were only thirty or forty yards apart, and both on handheld radios.

We are chatting away about this and that—and finding out that as we were sailing through the Lebanon void Spain had beaten Germany 1-0 in the World Cup semi-finals—when he must notice the camera hanging around Gillian's neck.

"Captain, your crew is not allowed to photograph any Israeli Navy vessel." I assure him she hasn't done so. A moment later he says lightly, "I like your boat. What is she?" I explain, then he laughs: "Nice, and I have photographed yours." I say I had already assumed that and we give each other a friendly wave goodbye.

In Haifa we see several more Israeli Navy warships. Being a bit of a peacenik I've never really taken too much notice of warships before, but now I begin to understand why the Lebanese Navy elects to stay up north. Warships, as I used to glue them together at homework time, had big guns on turrets fore and aft, and some lesser guns running along the sides. These Israeli Navy warships forget about the guns and major on the missiles; dozens of them, stacked in rows and columns, some with enormous grey launching tubes, others with shorter more pugnacious black short range tubes. One extraordinary warship had a sharpish, almost chine, hull form, and was matt charcoal. Gillian obeys instructions about not taking photographs, although of course I cannot resist looking it up on Wikipedia later, and for any spy interested she is INS *Hanit*, a Sa'ar 5-class corvette.

And now for the last loop before entering Israel. Many people will have heard of the "Israeli passport stamp stigma", whereby an Israel stamp in your passport will impede entry into any number of Arab countries. The Israeli immigration people won't stamp your passport if asked not to do so, and we ask them not to do so. Then the questions begin.

Before arrival Gillian and I are not sure how to play this. The easy solution is just to say we are tourists, but our passports are riddled with Turkish, Syrian and Lebanese entry and exit stamps. *Vasco da Gama*'s logbook is a guide to the ports of the Holy Land. On board, our library is breathing in to cope with books about the region and its religions, not all of them well disposed towards Israel past or present. We had already decided to play it straight and go through the third degree.

"Why so many trips to Arab countries?" The immigration officer is a tall, healthy-looking young woman, with long and straggly mousy hair, heavy in breast (starboard breast crowned by her department's badge), full in tooth and zappy in air. One thing though—and do pay attention, 007—is that as her badge is on the starboard breast one would expect her to be a southpaw, but no, she writes right handed. Most curious. Someone must have pinned it on for her. Unless she did it in the mirror. Long night. Ah yes, "Why so many trips to Arab countries?"

"I'm writing an historical travel book about Asia Minor one hundred and fifty years ago—before Syria, Lebanon or Israel existed," I reply.

"And you, ma'am?"

"I'm the photographer and video person."

"What is your book about?" she asks looking me closely in the eyes.

"Mark Twain, the American travel writer. He was here in the Ottoman times."

"Oh, Mark Twain, I know all about him. He's neat. Sounds like a great project." She closes our unstamped passports with a toothy lunge and says, "Very well, enjoy your stay." We chat aimlessly about this and that for a few minutes, the subtext no doubt an extension of the interview. So much for the third degree; I am rather disappointed that all the carefully rehearsed answers will have to stay in the unused excuses drawer.

Why no third degree? Why no awkward questions? Why no checking on my mother's maiden name and Gillian's father's occupation (just as well on that, he *was* a spy)? Maybe it was the way I kept my eyes on her teeth, resisting all temptation to head south. But maybe there's a finer answer: as I will discover over the coming weeks Mark Twain is a bit of a folk hero in Israel. Why so? Well, you may have noticed in the first three chapters that he was none too impressed by the Arabs extant and wasted no time saying so. (Note to the faint of heart and correct of politics: worse is to come in the chapters ahead.) Over the years the Israeli Ministry of Information has frequently used Mark Twain's quotes from *The Innocents Abroad* as proof of how Israel "has made the deserts bloom". Schoolchildren are shown what the great American writer saw in Palestine then, and to contrast and compare what he might report about Israel now.

By early afternoon we are tied up at the Carmel Yacht Club, our umbilical cords of electricity and water connected to the dock. A deep siesta consumes the hours of lost sleep from the overnight passage. In the early evening a taxi takes us to the car hire station, and a piece of junk called a Kia Rio takes us back to *Vasco da Gama*, sundowners, showers and sleep.

Early the next morning, still discombobulated by the irregular sleeping patterns, two keen Strathcarrons, one new Ferguson—a young Italian Israeli, Bruno—and one reluctant Kia Rio are heading up through north-central Israel, across into the Golan Heights, up to the old border with Syria, past the landmine signs and burned out tanks, then north to the UNDOF station and the new border with Syria. We stop on the main road we saw from across the border, and look down onto the UNDOF checkpoints and watchtowers just below and the flattened remnants of old Quneitra close behind.

We drive up to the main gate. On the Syrian side the two soldiers by the barrier were loafing around in the shade playing backgammon. When we pulled up one held his hand out for our paperwork and, still sitting, waited for Samir to get out of the car and give him our documents while allowing us to photograph. Samir gave them a tip as one does. Now on the Israeli side there are four spick-and-span sentries standing to attention as we arrive. Bruno explains that we just want to drive a couple of hundred yards up to the UNDOF checkpoint. Why? I explain we are hoping to meet our caravanserai that had passed through here one hundred and forty-three years ago, turn around and follow them out—for the sake of the footsteps. Gillian holds up her camera and smiles.

We are told to wait. There are phone calls. We are still waiting. The sentries are still standing to attention. Heat shimmers off the tin roofs. A spruce new uniform wanders into the guard-room and they all look through the window at us. Another phone call. After twenty minutes I figure that dragoman Mohammed bringing up the rear would have passed by now. I jump out into the heat and ask the sentry for our passports, Bruno turns us around and we follow Mohammed up the hill. Even in the Kia Rio it doesn't take long to catch him up. Our footsteps are rejoined. The Detour has lasted five days, give and take an hour or two.

5: The Golan and the Galilee

Our new Ferguson/driver/dragoman is Bruno, the son of our biblical advisor in Jerusalem. His father, Massimo Fornaciari, is quite a *cause célèbre* in Israel: born into a high Catholic family in Turin, he converted to Judaism after studying theology at university. He now teaches theology at the Hebrew University. He claims he saw the Pauline light on honeymoon but Bruno later tells us that he only says that to placate his wife who remains resolutely Catholic and slides off back to Italy* at the drop of a *kippah*. Bruno has just finished university, studying Political Theory and Practice—"anything except theology," as he says—although I would have thought the two in Israel are hardly opposites—and is having some time off. The deal is that he drives us around for a month, "facilitates" where facilitating is needed, and then stays in our apartment in London for a month. The apartment is barely the size of a cupboard so we hope he won't be too disappointed. After Samir's wisdom-of-the-ancients approach to life, Bruno's brash impatience and general cockiness is a step backwards, and anyway there is precious little translating to be done in English-speaking Israel until we reach the Arabic-speaking Occupied Territories. In spite of Massimo's assurances, his son now tells he can't—or won't—speak Arabic anyway. Writing this at the end of the first day high up in the Golan Heights I'm thinking of "letting him go"—what a horrible euphemism that is, bad enough to stop me actually doing it—and trying to find a gnarled old Druze with some perspective on life and an axe to grind in his stead.

---

* They examine passports on the Italian frontier for fear an honest man may slip in. *Notebook 1878*

Mark Twain's lack of enthusiasm for the Syrian outback continued as he crossed over into the Golan Heights, the old biblical area of Bashan, still claimed by Syria if now firmly occupied by Israel. For many Israelis this recent addition to Israel is now their favorite part of the country, their own Scottish highlands: sparsely occupied, frontier territory, weekend-able, a hill station in summer and ski station in winter.

The Excursionists left Quneitra "very early in the morning, and rode forever and forever and forever". The route that they took, which then could be described as one "over parched deserts and rocky hills", is now scenic in the extreme, the parched deserts now green and yellow with farms and forests, the rocky hills now graced with olive groves, vineyards and almond orchards. To make matters worse they were "hungry, and with no water to drink".

Twain's next entry for that day reads: "At noon we halted before the wretched Arab town of El Yuba Dam, perched on the side of a mountain, but the dragoman said if we applied there for water we would be attacked by the whole tribe, for they did not love Christians. We had to journey on."

We are following Mark Twain's 1867 route on a 1922 British Mandate map but the 2010 track runs out some way below the top of a volcanic crater. The British map tells us that "Yuba" means crater and "Dam" means spring. Any pleasure we have taken solving this bloodhound detective work is tempered by the "Warning: Land Mines" signs on either side of the track. Bruno says the Syrians planted them pre-1967 and the Israelis have left them there to deter a Syrian attack. Bruno doubts if they worked even when the Syrians laid them, but just in case reverses the Kia Rio in the width of the track. Soon are we bouncing from one rock hard rock to another and take an eight-mile detour to reach the other side of the crater and the site of what was El Yuba Dam.

Today El Yuba Dam is the very opposite of a "wretched Arab town". In fact, nowhere better illustrates the remarkable transformation of the Golan Heights than Odem, El Yuba Dam's replacement. Odem is a *moshav*, an Israeli invention with no Western equivalent, but best understood as a co-operative village where the land is individually owned; the resources to service the land are shared in a kind of semi-capitalist kibbutz. Among other enterprises this moshav is the home of Odem Mountain Winery Ltd.

To reach it Bruno has to drive us around the crater and into the National

Park of Ya'ar Odem. We drive through a forest of Middle Eastern oak trees, the famous biblical oaks of Bashan, oak trees much shorter and stubbier than European ones. Later we learn that the Golan Heights used to be covered in oak trees but over the centuries the Turks stripped them bare, first for charcoal and fuel, then later to power their steam engines—the same ones quite probably that T. E. Lawrence enjoyed derailing. Apparently the Turks discovered that one thousand year-old oak tress made excellent furnace fuel, and of course it never occurred to them to replant. When Israel took over the Golan Heights in 1967 one of its first acts was to create a National Park for the oak forests and replant the hillsides with this most attractive and evocative tree.

The road through the National Park eventually leads in a cul-de-sac to Odem. Green, whole hews of it, forms the first impression; endeavor, whole rafts of it, the second. To one side are riding stables, on another four wheel drive safari quads and straight ahead the winery. A younger Kenny Rogers lookalike welcomes us at the shop. I explain what I want. He explains what I want to a phone, then points to a factory next door and says, "Go right through, my father is waiting for you."

An elder Kenny Rogers beckons me in, and pulls up two stools. "I'm Michael Alfasi. We're just finishing lunch. Come and join us." He introduces his other son, Yishay, and two daughters, Zvia and Michal. "Between us we run Odem Mountain Winery. Now what do you say this place was called?"

"El Yuba Dam," I reply.

"Not in my time. I arrived here thirty-five years ago, two years after the Yom Kippur War. It was a desolate scene. Rocks and scrubs. We got some Arab goat flocks up on the hill. That hasn't changed. But everything else has. Me and some other pioneers formed this moshav and you can see how it looks now. Look, I was about to leave, my son Yishay here will show you around."

Yishay shows me through a window the gleaming new stainless steel vessels and copper tubes and oak casks and unfilled bottles all lined up in rows. It is more like a laboratory than a winery. If there was a sandwich to hand it could be eaten off the floor. Yishay's business card reads "Winemaker". Yishay says, "We don't grow grapes, we grow wine".

"So how's it done? How can you miss out the vine stage?"

"Well we have vines of course. But what we really have here is the perfect climate, the perfect height, the perfect slopes and around here the volcanic soil. That's perfect too. All we needed to add was water. That's the value of a moshav. We all needed water, so we engineered it from a reservoir we created one hundred meters below. We have to push the water uphill, but we've got it. We yield four kilos a vine, whereas normally you'd figure two kilos."

"And it's still expanding?"

"Eight years ago we made seven thousand bottles and last year over seventy thousand, so yes."

"Your brother said all the wine was kosher. How does that work?"

"It's not really to do with the raw materials, more the add-ons, the finings and sulfates, and the casks and of course only Jews handling the product. It's why I can't show you around, why you had to look through the window— only Orthodox allowed inside. Although it's an expense, it does mean we automatically pass any quality standard anywhere in the world."

After an agreeable sampling of one of last year's seventy thousand bottles of Cabernet Sauvignon I have to ask: "This whole Golan Heights area is still in dispute. I've read that under the Oslo Accords your government had agreed to hand it back to Syria, and many people reckon Oslo 2 is the only way forward. Yet your family and the moshav are investing enormously in this area. You've created a kind of paradise. Aren't you worried that the Syrians will just take land over and kick you out? That all this will be for nothing?"

"Look, you can't live your life worrying about politics. What happens if this, what happens if that? When we gave the Arabs back Gaza they smashed up all the Israeli investments. I'd hate to think of them doing that here, but you know we make alcohol so... let's hope the mullahs don't get here first. But in the meantime we'll just love this land, love growing our wine on it and love being part of the moshav. We're our own state up here, beyond Israel in a way. So just love every second. Just in case..."

He has a point about the vandalism. When the settlers were paid off in Gaza the Palestinians asked the Israeli forces to destroy the houses, saying they did not want or need single family seaside villas but needed land to build high-rise refugee camps. In the event not all the houses were destroyed and those left were grabbed by party leaders for themselves. No new housing for the refugees was even started on settler land. The Israeli greenhouses and farms were all destroyed; in their place Hamas installed rocket launchers.

Unlike the writer the Excursionists were turned away thirsty from El Yuba Dam/Odem and they pressed on higher and higher and at 2.00 p.m. they

reached what is now known as Nimrod's Fortress, but back then was still
known by its Arabic name Qala'at Namrud, Castle of the Large Cliff. More
recently Judaic enthusiasts, noting the similarity between the Arabic Namrud
and their own Nimrod, have grafted the Genesis legend onto the castle—and
indeed have had him buried at nearby Quneitra where we were last night.
A new plaque from Genesis 10 proves the point beyond reasonable doubt:
"And Cush begat Nimrod: he began to be a mighty one in the earth. He was
a mighty hunter before the Lord: wherefore it is said, Even as Nimrod the
mighty hunter before the Lord."

Mark Twain was told that "It is of such high antiquity that no man knows
who built it or when it was built," but since then archaeologists have been
digging and sifting and we now know it is comparatively recent, from the
mid-thirteenth century. By the standards of the castles hereabouts this one had
a short and peaceful working life. It was built by Salah al-Din's nephew Al-Aziz
to pre-empt the expected assault on Damascus from Acre by the Sixth Crusade.
But the attack never came: by then the whole crusade movement had degenerated into a religious cover for piracy and after having spent a year in Cyprus
squabbling among themselves, the by now thoroughly disreputable crusaders
forsook Damascus and headed directly for the easy pickings of Egypt. Within
a hundred years the last crusader stronghold at Acre, only forty miles away
on the coast, had been abandoned and the castle started to fall into disrepair.
When the conquering Ottomans arrived two hundred years later they used the
castle as an up-market prison for disfavored officers and gentlemen.

The most amusing display now is the blood curdling English translation of the
builders' inscription:

> The inscription dated 1275 commemorates and glorifies the construction of
> this castle, and for the holy cause that inspired it, and to bring Death to the
> Unbelievers who venture towards it, and to preserve the lives of those who
> defend it.
>
> In the name of God, the Merciful, the Compassionate, this sacred tower was
> renewed by the Grace of our Lord, the Sultan Al-Malik, the most splendid
> Master, the Scholar, the Just, the Fighter of the Holy War, the Warrior on
> the Border, the Heavenly Assisted, the Victorious, Sultan of Islam and the

Muslims, Killer of rebellious deviators, Renewer of justice in the whole
world, the Partner of the Commander of the Faithful, Orderer of this work,
the Sir, the honorable Lord, the noble Sir, the great officer the Sultan Al-Zahir,
the most Glorious, the most Felicitous, Lofty, the well served, the splendor
of Islam and the Muslims, Leader of the Army of the Monotheists, King of
Commanders in the whole world, Sultan Bilik, may God perpetuate his days.

Since then earthquakes, neglect and shrubbery have added to the castle's woes.
Twain spent an amusing, if not historically accurate, "three hours among the
chambers and crypts and dungeons of the fortress and trod where the mailed
heels of many a knightly Crusader had rang, and where Phoenician heroes had
walked ages before them." Today the old castle has a steady stream of visitors,
but compared to the magnificent crusader castles of nearby Syria this one is
hardly worth a clamber over.

They left Nimrod's Fortress in the late afternoon for the easy ride down to
Banias, or as Twain put it: "we entered this little execrable village of Banias
and camped in a great grove of olive trees near a torrent of sparkling water
whose banks are arrayed in fig-trees, pomegranates and oleanders in full leaf.
Barring the proximity of the village, it is a sort of paradise."

It still is a sort of paradise, at least the half of that is left, because, you've
guessed it:

> They paved paradise
> And put up a parking lot
> With a pink hotel, a boutique
> And a swinging hot spot

I seem to recall Joni Mitchell was talking about somewhere she had visited in
Australia, but it could have been right here in Banias. Even in the height of the
season there were no more than two coaches and half a dozen cars, so quite
what the thinking was in paving paradise is unclear.

Banias is interesting for four reasons. Firstly, has been a sacred site from the times of pre-history and like all sacred sites first became so because it was a site of natural wonder. At Banias numerous springs miraculously gush out of the rocks around a cavern; the springs bring water from Mount Hermon and go on to become the River Jordan, while the cavern is shaped, equally miraculously, like a temple. Secondly, it was later an ancient Greek—and even later Roman—sacred site where they worshipped the god Pan—hence the name of Banias derived from Pan-ias. Thirdly, it was the site of the Roman city of Caesarea Philippi. Fourthly, it is where Jesus said to Peter: "Thou are Peter; and upon this rock will I build my church."

Actually, this third point of interest can soon be discounted because as Twain said, "The ruins here are not very interesting," and they are not. The city was built by Herod the Great's son Philip who named it Caesarea Philippi partly in honor of the emperor Caesar Augustus and partly in honor of himself. One can only assume young Philip put it up in a bit of a rush as Roman ruins of far greater antiquity are still standing proudly all over Asia Minor, whereas his city is indeed just a pile of rubble. In Mark Twain's time the site was distinguished by "trees and bushes that grow above many of these ruins now; the miserable huts of a little crew of filthy Arabs are perched upon the broken masonry of antiquity, the whole place has a sleepy, stupid, rural look about it, and one can hardly bring himself to believe that a busy, substantially built city once existed here, even two thousand years ago." Now it is just fenced off and sad, only marginally more interesting than the enormous paved-paradise car park that lies alongside it.

The sacred aspect of Banias cannot be so easily discounted. Three hundred years before Herod and Philip, and soon after Alexander the Great conquered the tribal lands hereabouts, the Ptolemy clan built the Temple to Pan. Pan was the god of all that might be found near the temple: goats and deer, hunting and gathering, music and campfires. When not attending to matters pastoral he encouraged his flock to stampede into battle, causing, you've guessed it... pan-ic... and pan-demon-ium. Mark Twain saw that "niches are carved in the rocks still, and the Greek inscriptions". We know that the smaller niche housed a sculpture of Echo, the mountain nymph and Pan's consort, while the larger one on its right housed a statue of Pan's father, Hermes, son of nymph Maia. Inscriptions in the niches mention those citizens who gave large donations.

But for the Excursionists the most relevant spot was where Jesus told Peter about the rock and the church. Mark Twain does not mention an exact spot where the famous pronouncement took place, but I hear two tour guides being quite specific about it being "right here", next to a small boulder in front of Echo's niche. Who knows? And more to the point who knows what Jesus meant by rock? For Protestants like the New Pilgrims, and of course Twain himself, the meaning was clear: Jesus meant that he would build his church (not yet in the building sense of the word) on the foundation of faith that He was the Christ and the Son of God. The Catholic view is that Jesus was saying that He would build His church on the apostle Peter himself. For Orthodox Christians, having the benefit of precise ancient Greek meanings and nuances, the rock refers to the Apostolic calling as a whole.

Twain reverted to the anti-Catholic position: "The place was nevertheless the scene of an event whose effects have added page after page and volume after volume to the world's history. For in this place Christ stood when he said to Peter: 'Thou art Peter; and upon this rock will I build my church, and the gates of hell shall not prevail against it. And I will give unto thee the keys of the Kingdom of Heaven; and whatsoever thou shalt bind on earth shall be bound in heaven, and whatsoever thou shalt loose on earth shall be loosed in heaven.' On those little sentences have been built up the mighty edifice of the Church* of Rome; in them lie the authority for the imperial power of the Popes over temporal affairs, and their godlike power to curse a soul or wash it white from sin. To sustain the position of 'the only true Church,' which Rome claims was thus conferred upon her, she has fought and labored and struggled for many a century, and will continue to keep herself busy in the same work to the end of time."

They camped overnight in Banias and "during breakfast, the usual assemblage of squalid humanity sat patiently without the charmed circle of the camp and waited for such crumbs as pity might bestow upon their misery. These people about us had other peculiarities, they were infested with vermin, and the dirt had caked on them till it amounted to bark."

By now his patience with the local lack of initiative was wearing thin. He had noticed the high number of children with sore eyes and the high number

---

* Concentration of power in a political machine is bad; and an Established Church is only a political machine; it was invented for that; it is nursed, cradled, preserved for that; it is an enemy to human liberty, and does no good which it could not better do in a split-up and scattered condition. *A Connecticut Yankee in King Arthur's Court*

of blind adults, and concluded that one led to the other, but couldn't square why nobody did anything about it. "And, would you suppose that an American mother could sit for an hour, with her child in her arms, and let a hundred flies roost upon its eyes all that time undisturbed? I see that every day. It makes my flesh creep. Yesterday we met a woman riding on a little jackass, and she had a little child in her arms—honestly, I thought the child had goggles on as we approached, and I wondered how its mother could afford so much style. But when we drew near, we saw that the goggles were nothing but a camp meeting of flies assembled around each of the child's eyes, and at the same time there was a detachment prospecting its nose."

While there he had an insight into Christ's role as a healer: "As soon as the tribe found out that we had a doctor in our party, they began to flock in from all quarters. Dr. B [Doctor George Birch, a fellow Excursionist] had taken a child from a woman who sat near by, and put some sort of a wash upon its diseased eyes. That woman went off and started the whole nation, and it was a sight to see them swarm! The lame, the halt, the blind, the leprous—all the distempers that are bred of indolence, dirt, and iniquity—were represented in the Congress in ten minutes, and still they came! Every woman that had a sick baby brought it along, and every woman that hadn't, borrowed one.

"What reverent and what worshiping looks they bent upon that dread, mysterious power, the Doctor! When each individual got his portion of medicine, his eyes were radiant with joy—notwithstanding by nature they are a thankless and impassive race—and upon his face was written the unquestioning faith that nothing on earth could prevent the patient from getting well now.

"Christ knew how to preach to these simple, superstitious, disease-tortured creatures: He healed the sick. The ancestors of these—people precisely like them in color, dress, manners, customs, simplicity—flocked in vast multitudes after Christ, and when they saw Him make the afflicted whole with a word, it is no wonder they worshiped Him."

∽≫

They left Banias after breakfast and Dr. Birch's impromptu surgery and five miles later found themselves in the ancient pile of Old Testament stones known as Dan. Since Twain's time the site has since been extensively investigated by archaeologists and incorporated into the Tel Dan Nature Reserve.

The Nature Reserve is a lovely place to meander around, with paths through its ancient forests surrounded by wildflowers and birdsong, rushing water and leaping barbel. The springs emanating from the rocks at sacred Banias have now been joined by others from nearby hills and a veritable torrent gushes through the center of the Nature Reserve even in mid-summer. Here and there one stumbles across Old Testament stones piled high into a wall of sorts but unless one is an enthusiast for the more arcane aspects of first millennia BC inter-tribal smiting and smoting and weeping and wailing and girding of loins and gnashing of teeth—and neither Mark Twain nor the writer are—it is hard to summon up much enthusiasm for the archaeologists' endeavors.

For me the most interesting non-floral, non-faunal part of the Tel Dan Nature Reserve is the site of the 1964 Pencil Line War on the Reserve's northern edge. This also marks the pre-1967 Six Day War border with Syria. Here is what happened. In 1923, when the British and French were carving up Asia Minor into the countries we know today, they disagreed on this part of the border between Syria and Israel. The British wanted part of their mandated land to have some bearing to theoretical Israel and so follow the old biblical boundaries from "Dan to Beersheba", while the French wanted their mandated land of Syria to cling to more secular, geographical features. They reached a compromise and drew a line, by repute with a 9B grade pencil, on a map. On the ground this 9B line represented one hundred and thirty yards, and not just any old one hundred and thirty yards but the one hundred and thirty yards through which flowed one of the three sources of the River Jordan.

Naturally enough both sides claimed the water source, both sides set up military posts one hundred and thirty yards apart and there were frequent skirmishes. In 1964 the Syrians joined forces with the Lebanese to physically divert the water away from Israel; Israel responded as she usually does—explosively—and all was quiet for a while as the Syrians licked their wounds. Then on 13 November 1964 the Syrians shelled the nearby Kibbutz Dan, and the Israelis responded with air and ground assaults, knocking out the Syrian position and moving their forces one hundred and thirty meters forward. A burned out Syrian tank can still be seen *in situ* as a war-trophy-cum-tourist-attraction. The Pencil Line War was over in an afternoon and was finally settled forever when the old border was lost in the Six Day War.

I apologize for this lengthy aside, only justified by it being the kind of story about the absurdity, the arrogance, the pomposity of Empire that Mark Twain would have loved—and loved laying into.

And so we head south. There are now wide gaps opening up between Twain's descriptions of how the land lay then and how the land lies now. The cities in the old Ottoman provinces that had become Lebanon and Syria have changed—or more accurately grown—enormously but the barren landscapes he described then are still recognizably the same forlorn landscapes we have seen over the last two months. Here in what has become Israel we are seeing the opposite; the desolation and squalor of 1867 have been transformed into a fertile plenty. Having been wonderstruck at the winery and delighted at the Tel-Dan Nature Reserve we are about to be spellbound by Agamon Hula.

When Twain saw what he knew as Lake Hula and what the Bible calls the Waters of Merom, he first saw it after "we traveled a long stretch of miserable rocky road, overrun by water, and finally turned and followed down the other side of the valley, along a vast green swamp that occupies the whole width of the valley. We camped at last at a fountain and a mile down abreast of Lake Hula."

By now we have impressed upon Bruno that we like to travel at caravanserai speed, with frequent stops for atmosphere and tea.* The track that the Excursionists took has been absorbed by agriculture. A shiny new highway sweeps around the "miserable rocky road" and halfway up the side of the valley so the first sight one sees of the "vast green swamp that occupies the whole width of the valley" is from a high vantage point; this makes the unfolding viridescent abundance even more spectacular. It is clearly a man-made phenomenon and there and then I ask Bruno to make some phone calls so I can meet the man behind the scene in front.

It has been unusual in the Middle East for the writer to meet a man taller than himself or to greet one whose handshake swamps his own but in Aviram Zuck the writer meets the man. I explain about the Mark Twain project and he interrupts me with: "Oh, I know all about Mark Twain. Whenever I'm giving a reforestation presentation I open with a slide of Mark Twain quotes about the area!"

On the wall I see a large-scale version of the same 1922 British Mandate map we are using. I ask what he uses it for.

"In this case to recreate the River Jordan." I must be looking surprised. "Yes, we recreated it, every twist and turn."

"Why did it need recreating, it must have been quite happy since time began?"

---

* There ain't no surer way to find out whether you like people or hate them than to travel with them. *Huckleberry Finn*

"Come." We walk over to the wall and next to the map are several other maps and photographs and graphics. For half an hour Aviram tells the story of the Hula project. I scribble down notes and now this evening I'm deciphering them while they are still fresh. Here goes: In the 1950s after Israel was founded the farmers in the Hula valley were desperate for land and water and looked down enviously at the three thousand hectares—or eleven square miles—of pale green swamps and marshes below. At the time the government wanted to make a grand political gesture and to create farmland from swampland seemed like one. The drainage of the swamps seemed like a good idea at the time, but like all good ideas at the time was certain to run into our old friend TLUC.

It was an agricultural and ecological disaster. Over six feet of peat topsoil were lost and the effluents flowing into the Sea of Galilee did untold damage to its ecosystem. By the 1990s the situation was so ruinous that a major new vision for the area was needed, and under the auspices of the Jewish National Fund "Hula 2" was envisioned.

And vision is the word. Three thousand hectares worth of vision, of thinking the impossible and making it happen. Two new north-south canals were built, the poor old River Jordan re-established, a dozen cross canals intersecting them at each junction with water level barriers. New peat topsoil was laid down and vast spraying machines sprinkle it with exactly the right amount of water.

"The farmers love it because they can grow pretty much anything they want. It's as fertile as any piece of land in the world. Peanuts and potatoes are the big cash crops here now," Aviram explains. "But the real start of the show is the Nature Reserve."

We jump in his pick-up truck for a tour. In the center of this artificial agricultural paradise they have created a bird sanctuary. "The Hula is on the main migration route. Before Hula 2 they had almost stopped using this route. Now we have five hundred million birds flying through every year, three hundred and fifty different species. This is now one of Israel's major tourist attractions, and birdwatchers come from all over the world in the spring and fall."

A tractor chugs by the other way. The driver is oriental and so are the workers in the trailers behind. "Where are they from?" I ask.

"Thailand," Aviram replies. "They come over here for three years then go home and buy a house. We look after them really well."

"Mark Twain stayed at a village called Ain Mellahah, that's obviously gone," I suggest.

"Partly gone, it's now the Mellahah pumping station, over there on that small hill. And what would Mark Twain think of all this?"

"He would have loved it. He was a great technocrat and loved engineering solutions. Above all he would have loved the vision and willpower behind all this. He strove for progress and improvement. He never accepted that just because things had been done *this* way there wasn't a *that* way."

Agamon Hula is a paradise for birds and birdwatchers, yes, but I can't help but see TLUC hovering like a ruby-throated hummingbird. The swamps and marshes had evolved there since forever; the first attempt at improving nature had been a disaster; this second attempt at improving nature is clearly not a disaster in any obvious sense at all, and yet, and yet. For a start—if you were a crane and halfway between Europe and Africa there was a Disneyworld paradise pit stop with unlimited peanuts and fresh water and nice people in sensible hats taking photographs of you, wouldn't you be inclined to forget Europe and Africa and the hassle of flying backwards and forwards and stay firmly put?

This evening we are staying at the Cosasu family's guesthouse in Rosh Pinna at the southern end of the Hula experiment. Of course, they know all about Hula 1 and Hula 2, but their own story is illustrative of how Israel has "made the deserts bloom" to use the phrase that so annoys the Palestinians. They arrived from Romania in 1953, both in their mid-twenties, both penniless but educated: Levana was a teacher and Yaron was halfway through his architecture degree. They arrived at Jaffa and were unceremoniously put on a bus to a kibbutz. "They told us we were farmers now, the country needed farmers not teachers and half-architects," Levana explains. "But in many ways not knowing anything about farming was good as all of us looked at farming as engineers or scholars. We made water flow, we helped seeds grow fuller. And communist! It was more communist than Romania. We worked and worked and worked. We worked so hard on that kibbutz in those early days," she says looking rather wistfully at Bruno with his smooth hands and easy care clothes. And teaching, and architecture? "Yes, later, five years later, they let us go."

＊＊＊

It only took the Excursionists and their caravanserai the next morning to ride the fifteen miles to Capernaum. When first reading *The Innocents Abroad* I was surprised that Mark Twain didn't make more of Capernaum, didn't stay longer. It is after all the first place where Jesus can be said to have landed; nothing certain of His life up to then—in His mid to late twenties depending on where you plant His birth—can be said to be known. It is only after His ministry started in Capernaum that His life as a traditional biography can really be attempted.

For Twain Capernaum "was only a shapeless ruin. It bore no semblance to a town, and had nothing about it to suggest that it had ever been a town." This it still is now, and it takes a leap of imagination to see the site as the busy fishing town of twenty thousand people that it was. Indeed, the same can be said all along the shores of the Sea of Galilee, now largely empty, then very much peopled—the reverse in fact of Nazareth to where we are heading, which two thousand years ago would have been a tiny village and is now a bustling town bursting with multifaith life.

Capernaum was a prosperous town in a rich and fertile area. The reliable historian Josephus, writing thirty years after Jesus died, recorded that "the whole area is excellent for cattle and crops and rich in forests of all kinds, so that by its adaptability it invites even those least inclined to work the land. Consequently every unit has been cultivated by its inhabitants and not a corner goes to waste. It is thickly studded with towns, and thanks to the natural abundance the innumerable villages are so densely populated that the smallest has more than fifteen thousand inhabitants."

The whole area fell into disrepair with the Muslim triumphs of the seventh century and by the time of Twain's visit it must have been near its lowest ebb. Sitting in the shade at Capernaum I hear a guide tell a Christian tour group that until the British Mandate of 1917 Galilee had been a sort of Wild West, a lawless land used only for plunder by the Bedouin and taxes by the Turks. Apart from the incorrect date (the British Mandate started in 1922) it seems like a correct analysis and ties in with Twain's own description of Capernaum and its surroundings.

Since his visit in 1867 archaeologists have been finding out much more about the Capernaum that was Jesus' home—or more accurately His base—for those three or four years. The remains of the large synagogue are from the fourth century, but under that they have discovered an earlier, first-century synagogue. This earlier building was uncommonly substantial too, built with

Greco-Roman influences. The latest guesswork is that it was built by a Jew who had traded abroad successfully, returned with funds for the synagogue and had it designed along the lines of a particular temple he had seen in his travels. It would have been in this synagogue that the Synoptic Gospels tell us that Jesus preached—and in particular healed.

Of course, this cannot be seen by the tourist today, but still there *is* something in the air. Mark Twain said that "all desolate and unpeopled as it was, it was illustrious ground. From it sprang that tree of Christianity whose broad arms overshadow so many distant lands to-day. After Christ was tempted of the devil in the desert, he came here and began his teachings; and during the three or four years he lived afterward, this place was his home almost altogether." Although the site has been developed as far as it can be since then, Twain's summary still holds true. On the one hand there really isn't that much to see, while on the other its evocative reverberations for anyone brought up anywhere near Christianity is profound: this really is where you can walk in His footsteps in hallowed ground.

A few miles beyond Capernaum lies the new Israeli village of Migdal on what was once the site of Magdala, and by tradition the birthplace of Mary Magdalene. It was bought by Russian Zionists in 1910, and so for an Israeli village it has some pre-independence provenance. It is in fact a very sound suburban settlement, not big enough to be called a town and not dead enough to be called a dormitory. The streets are wide, swept clean and speed bumped, the houses plentifully spaced, two-storied with copious foliage and individually designed, swimming pools sunbathe in the gardens, the children play on the streets and in the bright plastic colored playground. Even the birds keep their voices down. Stultifying respectability is Migdal's message.

This is Migdal today; this was Magdala in 1867: "Magdala is not a beautiful place. It is thoroughly Syrian, and that is to say that it is thoroughly ugly, and cramped, squalid, uncomfortable, and filthy. The streets of Magdala are any where from three to six feet wide, and reeking with uncleanliness. The houses are from five to seven feet high, and all built upon one arbitrary plan—the ungraceful form of a dry-goods box. There are no windows to a Syrian hut, and no chimneys.

"As we rode into Magdala not a soul was visible. But the ring of the horses' hoofs roused the stupid population, and they all came trooping out—old men and old women, boys and girls, the blind, the crazy, and the crippled, all in ragged, soiled and scanty raiment, and all abject beggars by nature, instinct and education. How the vermin-tortured vagabonds did swarm! They hung to the horses' tails, clung to their manes and the stirrups, closed in on every side in scorn of dangerous hoofs—and out of their infidel throats, with one accord, burst an agonizing and most infernal chorus: 'Howajji, bucksheesh! howajji, bucksheesh! howajji, bucksheesh! bucksheesh! bucksheesh!' I never was in a storm like that before."

Later that day he could not resist one final dig and wrote in his notebook: "The people of this region in the Bible were just as they are now, ignorant, depraved, superstitious, dirty, lousy, thieving vagabonds."

Having got that off his chest Mark Twain and the caravanserai ventured two hours further south to Tiberias, then as now the main town on the Sea of Galilee. They camped overnight in what must have been somewhat less than a town. He wasn't too impressed with Tiberias either: "Squalor and poverty are the pride of Tiberias." The only squalor and poverty there now refer to the architecture. Tiberias was unfortunate enough to be declared by the early Israeli government of the 1950s as a holiday resort and so is covered in horribly ugly Soviet-style hotels to which early developers have added some equally ugly 1960s package tour-style hotels and then later developers filled up the outskirts with some equally ugly 1970s Spanish Costa-style hotels. After that they all gave up, as indeed have the tourists. Tiberias today is a tourist ghost town, all dressed down with nothing to show.

～

I wish Mark Twain could have been in Tiberias seventeen years later when he would have come across a remarkable twenty-three-year-old Scotsman called David Torrance. Torrance was a Church of Scotland enthusiast and a newly qualified doctor. The Church of Scotland, like many other Protestant churches, had taken it upon itself to convert the wayward Jews to Christianity. Tiberias was, and is, one of the four most important centers of Judaism and yet there was no hospital. Torrance decided to build this hospital, with a Church of Scotland kirk alongside it, and duly bought Ottoman permission to do so.

This hospital evolved and expanded and was the major care center in Galilee until the new Israeli government built a state hospital in Tiberias

The Golan and the Galilee 117

in the late 1950s. The Church of Scotland decided to convert the hospital into a hotel, and to use any profits to improve the missionary work of the kirk. Today the hotel stands proud in the prime position in Tiberias, within its own tropical grounds complete with pool and in fact does not look as incongruous as one might imagine: the Scottish baronial manse-style is uncannily Ottoman—only the saltire and an almost-kitsch St. Andrew (himself a Galilean) statue in the garden give the game away on first acquaintance.

It was in Tiberias later that day that Mark Twain had his first sighting of the ultraorthodox Jews, the *haredim*: "They say that the lanky, dyspeptic-looking body-snatchers, with the indescribable hats on, and a long curl dangling down in front of each ear, are the old, familiar, self-righteous Pharisees we read of in the Scriptures. Verily, they look it. Judging merely by their general style, and without other evidence, one might easily suspect that self-righteousness was their specialty."

It's not known whether he ever saw any body-snatchers in the US before he left; he certainly never wrote about them. There were two synagogues in San Francisco when he lived there in the early 1860s, founded simultaneously as the congregation could not decide whether to follow the German or Anglo-Polish patterns of worship. There was only one, on 19th Street, in New York when he was there just before the *Quaker City* sailed. If he had seen any ultraorthodox Jews they would seem not to have made the same impression on him on home soil as they did here in Holy Land.

Before leaving England to follow in Mark Twain's footsteps and write this book I wanted to clarify the Jewish phenomenon in my own mind. We have probably all seen the junk email about the Jews and the Muslims and the Nobel Prizes: how the Muslims are twenty per cent of the world's population and have seven Nobel Prizes (including, bizarrely, one for that ghastly murderer Yasser Arafat, or as Bruno says on hearing this, WTF?) while the Jews[*] with 0.02 per cent of the world's population have one hundred and twenty-nine Nobel Prizes. Why so? And beyond the hallowed halls of Nobel why in any sphere of human endeavor—the arts, scholarship, the sciences, business, politics, the law, the media, entertainment (but not, interestingly enough, sport) do the Jews excel way beyond any statistical justification for their achievements? Why, in other words, do they seem to us Gentiles as being programmed to excel?

In London I put all this to my worldly-wise friend Saul Isaroff, to my

[*] It's a marvelous race—by long odds the most marvelous that the world has produced, I suppose. *Letter, 1897*

son's best friend Dominic Roter and to my old school friend and rabbi's son Robert Armstrong. Between them they hold an encyclopedic knowledge of Jewry whether Israeli or diasporic, ultraorthodox or long lapsed, historical or current. Saul is a collector of Jewish facts and folklore from near and far; Dominic was brought up in a Jewish home and has what I imagine is a typically modern secular approach to Jewry: he knows the Orthodox ropes when needed but isn't averse to a bacon sandwich when he pops over to us for breakfast. Robert was brought up in a household of Twainian piety; and like the young Twain he rebelled when his mind was old enough to think freely and for itself.

So why, I asked all my friends, why all this excelling? Well, firstly to say this is a short book, and we are already veering off-subject, so bear with me and some sweeping generalizations. The answers can be boiled down to religion and upbringing. The religious aspect is divided between the written law and the oral law and this encourages the central Jewish phenomenon of debate and questioning. A child growing up will be encouraged to question everything, secular as well as religious, and it is a given that a Jewish mind should be an enquiring mind. Religiously this leads to endless schisms. Some take the written law literally as God-given; others take it poetically as inspired by wisdom—but not by God; others view it as a man-made survival technique—and none the worse for that, just leave out the divinity. The former aren't inclined to let the latter live and let live, and to be one side or the other of this fence is another part of the Jewish phenomenon.

The upbringing aspect reflects the Jewish experience in the last two thousand years in exile. At different times and in different places all over Europe Jews were forbidden from owning property or practicing certain professions or practicing their religion—after all, it wasn't until twenty years after the Second World War that the Vatican finally accepted that Judaism as a whole was not to be held responsible for the death of their Catholic Christ. With this experience of discrimination and deprivation—and one of which the Holocaust was a climactic conclusion—survival inevitably meant self-succor, education and excellence, and excellence inevitably led to achievement and achievement inevitably led to jealousy and jealousy inevitably led to the pogroms and the circle was—equally inevitably—repeated.

These are causes and effects: the religion and the upbringing, the questioning and the excellence and both can be seen as alive and well in Israel now, as indeed can be seen the less attractive side-effects of intensity and fervor and a lack of what used to be called gaiety and what is still called charm. In

Syria, when I said we are going to Israel I was met by blank looks of incomprehension and disinterest; I might as well have said I was going to the rogue planet Cha 110913-773444. In Israel, when I say I have just come from Syria the questions start straight away. How much is a falafel? Did they have many newspapers? Internet? What, wifi or cable? Is there sales tax or is it all cash? Even with a credit card no tax? No credit card? ATMs? Anyone speak English? Likewise when I arrive in Israel by sea and the *marinistas* see *Vasco da Gama*. She has an unusual rig. In marinas in Turkey, Syria and Lebanon people looked, paused for a second and passed on. In Israel it's: what's the advantage? If it's simpler why is it more expensive? Which came first, wishbones or windsurfers? Wishbones? So why does it look like a windsurfer? And so on. Later in Jerusalem I overheard a guide tell his (Christian) group that the Jews were wonderful tourists because they asked so many questions about the country they had come to live in, whereas the Arabs either thought they knew it all or were not interested.

A fascinating consequence of the constant questioning—and I'm sorry, we'll return to Mark Twain in a moment—is its effect in the military. Every boy and girl, and until forty-five every man, is what is called "a fighter". When they start soldiering the questions start too, and as any officer will affirm, unquestioning acceptance of fighting orders once the fighting starts is better than starting a debate about the orders. There's a special unit in the army to deal with this phenomenon—and beyond that a facility for any fighter to question a superior once the fighting stops.

Now back to Mark Twain: unless any reader reading his comments about the body-snatchers thinks that he was anti-Semitic I can assure them that this is simply not the case. Later in life he wrote that: "I am without prejudice. It is my hope that both the Christians and the Jews will be damned; and to that end I am working all my influence. Help me pray... If I have any leaning it is toward the Jew, not the Christian. Christianity has deluged the world with blood and tears—Judaism has caused neither for religion's sake."

Less flippantly he remarked: "A few years ago a Jew observed to me that there was no uncourteous reference to his people in my books, and asked how it happened. It happened because the disposition was lacking. I am quite sure that I have no race prejudices, and I think I have no color prejudices nor caste prejudices nor creed prejudices. Indeed, I know it. I can stand any society. All that I care to know is that a man is a human being—that is enough for me; he can't be any worse.

"The Jew is not a disturber of the peace of any country. He is not a loafer, he is not a sot, he is not noisy, he is not a brawler nor a rioter, he is not quarrelsome. In the statistics of crime his presence is conspicuously rare—he is a stranger to the hangman.

"That the Jewish home is a home in the truest sense is a fact which no one will dispute. The family is knitted together by the strongest affections; its members show each other every due respect; and reverence for the elders is an inviolate law of the house. The Jew is not a burden on the charities of the state nor of the city; these could cease from their functions without affecting him. When he is well enough, he works; when he is incapacitated, his own people take care of him. And not in a poor and stingy way, but with a fine and large benevolence. His race is entitled to be called the most benevolent of all the races of men."

But there's no doubt that Twain found the body-snatchers disagreeable, partly because he couldn't agree with their Pharisee-ish self-righteousness and partly because he couldn't follow how they could believe in a doctrine of divine preference. Twain's—and the writer's—view of a personal god, a male god, a separate being that had to be worshipped and obeyed, a god distinct from his creation and not an integral part of it, within us all, can be summarized thus:

> The best minds will tell you that when a man has begotten a child he is morally bound to tenderly care for it, protect it from hurt, shield it from disease, clothe it, feed it, bear with its waywardness, lay no hand upon it save in kindness and for its own good, and never in any case inflict upon it a wanton cruelty. God's treatment of his earthly children, every day and every night, is the exact opposite of all that, yet those best minds warmly justify these crimes, condone them, excuse them, and indignantly refuse to regard them as crimes at all, when he commits them. Your country and mine is an interesting one, but there is nothing there that is half so interesting as the human mind.

Twain could not intellectually grasp the concept behind: "a God who could make good children as easily as bad, yet preferred to make bad ones; who could have made every one of them happy, yet never made a single one happy;

who made them prize their bitter life, yet stingily cut it short; who gave his angels eternal happiness unearned, yet required his other children to earn it; who gave us angels painless lives, yet cursed his other children with biting miseries and maladies of mind and body; who mouths justice and invented hell, mouths mercy and invented hell, mouths Golden Rules and forgiveness multiplied by seventy times seven, and invented hell; who mouths morals to other people, and has none himself; who frowns upon crimes, yet commits them all; who created man without invitation, then tries to shuffle the responsibility for man's acts upon man, instead of honorably placing it where it belongs, upon himself; and finally, with altogether divine obtuseness, invites his poor abused slave to worship him!"

The writer has the same trouble squaring the Abrahamic circle today. Granted, up to a point, Mark Twain' view: "The Jews have the best average brain of any people in the world. They are peculiarly and conspicuously the world's intellectual aristocracy." Fine, but if so, how can the "body-snatchers", the religious vanguard who have kept the candle, real and metaphorical, burning all these centuries actually believe that three thousand illiterate and superstitious years ago Moses was given a covenant from a god who became not one god for all humanity—a strange enough concept in itself—but a divisive god, a racist god, a sadistic god, a vengeful god, a sexist god, a god that if alive today would be arrested on the spot?

It is not really even possible to suggest that those unlettered tribesmen believed all this three millennia ago, as they understood life through what the Greeks called *mythos* and not what the same Greeks called *logos*. Like all ancients they used *logos* to sharpen their weapons, to observe the movements in the night sky and ultimately to survive. But *logos* could never explain the inexplicable, what we still call the mysteries of life, either personal emotions or natural phenomena. For that they used *mythos*. Myths were never intended to be factually correct as they were, by definition, dealing with layers of understanding beyond the factual, the explicable. It would never have occurred to the authors of the Old Testament that the texts would be taken literally.

But now that we know that Exodus is largely *mythos*, that the best archaeologists in the world have sifted all through the Sinai and Canaan and no evidence exists that there was ever any flight from Egypt, and no conquest of the Promised Land. So why the ultraorthodox denial of science and reason? Why the flat-earth insistence on the literal meaning of ancient words never meant to be taken literally? Could it be that the incessant questioning has led to the abandonment of the *mythos* source and the application entirely of *logos*, after all the very language of dialectic—and questioning? Has logic tied itself in a Gordian knot and the more it picks at it the tighter the knot becomes?

Modern secular Israelis, in other words the vast majority of Israelis, are embarrassed when you ask them about the ultraorthodox. In the car Bruno adds on at least thirty mph before he finishes his rant against them. The former are irked that they have to pay for the latter "studying" away their adult lives and not working; that they don't have to join the military (although always vote for war)*; that they have a virulent birth rate; that they behave with an arrogance that they are not only the chosen ones but verily chosen among the very chosen. Politically, although they only make up a tenth of the population, in a proportional representation system they have a disproportionate—and generally intransigent—role to play. Ironically, in view of recent Jewish history, the default position of the religious-right on most issues would not embarrass Mussolini. Certainly the images ones sees of them on Israeli TV, the images of hatred on screwed-up faces as they throw bricks at plasma TV screens, or abuse at fire-fighters trying to rescue an imprisoned woman, are directly comparable to the baying mobs of Muslim maniacs in Pakistan or Iran. Bruno calls them Judeofascists, no better than Islamofascists, but Bruno is young and inexperienced and throws words like fascist around with no experience of what they stand for. But he does tell me the rather shocking fact that the children of the ultraorthodox do not have to be educated in any subject expect religion, again at the state's expense; no science; no languages; no arts, nothing except religion. Is it any wonder that they behave as adults like Islamic fundamentalists when they are schooled at madrassah seemalikes?

Mark Twain was twenty years older than Sigmund Freud. When they met in Vienna in 1898, Mark Twain was sixty-two. As an admirer of the Jewish intellect one imagines our man was on good behavior in the presence of the pinnacle, but unfortunately no record of their conversation exists. We can be sure, however, that they agreed that religion was a man-made and not a divine phenomenon, and one made to satisfy primitive survival yearnings in an unpredictable world an awfully long time ago. In fact, Freud thought

---

* To be a patriot, one had to say, and keep on saying, "Our country, right or wrong," and urge on the little war. Have you not perceived that that phrase is an insult to the nation? *Glances at History, 1906*

that religion* was a neurosis that bordered on insanity, and that the yearning for a personal, male and above all immortal god was "so patently infantile, so foreign to reality, and to anyone with a friendly attitude to humanity, it is painful to think that the great majority of mortals would never be able to rise above this view of life." One hesitates to add to the same paragraph as Sigmund Freud, save to observe that in the time spent in Israel I have yet to see a haredim laugh, or even smile. I have been with Vedantic gurus, and the Dalai Lama, wise men all, and they dance through the bliss of life and take you dancing through the bliss with them.

(Talking of Freud reminds me of Carl Gustav Jung—why do they always crop up together? It was Jung who pointed out the central paradox in every personal God belief system: if you could logically prove there is a personal god there would be no need for faith, yet faith is what hold these monotheistic religions together. For Jung religion actually prevented spiritual experience as it reduced the transcendent to a man-made concept.)

And talking of dancing bliss, I wish Mark Twain could have stumbled across this gem of a story and I wish I could see him shake his head and wonder. I'm sure a version of it would have found its way into *Pudd'nhead Wilson* as a counter-story. We start with Exodus 12:15, which for no clear reason instructs that for seven days "ye shall eat unleavened bread" and ends by threatening transgressors: "thy soul shall be cut off from Israel." It's not as simple as no bread for the week as the rabbis have taken it to mean no pasta, no peanuts (eh?), no cereals, no burger buns, no cakes, no biscuits, no couscous, no pizza, no pitta, no rice, no beans, no pulses, no whiskey. No bakery or supermarket is safe from patrolling rabbis. Many restaurants find it easier just to shut for a week. Secular Israelis, at least the ones I met, either take a holiday abroad for a week or use up the bread, etc in the freezer and eat what they like at home all week.

Now then, one way or another the State of Israel cannot help but be a large holder of leavened products in its schools and hospitals and barracks and, well everywhere, including all the embassies abroad. It is clearly impractical to dump them or sell them so the government and the rabbis have come up with this ingenious wheeze. A Gentile buys all these tons of government-held stock for a week for a nominal sum on option, then at the end of the week lapses his option. Result: legal niceties and religious purity preserved and one coopera-

---

* Religion consists in a set of things which the average man thinks he believes, and wishes he was certain. *Notebook, 1878*

tive *goy* slightly richer. For many years this was a Mr. Moghrabi, an Arab lawyer[*] from East Jerusalem. One year, a jesting journalist did a background check and found out that he was partly Jewish and on the female side. Pandemonium! Rushing-around rabbis tying themselves in knots, frantic digging in the Exodus archives for a loophole, much weeping and wailing and gnashing of teeth—and sadly, no more delicious story for Mr. M. to dine out on.

Enough religion already. The Excursionists left Tiberias the following morning and the caravanserai "jogged along peacefully over the great caravan route from Damascus to Jerusalem and Egypt, past Lubia and other Syrian hamlets and came at last to the battle-field of Hattan."

I have been on a number of battlefield tours in Europe and Africa and wish there was one here: the site where was fought the decisive battle that regained Jerusalem from the crusaders, and was indirectly the beginning of the end of the crusades altogether. Time for a Mark Twain history lesson, this one factually accurate. The date is 4 July 1187.

> Here the peerless Saladin met the Christian host and broke their power in Palestine for all time to come. There had long been a truce between the opposing forces but Raynauld of Chatillon broke it by plundering a Damascus caravan, and refusing to give up either the merchants or their goods when Saladin demanded them.

> This conduct of an insolent petty chieftain stung the Sultan to the quick, and he swore that he would slaughter Raynauld with his own hand, no matter how, or when, or where he found him. Both armies prepared for war. Under the weak King of Jerusalem was the very flower of the Christian chivalry. He foolishly compelled them to undergo a long, exhausting march, in the scorching sun, and then, without water or other refreshment, ordered them to encamp in this open plain.

> The splendidly mounted masses of Moslem soldiers swept round the north end of Tiberias, burning and destroying as they came, and pitched their camp in front of the opposing lines. At dawn the terrific fight began. Surrounded on all sides by the Sultan's swarming battalions, the Christian Knights fought

---

[*]   They all laid their heads together like as many lawyers when they are getting' ready to prove that a man's heirs ain't got any right to his property. *Letter, 1856*

on without a hope for their lives. They fought with desperate valor, but to no purpose; the odds of heat and numbers, and consuming thirst, were too great against them.

The doom of the Christian power was sealed. Sunset found Saladin Lord of Palestine, the Christian chivalry strewn in heaps upon the field, and the King of Jerusalem, the Grand Master of the Templars, and Raynauld of Chatillon, captives in the Sultan's tent. Saladin treated two of the prisoners with princely courtesy, and ordered refreshments to be set before them.

When the King handed an iced Sherbet to Chatillon, the Sultan said, "It is thou that givest it to him, not I." He remembered his oath, and slaughtered the hapless Knight of Chatillon with his own hand.

Two touches Mark Twain left out were that Salah al-Din had his army light bush fires upwind of the Christian soldiers to make their thirst worse, and then had his water camels bring fresh water from the Sea of Galilee half a mile away and empty their water vessels onto the ground to increase the Christian anguish.*Twain might also have mentioned that relations between Christianity and Islam never recovered from the carnage of the crusades. The site of the battlefield is still as he described it, "a grand, irregular plateau, that looks as if it might have been created for a battle-field". It is now irrigated around the edges and growing almonds and olives on the higher ground, where Salah al-Din encamped, and below newly planted citrus groves, all in uniformly neat rows, rather as the Christian host might have stood.

~~~~~~~

Actually there was another battle at Hittin, much more recent and far less significant, but one that in its tiny way helps explain the Israel that is today. It was fought between Jews and Arabs on 17 July 1948—fought is probably too strong a word as after the initial round of firing by the Israelis the Arabs fled across the valley to Jordan and the Israelis walked into an abandoned village.

After finishing retracing the Excursionists' tour around the Holy Land I am planning to finish this book with an epilogue called "Dear Sam", a journalist-to-journalist letter to Sam Clemens, about what happened to the Holy Land after he left it, what he would find here now, and what on earth anyone can do about the holy mess that various rabbis, imams, priests, dictators,

* As near as I could make out, most of the folks that shook farming to go crusading had a mighty rocky time of it. *Huckleberry Finn in Tom Sawyer Abroad*

generals, scoundrels, foreign governments and NGOs have managed to make of it. For now, as we are about to enter the West Bank, please bear with me as I summarize as succinctly as possible events that led up to this second battle at Hittin—and to the birth of Israel and the crisis of Palestine.

When Mark Twain was here there were around five thousand Jews in this Syrian part of the Ottoman Empire—mostly body-snatchers and mostly in Jerusalem, but also in Safed, Hebron and as he had just seen, in Tiberias. Fifteen years after his visit here the Orthodox Church* in Russia instigated anti-Jewish pogroms and these coincided with the birth of political Zionism, the desire of the diasporic Jews to return to the lands of their Bible. The Russian Jews fled to the Holy Land and settled in country very much as Mark Twain described: "There was hardly a tree or a shrub anywhere. Even the olive and the cactus, those fast friends of a worthless soil, had almost deserted the country... The only difference between the roads and the surrounding country, perhaps, is that there are rather more rocks in the roads than in the surrounding country...

"We traversed some miles of desolate country whose soil is rich enough, but is given over wholly to weeds—a silent, mournful expanse, wherein we saw only three persons—Arabs, with nothing on but a long coarse shirt like the 'tow-linen' shirts which used to form the only summer garment of little negro boys on Southern plantations... A desolation is here that not even imagination can grace with the pomp of life and action."

By the turn of the century the Jewish population had doubled to twenty thousand and as the Zionist message spread throughout the Diaspora it had doubled again by the outbreak of the First World War. During that war their hosts, the Ottoman Turks, decided to back the losing German side, and when it was clear that they would lose not only the war but the remains of their empire the British, French** and Russians met secretly to carve it up among themselves. This was far from being the most glorious episode in the history of the British Empire as it had already promised the Arabs an independent Greater Syria if they helped the allies defeat the Turks in Arabia, and it was about to promise the Jews an independent homeland in the self same space— clearly incompatible and expedient promises it had no intention of honoring.

The League of Nations then deemed the area best run by the British and

* The church is always trying to get other people to reform; it might not be a bad idea to reform itself a little, by way of example. *A Tramp Abroad*

** In certain public indecencies the difference between a dog & a Frenchman is not perceptible. *Notebook, 1879*

the French and thus was born the Mandate era. The French were given what would become Syria and Lebanon and the British what would become Israel, the West Bank, Jordan and Iraq. Thus although the Syrians wanted one large independent country the British divided it up into mini-Syrian pieces; and although the Iraqis wanted to stay loosely and tribally federated the British told them they were one country and foisted the ex-King of Syria on them after the French had kicked him out of Damascus.

By the time of the Second World War all these artificial borders, shifting alliances in shifting sands, broken promises and imperial hidden agendas, continued mass emigration of both Jews and Arabs into the now more affluent Holy Land and the rise of recognizable Arab nationalism brought many an imperial chicken home to roost. Eighteen months after the war, the British, having managed to betray and upset all sides equally, threw their hands up in the air and handed the whole mess over to the newly created United Nations.

We are now only thirteen months away from the second battle of Hittin. The UN proposed two more or less equally populated states: Israel and Palestine. The Israelis accepted it reluctantly; the Arabs rejected it whole-heartedly. It was to be the first of a series of disastrous decisions that the Arab side, in various guises, was to make over the next sixty years. Two months after the UN declaration, in early 1948, the Arabs attacked and in the period up to Israel's Declaration of Independence in May 1948 a series of skirmishes brought Israeli gains with every skirmish.

It wasn't until after Israel's declaration that the real War of Independence started. Five armies from Egypt, Syria, Transjordon, Lebanon and Iraq attacked Israel from all sides. In retrospect it seems they were more interested in grabbing land for themselves than helping establish Palestine—and this is exactly what Jordan did. The Arab side had a five to one numerical advantage, but they also had three decisive factors working against them. Firstly, unlike the Jews, they were not fighting for their long promised homeland and indeed for their very survival. Secondly, much as we love the Arabs we have to say they are not much good at soldiering—maybe that's why we love them. Thirdly, their leaders were more interested in stabbing each other in the back than stabbing the Israelis in the front. In fact, these same leaders, by ordering the resident Arabs to flee until the imminent and certain victory would enable them to return, were also largely—but not wholly—responsible for the massive refugee crisis which the war brought on: about seven hundred thousand Arabs fled the future Israel and six hundred thousand Jews fled from their surrounding Arab countries as retribution followed defeat.

The decision to invade Israel had been a disaster. The Arabs ended up with less territory than when they started the war, while Israel had increased hers by over thirty per cent and now had contiguous territory. There was still no Palestine. They had lost half of Jerusalem. They had created one and a half million refugees, the Arab half of which now number four million and are still stateless. Eighty-five per cent of the Arabs who were in what would become the new Israel had fled or were ethnically cleansed. Four out of the five hundred Arab villages were sacked or re-inhabited by Jews. Only Jordan won anything, and that was only because it colonized over half of what was supposed to be Palestine, the West Bank.

By 18 July 1948 the Arabs at Hittin had already largely lost heart. An Arab soldier's account in the *Palestine Study Journal* says that "we saw the Jewish armored unit advancing... we were too few and had too little ammunition. During the first Jewish attack we retreated to the village and with the few remaining villagers we fled north." The descendants of the village are now seething in Lebanon, ignored by Israel, forgotten by the Arabs. The village itself is a pile of rubble with only the minaret just about standing; wild mulberry, fig and eucalyptus trees, and random cactus plants grow around it. A small nearby stream supports aquatic plants. Butterflies flutter around, blissfully unaware of early dramas. Ironically, one can say only to oneself, the old village of Hittin has probably never looked prettier.

～～～

A few hours later, barely halfway through what must have been an exhausting day of sightseeing, the Excursionists found themselves on top of Mount Tabor. "Tabor rises some fourteen hundred feet above the surrounding level, a green, wooden cone, symmetrical and full of grace—a prominent landmark, and one that is exceedingly pleasant to eyes surfeited with the repulsive monotony of desert Syria. We climbed the steep path to its summit, through breezy glades of thorn and oak. The view presented from its highest peak was almost beautiful."

Today there's a single-track road that does the climbing up the steep path and it is so precipitous that the tourists' buses have to stay in a car park at ground level 2,000 feet below and decant their pilgrims into a caravanserai of minibuses. We are still actually only 1,600 feet above sea level; the Sea of Galilee is some 700 feet below sea level.

In Twain's time there was precious little to see on top of Mount Tabor. "There is nothing about Tabor (except we concede that it was the scene of the Transfiguration,) but some gray old ruins, stacked up there in all ages of the world from the days of stout Gideon and parties that flourished thirty centuries ago to the fresh yesterday of Crusading times. It has its Greek Convent, and the coffee there is good."

〚

Things have perked up on Mount Tabor these days. One does not like to be picky, but biblical scholars now place the Transfiguration—the moment when Peter, James and John saw Jesus transfigured in a vision to standing alongside Moses and Elijah—as being on nearby Jebel Jermuk rather than on Mount Tabor, which was first referenced several hundred years after the event. At that time Mount Tabor was going through its most illustrious period, with an enormous Byzantine church dedicated to the Christ Transfigured and two smaller out-riding churches dedicated to Moses and Elijah—an unusual New Testament/Old Testament juxtaposition. For several hundred years Tabor attracted pilgrims from all over Europe, and its glory was only terminated after the above-mentioned Battle of Hittin. The next day the victorious Saracens marched the same few miles as Mark Twain had done, climbed up the same steep path and sacked and slaughtered all before them.

Ruin and desolation befell Mount Tabor until six years after Twain's visit when the Franciscans bought permission from the Ottomans to colonize it again. Initially lack of funds prevented serious excavation or renewals and it was not until 1921 that a rich American benefactor enabled work to start on a new basilica. Using many of the ruins that were lying around during Mark Twain's visit, and copying as far as could be known the original design, the basilica took twenty years to complete.

It is a wonderfully gracious design, a truly spiritual space—and, as the Franciscans themselves say, a sort of transfiguration in itself. One enters between two towers that rise to form an arch. The vault is sky blue and all the space around is lit by a complex of tripled windows, a direct copy of the original Byzantine design. Incorporated into each side of the basilica are chapels to Moses and Elijah, the latter with a mosaic floor excavated from the original, and both surrounded by sympathetic modern frescoes. There are three naves which can all be seen immediately and in full on entering the basilica. Below one can see the crypt which still has the original walls and a copy of the original altar, rising to the altar in daily use and above that in the upper apse a glowing mosaic of the Transfiguration itself. It is a fine space in which to experience the sublime and a very far cry from the modern monstrosity in Nazareth we shall see tomorrow.

It is also a fine place to sit and watch the pilgrim groups come and go. The Nigerians this afternoon are especially enthusiastic and hold a beautiful unaccompanied sung service with their own priest and his assistant, female, who travel with their own vestments. The Italians are chattier and less reverential until the service starts, when they all fall into place and sing as boisterously as the Nigerians had rhythmically. An American group comes and goes in a hurry, leaving enough time only for the tour guide, Bible* raised in right hand, to give rather a haranguing—and inaccurate as it happens—lecture on the New Testament account of the subject in hand. As I am leaving I ask one of the monks, rhetorically, if they ever have the place to themselves. In Italish we joke that thirty years ago we would have been able to have this conversation in Latin, a skill recently lost to both of us. The answer is yes, at sunset the forty monks reclaim their basilica and enjoy the silence.

By the way, the Greek Orthodox church mentioned in Twain's account, "It has its Greek Convent, and the coffee there is good,"*is* still very much there if tucked away around the corner. In spite of trying twice to sample the coffee I find the place occupied by Orthodox monks but locked.

At the bottom of Mount Tabor one finds, then as now, the village of Endor. Endor of now is a top security gated ghetto. On the map it promises to house a museum in its midst—presumably having some relation to the biblical Witch of Endor.**. One follows the usual brown museum sign and soon comes across a large yellow reinforced sliding gate. There's a sentry box but no sentry. A telephone number lies across the gate. One dials accordingly.

"Hello, I'm at the gate. I've come to see the museum."

"Who are you?"

* The Bible is full of interest. It has noble poetry in it; and some clever fables; and some blood-drenched history; and some good morals; and a wealth of obscenity; and upwards of a thousand lies. *Letters from the Earth*

** There are no witches. The witch text remains; only the practice has changed. Hell fire is gone, but the text remains. Infant damnation is gone, but the text remains. More than two hundred death penalties are gone from the law books, but the texts that authorized them remain. "Bible Teaching and Religious Practice", *Europe and Elsewhere*

"My name is Ian. I'm a tourist. To see the museum."

"No, we don't want." Click.

Possibly they suspect I'm an unsympathetic historian; the Arabs of Endor were subjected to some particularly unpleasant ethnic cleansing by the Israeli Golani Brigade on 24 May 1948.

It sounds just as grim back then, even if from a different end of the grim scale: "We found ourselves at Endor, famous for its witch. Her descendants are there yet. They were the wildest horde of half-naked savages we have found thus far. They swarmed out of mud bee-hives; out of hovels of the dry-goods box pattern; out of gaping caves under shelving rocks; out of crevices in the earth. In five minutes the dead solitude and silence of the place were no more, and a begging, screeching, shouting mob were struggling about the horses' feet and blocking the way. 'Bucksheesh! bucksheesh ! bucksheesh! howajji, bucksheesh!' It was Magdala over again, only here the glare from the infidel eyes was fierce and full of hate.

"The population numbers two hundred and fifty, and more than half the citizens live in caves in the rock. Dirt, degradation and savagery are Endor's specialty. We say no more about Magdala now. Endor heads the list.

"A spring trickles out of the rock in the gloomy recesses of the cavern, and we were thirsty. The citizens of Endor objected to our going in there. They do not mind dirt; they do not mind rags; they do not mind vermin; they do not mind barbarous ignorance and savagery; they do not mind a reasonable degree of starvation, but they do like to be pure and holy before their god, whoever he may be, and therefore they shudder and grow almost pale at the idea of Christian lips polluting a spring whose waters must descend into their sanctified gullets.

"We got away from the noisy wretches, finally, dropping them in squads and couples as we filed over the hills—the aged first, the infants next, the young girls further on; the strong men ran beside us a mile, and only left when they had secured the last possible piastre in the way of bucksheesh."

At the hotel that night Bruno is leafing through a rather smudged coffee table book of nineteenth-century paintings of Asia Minor. The scenes are idyllic: camels standing or kneeling, kindly camel-herds tending them, happy children laughing around the donkeys and unmasked straight-backed maids carrying water pots on their heads heading to and from the well. In the background well dressed and well fed Arabs are reclining and smoking narghiles, in the foreground goats and sheep graze on the luxuriant grasses. "A far cry from Mark Twain's view," Bruno says. "Hang on," I reply, remembering a particular passage from *The Innocents Abroad*. A few minutes later I hand him my equally smudged copy of the book and he reads aloud: "Here was a grand Oriental picture which I had worshiped a thousand times in soft, rich steel engravings! But in the engraving there was no desolation; no dirt; no rags; no fleas; no ugly features; no sore eyes; no feasting flies; no besotted ignorance in the countenances; no raw places on the donkeys' backs; no disagreeable jabbering in unknown tongues; no stench of camels; no suggestion that a couple of tons of powder placed under the party and touched off would heighten the effect and give to the scene a genuine interest and a charm which it would always be pleasant to recall, even though a man lived a thousand years. Oriental scenes look best in steel engravings. I cannot be imposed upon any more by that picture of the Queen of Sheba visiting Solomon. I shall say to myself, You look fine, Madam but your feet are not clean and you smell like a camel." And for the first time even the sullen Bruno laughs out loud. "Awesome."

Early next morning:

> I pulled into Nazareth, I was feelin' about half past dead;
> I just need some place where I can lay my head.
> "Hey, mister, can you tell me where a man might find a bed?"
> He just grinned and shook my hand, and "No!", was all he said.

Sorry about that, these old tunes keep coming into my head. When Jesus lived in Nazareth it was a tiny village, when Mark Twain visited Nazareth it was still a village but one now with a church and grottoes and a multitude of recent relics, and when we roll into Nazareth it is vibrant and most welcoming city of 75,000 people, at the last count. After our recent biblical wanderings Nazareth is so modern, its people so young, its traffic so blaring, its street so alive. We are rejuvenated by big city life as Bruno double parks and we scamper off to seek out the annunciation scene.

Mark Twain only spent a morning here and probably had to stretch that out. They saw the chapel "tricked out with tapestry hangings, silver lamps, and oil paintings" built over the spot where Mary was annunciated and were shown the recess from which the angel Gabriel stepped. But for Twain, if not for the New Pilgrims, it was all too reminiscent of the relic trade of Catholic continental Europe:

> These gifted Latin monks never do any thing by halves. They have got the "Grotto of the Annunciation" here; and just as convenient to it as one's throat is to his mouth, they have also the "Virgin's Kitchen", and even her sitting-room, where she and Joseph watched the infant Saviour play with Hebrew toys eighteen hundred years ago. All under one roof, and all clean, spacious, comfortable "grottoes". It seems curious that personages intimately connected with the Holy Family always lived in grottoes—in Nazareth, in Bethlehem, in imperial Ephesus—and yet nobody else in their day and generation thought of doing any thing of the kind.
>
> When the Virgin fled from Herod's wrath, she hid in a grotto in Bethlehem, and the same is there to this day. The slaughter of the innocents in Bethlehem was done in a grotto; the Saviour was born in a grotto—both are shown to pilgrims yet. It is exceedingly strange that these tremendous events all happened in grottoes—and exceedingly fortunate, likewise, because the strongest houses must crumble to ruin in time, but a grotto in the diving rock will last forever.
>
> It is an imposture—this grotto stuff—but it is one that all men ought to thank the Catholics for. If it had been left to Protestants to do this most worthy work, we would not even know where Jerusalem is today, and the man who could go and put his finger on Nazareth would be too wise for this world. The world owes the Catholics its good will even for the happy rascality of hewing out these bogus grottoes in the rock; for it is infinitely more satisfactory to look at a grotto, where people have faithfully believed for centuries that the Virgin once lived, than to have to imagine a dwelling place for her somewhere, any where, nowhere, loose and at large all over this town of Nazareth.

Today the Christian aspect of Nazareth disappoints for different reasons. It is hard to believe that the same Franciscan order that oversaw the wonderful basilica on top of Mount Tabor was also responsible for the hideous Basilica of the Annunciation that dominates the Nazarene skyline today. It is the largest church in Asia Minor, is built on one of Christianity's holiest shrines and yet somehow manages to have absolutely no spiritual bearing whatsoever.

Catholic communities from all four corners of the world contributed artwork with which to decorate the walls around the extended courtyard. All are indescribably puerile, the less puerile tacky, the less tacky politically correct, the less politically correct just plain bad. Inside the basilica is worse. The architect is clearly not a Christian, although that in itself is no restriction as long as he has some spiritual awareness—and this one has none. The whole point of a spiritual building is to maximize the space within its physical bounds thereby removing as far as possible the physical restrictions on what one hopes will be a transcendental experience. To have concrete girders fly by just above one's head rather negates the whole object of going to a spiritual building in the first place. I keep thinking I'm in Stuttgart airport and about to miss my flight.

Nazareth escaped the worst of the ethnic cleansing during and after the 1948 war because there were so many Christians as well as Muslim Arabs living there. The Israelis sensibly preferred not to have an international outcry about Christians being forced to flee and so the Muslim Arabs survived there. Nazareth is now Israel's largest Arab city.

And what a relief to be back in an Arab city! After marveling at Israel's achievements over the past two weeks, and coming to believe there is something superhuman about the Israeli endeavor and not being able to avoid being overwhelmed by what they have achieved—overachieved by any applicable standard—it was a relief to be back among the poetry and humor and *joie de vivre* and frail humanity of Arab street life. No Endors or endomorphs here! The pavements themselves seem animated with the fripperies of conversation, the air resounds to shouted emotions and faux-shock responses—and there are cats and dogs and shrieking birds and bad tempered taxis and scampering children and fluttering chickens, and all of this all at once.

I'm enthusing about the street scenes with Bruno over Turkish coffee (for Gillian and me) and Diet Sprite (for him). He is relentlessly unimpressed by all before him and can barely hide his disdain for what he sees: dirt and danger. Then he light-bulbs and asks: "OK, Ian, you are stuck on a desert island, shipwrecked, no way out. Who would you rather have with you: twelve Jews or twelve Arabs?"

A sip of Turkish coffee, then: "Interesting question. I'm assuming this desert island is a bit of a dump and I actually want to get off it. So, if I thought there was any chance at all, even the remotest, vaguest, the most intangible possibility I'd choose the twelve Jews. I'd know that somehow they'd figure a way of getting me off there. But if we're all stuck together on a desert island they'd have to lighten up a bit."

"That's a condition," says Bruno. "No conditions, just twelve random Jews or twelve random Muslims."

"And if the Jews there were any fun they wouldn't be the type who'd be able to get you off the desert island anyway," says Gillian.

"True," I reply. "Twelve earnest Jews it is. But let's say there was no hope of escape, that we were so far off planet that not even twelve Einsteins could conjure up a way out, then I'd rather go down with the Muslims. Leave it all to Insha'Allah and hope for alien assisted escape. But no Korans."

"No conditions, remember," says Bruno. "You could choose Christian Arabs."

"What if they're Maronites?" I reply. "No, I'll go down with the Muslims, Korans and all. There'll be poetry in our demise, laughter at our helplessness. We'd be charming to each other as one by one we perish. The others will be waiting hospitably in heaven* to welcome me. I'll feel at home with fellow chronic underachievers. I'll even give up my share of the virgins."

"So the answer is?" Bruno insists

"Stay clear of desert islands."

"No, seriously."

"OK, I'd take twelve Jews and tell them six are to be excused. Ditto the Arabs. The ones who stay can select the other ones to leave. I'd make the Jews an escape committee, surround them with books and kosher grub and leave them alone. Of the Arabs, three would have to be women who'd do all the work. The other three, the men, would play backgammon and smoke narghiles and drink coffee and discourse about life's injustices with me all day. We'd have the women bring the Jews whatever they wanted whenever they wanted it."

"But I'm a Jew," says Bruno, "and I know what would happen. Your six smart guys planning the escape would say it's easier for six to leave than

---

* Heaven goes by favor. If it went by merit, you would stay out and your dog would go in.
Mark Twain, a Biography

twelve, and anyway what have these bums done to deserve a free ride? That's how it would go."

"Yes, I suppose," I reply, "and I guess the Arabs would say it's all a Zionist plot to take over the island. They'll get us all into a boat and reckon that as the Koran hasn't told us if we are allowed to swim, let alone how to swim, they could just push us off and we'd all drown, and we would. Then they'll turn round and take over all the island."

"So there's no hope," says Gillian.

"No, none really," Bruno agrees.

6: The West Bank

We are more than unusually trepidatious about what lies ahead as we leave Israel and enter the West Bank. Bruno cannot accompany us (merciful gods, your pity is well placed!) as Israeli citizens cannot drive on many of the West Bank back roads. Instead he has been building straw dogs, hamming up the dangers with a little too much glee and some of it has stuck. Other Israelis have warned us that "it is outlaw country", "not like here at all", "do be careful" and "don't stop for anyone". As we drive up to the border area the Israeli side of the Galilean countryside seems to give off one last triumphant blast of luxuriance.

The famous barrier—the Apartheid Wall or the Security Fence, depending on which side of it you find yourself—seems a bit half-hearted at this crossing, and there's hardly any movement at all, in or out. To the right is an imposing concrete IDF barracks, complete with the usual turrets and watchtowers, liberally laced with razor wire and menace. Bruno drops us off with a final, cocky "take care over there" and we agree to meet at the Qualandia checkpoint just north of Jerusalem a week later.

"You are spending twice as long as Mark Twain in there," he says. This is true, but by then even the most enthusiastic Excursionist was keen to press on, put the desert and deprivation behind them and arrive at the mother lode, Jerusalem.

"I know, but there's something about a warzone that pulls me back to them," I reply. "Look, if it's too weird I'll give you a call. As the good Doctor said, "when the going gets weird, the weird turn pro." It's hardly as if we're going to Outer Mongolia."

"Ha, Outer Mongolia, you should be so lucky."

Outside the car is air is stagnantly hot and heavy—and rather bored.

All over Israel there are signs in three languages: Hebrew, English and Arabic, but here at the Wall/Fence there are none. We see an elegant Arabic

woman and her skipping children come out of a railed-off area and head for
a waiting Audi. Hats and shades on against the heat and glare we head for the
turnstiles under a raw concrete lintel stretching across the entry zone. Still
no signs, but one route turns *this* way only and the other route turns *that* way
only—but up close *that* way only has a concrete slab blocking it, so we take
Hobson's Choice and choose the one that turns *this* way only. The turnstiles
are thick and functional, heavily galvanized and heavily sprung. There is just
enough room in each turnstile quarter for one person; you have to put your
luggage in the quarter in front and push it through, or in the quarter behind
and pull it through. Gillian isn't strong enough—and she's hardly a weedy
weakling—to push against the turnstile and push herself and her bag through
in tandem, so I have to tango the turnstiles to take our mini caravanserai
through. With much scraping of bags and scuffling of shoes and cusses of
profanity we manage to pull and push our way through the first turnstile.

"That was tight," I say, "I wonder how a heifer gets through."

"There aren't any heifers," Gillian replies. This is true, we haven't seen one
obese person all the time we've been in Asia Minor. The philosophy of *Bella
Figura* is alive and well in the Middle East.

We shuffle forward to the next turnstile. Still no signs and no one around;
various cameras stare unfeelingly towards us. We repeat the ungainly exercise
of manhandling two Anglo-Saxons with their hand baggage and luggage
through the obstacle course.

"Weird," I say, "I presume those camera are working."

"I hope not, we must look a terrible sight by now." She's right, we must.

Five minutes later we are out of Israel and into the West Bank. We have
just passed through three turnstiles and seen no one. It is rather disappointing,
having prepared for an in-depth interview and been shown an open door, or
at least three open turnstiles and an obstacle course.

I look around for the promised white Chevrolet Nubira. Of course,
I grumble to Gillian, it isn't a Chevrolet at all but a horrible thing called
a Daewoo built in Korea. Some bright suit at GM thought they'd sell the
Chevrolet brand short on the off-chance of shifting some dodgy Daewoos.
She tells me not to be so obsessively, compulsively disordered, or something
like that.

The first car we see is in fact the Daewoo masquerading as a, oh never
mind. First person we see is our new Ferguson, Mr. Farki. I had contacted
a friend of a friend in the British Embassy in Amman, Jordan, and asked him
about a Palestinian driver and interpreter. He had suggested Mr. Farki, a fine

man used by the Brits whenever they need a driver. Mr. Farki and I had spent so much time haggling on the phone that it would have been cheaper to pay him what he wanted in the first place rather than to have to pay half as much to Vodafone as well.

As Bruno said, the New Pilgrims moved through the West Bank at a good pace and all we heard from Mark Twain about our first stop, Jenin, was that he arrived there late one evening, Saturday 21 September to be precise, and left early the next morning. We can see from contemporaneous prints that Jenin then was a tiny village of a mosque and a few shacks, but just before entering Jenin there is still standing a Greek Orthodox Church in the village of Birkin. Knowing the New Pilgrims' habits I imagine they would have stayed there, and Mr. Farki's first stop is Birkin. Like all good Greek Orthodox churches this one is locked; it is also clearly unused as is the village of Birkin. No sign of bomb damage; no sign of a plague; no sign of ethnic cleansing, just no sign of life. Mr. Farki reckons they've all up and left for Jenin.

I'm convinced this is where they camped. It's an old village so there must have been a well. It's on a main road—in fact the old trunk route from Damascus to Jerusalem. The church has decent grounds and they would have felt safe there. The curious, well quite curious, point about Birkin today is that somebody clearly looks after the church's grounds. All around is dust and decay, the flags on the church's poles are barely hanging by their last threads, the locked gates are down to the rust, yet the garden is kempt, the courtyard swept and the shrubs tended. Curious, but only quite so. Like the Excursionists, on we press.

Mr. Farki is about seventy, has worryingly thick glasses for a driver and wonderfully thick white hair for a seventy-year-old. In spite of his looks he isn't at all absent-minded and is as learned on matters Middle East as a professor. He always wears a waistcoat a size too big for his wiry frame. He speaks excellent English, thank heavens.

He grew up and qualified as a "financial supervisor" in Jordan and moved to Jerusalem when it was still part of Jordan and when Amman was still "very much the backwater". He was twenty-five; two years later Jordan was part of the losing team in the Six Day War; it lost Jerusalem and had the West Bank annexed. Unable to guide in Jerusalem he moved to Ramallah, the proxy capital of Palestine. He still has a Jordanian passport. Did he ever think of moving back to Jordan? Oh, he goes back every year to see his family but he prefers it here, intifadas and all—too many Palestinians in Jordan, he says with a straight face. And financial supervising? He shrugs, "That seems like a lifetime ago when all I wanted was money. Now I am a tour guide and Nosy Parker. Guiding is more enriching at my age." An Arab with irony; I can see we are going to get along.

Yes, and we are now on the outskirts to Jenin. No longer a one-mosque-and-three-shack village, Jenin is a bustling market and administrative town of a hundred thousand souls, half of whom seem to be pre-teen and laughing about it. The night before I had read that the West Bank has the highest reproduction rate of anywhere in the Arab world. Sometimes one sees a statistic and thinks "that's a damn lie", but here seems to be the proof.

Ah, and it's good to be back in an Arab traffic jam. The noise, the fumes, the blaring horns, the shouting drivers, the laughter, the feigned insults, the gestures. In Israel traffic is well ordered in a strangely Hunnish way. Each car has its solo driver, its windows up, its aircon on; the roads have painted lanes, to which the cars adhere. Verge-side flowers are planted and automatically irrigated. Coming in to Jenin we see each car packed with families yelling through open windows, the roads are covered in litter—whoops! there goes another Coke tin—and the sidewalks, well there are no sidewalks and if one does manage to appear it will soon have a car parked right across it. Near the center we see a skip, but it is so overloaded with rubble and rubbish that it would take an archaeologist to level it off. Later we find that rubble and rubbish are the West Bank motif. The whole chaotic scene is positively heaving with life—and the humor and futility that defines human endeavor; Mark Twain source material, in other words.

Nearly twenty miles ahead of us lay our second Excursionists' stop, what was then still known by its ancient Roman name of Samaria, but is now called Sebastia. The Excursionists "climbed a high hill to visit the city of Samaria from whence, no doubt, came also the celebrated Good Samaritan. Herod the Great is said to have made a magnificent city of this place, and a great number of coarse limestone columns, twenty feet high and two feet through, that are almost guiltless of architectural grace of shape and ornament, are pointed out by many authors as evidence of the fact. They would not have been considered handsome in ancient Greece, however."

Quite. One becomes rather blasé about Roman ruins and expects them to be in a state of at least imaginable repair, but preservation has not been too kind to poor old Samaria. Mark Twain wrote that "There was nothing for us to do in Samaria but buy handfuls of old Roman coins at a franc a dozen".

It is in the token souvenir shop that I find out what has happened. The man behind the counter is trying to sell me old Roman coins but at a little more than a franc a dozen. I wonder if they are the same coins that Mark Twain was offered. The seller speaks excellent English and is a seamless authority on his coins. "This one is from the time of Agrippa the First, but this one, now this is a Widow's Mite from the time of Jesus. I have a bigger Widow's Mite here, but it's older so less valuable." How valuable? "Eighty dollars. Three years ago it was worth sixty dollars; they are an excellent investment." Not as good an investment, I thought unkindly, as the little chap out the back knocking them up for you.

"I'm not interested in coins," I say, "but I am interested in you. You speak such good English. How come?"

He unburdens himself over Arabic coffee. I love the way there is always time to spare in Arabic cultures. He is Ibrahim Sharif, a Lebanese citizen. He worked in his uncle's hotel in London for twenty years. When the Israelis took over here in 1967 they made Samaria a proper Archaeological Park, and his sister-in-law, a young widow, already had a stall here. She was in the right place at the right time. With Ibrahim's help her coffee stall became a restaurant and souvenir shop. There were coach loads of tourists for twenty years. Then in the mid-1990s came the Oslo Accords and Israel had to give Samaria, now Sebastia, to the Palestinians. Not for the first time I hear that when an Arab inherits an Israeli project he destroys it and so it was with the Archaeological Park—but not so much destruction, I suggest to Ibrahim, as neglect, death by a thousand cuts.

Now the archaeological site is in a sorry state and becoming sorrier. Vandals have graffiti-sloganed the columns and one can see a process of archaeology in reverse: the dirt and dust are starting to reclaim the columns and capitals on the ground.

Some things have improved though; whereas Mark Twain noted that "The inhabitants of this camp are particularly vicious", one can have no such complaint today: apart from Ibrahim and his family there are no inhabitants. But there are inhabitants above: the new conquerors—the new Romans—the

Israelis, who have built a conspicuous settlement above Sebastia. Mark Twain finished with: "We were glad to leave this hot and dusty old village and hurry on." Again, quite so.

Twain's version of "hurrying on" bears no resemblance to how we can hurry on today. Already only a few miles into our West Bank journey we are amazed at the quality of the roads and the infrastructure. Everywhere one sees the presence of foreign aid: USAID in particular, but also "Funded by the European Union" signs along the highways with individual projects from Holland, Italy and Spain—and these are just the ones we have seen on the first morning.

Mr. Farki explains that the aid taps are turned on and off by the donors' reactions to events on the ground. After Oslo in the mid-1990s aid increased dramatically as part of the process. The intifadas turned it off again. Then Yasser Arafat died and the taps turned on again. Then the Palestinians voted in Hamas and the taps were off again. Then they managed to restrict Hamas to Gaza and now aid to the West Bank is on again.

"Mr. Farki, would it be fair to say the Palestinians have a marked tendency to shoot themselves in the feet? I mean intifadas, Arafat, Hamas, Black September, always saying no to any peace proposal. It all seems rather counter-productive."

"Yes, Lord Ian, but don't forget the Palestinians are poets. Truth is a higher ideal than compromise. Better to lose with honor than win with shame. That's one of the reasons I like living here."

"Fair enough. By the way, how about I stop calling you Mr. Farki and you stop calling me Lord Ian?"

"What would you call me?" he asks.

"What is you first name?"

"You would not be able to say it, so Farki is easier."

"Well I could try, what is it?

"Hudhaifah al Din." A pause. "Lord Ian."

"As your prefer, Mr. Farki."

Zooming along the shiny new USAID road, with fertile agriculture all around and a large irrigation project being built by "the Friends of Palestine, Brazil", we reach Mark Twain's next stop, Nablus, in only half an hour. It would have been twenty-five minutes but Mr. Farki has a rather disconcerting habit of stopping in the middle of nowhere and whisking a well-used purple patterned prayer rug out of the trunk and performing his prayers by the side of the road. He's not alone in that regard.

Nablus, often but not always known as Shechem in Twain's time, was famous then for two reasons: it was—still is—the holy mountain of the Samaritan sect and the site of Jacob's Well. Now we must add a third reason; opposite Jacob's Well is the Palestinian refugee camp of Balata, run by the United Nations Relief and Works Agency (UNRWA), the largest single UN activity in the world.

The Samaritans held a particular fascination for Mark Twain: "I found myself gazing at any straggling scion of this strange race with a riveted fascination, just as one would stare at a living mastodon, or a megatherium that had moved in the grey dawn of creation and seen the wonders of that mysterious world that was before the flood."

The Samaritans follow an older religion than Judaism, and believe that their Torah was given directly by Abraham rather than a later, sanitized version—as they see it—given by Moses to the nomadic "Tribes of Israel". Their rules of religious and secular behavior are even more esoteric than those of ultraorthodox Judaism, or as Mark Twain wrote: "For thousands of years this clan have dwelt in Shechem under strict tabu, and having little commerce or fellowship with their fellow men of any religion or nationality."

The Samaritans today are just about clinging on: "This sad, proud remnant of a once mighty community still hold themselves aloof from all the world; they still live as their fathers lived, labor as their fathers labored, think as they did, feel as they did, worship in the same place, in sight of the same landmarks, and in the same quaint, patriarchal way their ancestors did more than thirty centuries ago"

Mark Twain was clearly suspicious about some of their claims: "Carefully preserved among the sacred archives of this curious community is a MSS. copy of the ancient Jewish law, which is said to be the oldest document on earth. It is written on vellum, and is some four or five thousand years old. Nothing but bucksheesh can purchase a sight. Speaking of this MSS. reminds me that I procured from the high priest of this ancient Samaritan community, at great expense, a secret document of still higher antiquity and far more extraordinary interest, which I propose to publish as soon as I have finished translating it."

Half of the only six hundred Samaritans remaining can be found in two villages on the foothills of Mount Gerizim, their sacred mountain, just outside Nablus. With their white robes and red fezzes the men make a numinous sight. Of the women there is no sign. Within the last generation their religious leaders, all hereditary, have countered the interbreeding problem by relaxing the rules on marriage for husbands but few modern Jewish women are willing to go through the degrading menstruation tabus* and childbirth stigmas, amongst many other humiliations, that are part of the Talibanesque Samaritan culture. It reminds one of how ghastly it must have been for women at the time of the invention of any of the patriarchal Abrahamic religions.

Recent internet-derived brides have come from Egypt, Ukraine and China; one wonders how the ad is worded. Maybe something like:

* WANTED: BRIDES FOR EXOTIC HOLY MOUNTAIN SECT.
* PRE-HISTORY ENTHUSIAST PREFERRED.
* ONLY SIX-MONTH TRIAL PERIOD BEFORE ACCEPTANCE INTO SECT.
*KNOWLEDGE OF LEVITICUS USEFUL BUT NOT ESSENTIAL.
* IDEAL POSITION FOR AGORAPHOBICS, TRAPPISTS OR MASOCHISTS.
* WE WELCOME REFORMED PRISON REFORMERS AND THOSE RESEARCHING
CAVE-DWELLING AND SLAVERY.
* NSOH RECOMMENDED. (PLEASE NOTE BRIDES WILL NOT BE ALLOWED IN
THE SYNAGOGUE OR TO TAKE PART IN ANY COMMUNITY BASED ACTIVITIES.
IF THEY LEAVE THEY WILL BE SENTENCED TO DEATH BY STONING.)

The husbands must still be hereditary Samaritans. The animal sacrifices remain, in accordance with Abrahamic ritual, and are now held off-camera to avoid Israeli activists who view pretty much all aspects of Samaritan culture as inhumane to man—which means to woman—and beast.

Jacob's Well can be dismissed, now as then, as a gimmicky hole in the ground; then "as a parcel of ground bought for a hundred pieces of silver", now as a bait for the gullible waiting for the rattling money tray of a Greek Orthodox impostor. But as one comes out a few shekels lighter one sees across the road the Balata Refugee Camp.

---

* The tabu was the most ingenious and effective of all the inventions that has ever been devised for keeping a people's privileges satisfactorily restricted. *Following the Equator*

One's image of a refugee camp is of rows of tents housing the victims of what one hopes is a temporary refugee crisis: Darfur, for example, or Haiti after the earthquake. Balata is a permanent fixture, now sixty years old, of concrete apartments and tarred roads, streetlights and wheelie bins: it is a suburb of Nablus, although there is nothing suburban about it. There's too much aid pouring in for it to be a slum, physically, but mentally it is very much a slum. Much against Mr. Farki's better judgment we walk through Balata, and in a low voice he gives me a running commentary: "the heaviest population in Arabia, about thirty thousand people, also, they say, the densest population of Israeli spies. In the first intifada the Israelis were caught by surprise, in the second they knew exactly which houses were making the rockets and blew them up. Didn't even wait for the bulldozers. More free money pouring in here than anywhere in Palestine, and that means anywhere else on earth. Look, UN everywhere, MSF, WHO, this-aid, that-aid spending money here everywhere. Best education, best health in the West Bank. Thirty thousand people live here, nearly all born here. Would you leave? It's a holiday camp not a refugee camp."

Well that seems a bit harsh. Certainly the evidence of aid is everywhere and it's easy to see Balata as a hotbed of victimhood—the sort of self-perpetuating cycle of dependency where the NGOs need the victims as much as the victims need the NGOs. The aid figures are indeed quite staggering: US$1.25 billion a year is being shoveled into Palestine as a whole for the benefit of four million people—and proportionately four times of that amount per person in the UN refugee camps. But there is real anger here too, even if self-defeating anger: posters of Yasser Arafat posing with Saddam Hussein (Arafat supported Iraq's invasion of Kuwait, among his many other great judgment calls), endless graffiti, Hamas, Hezbollah and Iranian ayatollah posters, listless youths loitering menacingly around. Menace is in the air; the youths cannot tell if we are Israeli rubberneckers or part of a new NGO and so, rather reluctantly, stand aside as we walk past.

We come across a proper organized tour: a dozen young idealists—I tell the tutting Mr. Farki there's no point in being young if you are not an idealist—from northern Europe. How do I know where they are from? I tell a disbelieving Mr. Farki that I know because they are wearing cotton not polysomething and so aren't American. He says he will remember that piece of useless information—and he will. They are being shown around by a young tall Palestinian tour leader wearing fatigues and a red keffiyeh. It's the Yasser Arafat look but without the gun. Mr. Farki says there'll be a gun somewhere on him—they're all armed, bored and armed. There are few cars but endless aid vehicles. Mr. Farki would have the whole farrago closed down tomorrow, and by tour's end he wasn't talking so softy. Time to move on.

Half way to the caravanserai's next camp, then known as Lubia but now called al-Lubban al-Sharqi, we pull over into a new roadside diner. Hannibal, Missouri in the Occupied Territories. After another prayer break and over coffee I ask Mr. Farki what is to become of the Balata refugees. He agrees that the brighter ones move out as soon as they can but they are still stuck in Palestine. The Arabs countries around have always talked up the Palestinian cause while ignoring it completely when the time comes to keep the promises. Jordan, the post-1948 occupying power, already has a Palestinian majority, and the Hashemite ruling minority emphatically don't want any more. Egypt refuses to have anything to do with the Palestinians in Gaza, although they have at least a moral responsibility for their predicament and could easily absorb them. Lebanon already has three million Palestinians and has such a delicate political and religious balance that it does not even allow them citizenship or the right to vote. Syria, while happy to arm them through Hezbollah in Lebanon, refuses any Palestinian refugees even though they have space enough to accommodate them. Israel certainly won't have them. The sad fact is that from 1922 when the British Mandate first mooted Palestine as a possible country—and there had been no mention of it as such at all up till then—the elusive country's Arab neighbors have at best let down and at worst betrayed their Palestinian Arab brothers at every turn.

As we turn off the new road and head a quarter of a mile up the dirt track to al-Lubban I pull some sheets of paper out of my portfolio and read them to Mr. Farki.

"This first is from Mark Twain, dated 22 September 1867. 'We got so far ahead of the tents that we had to camp in an Arab village, and sleep on the ground. We could have slept in the largest of the houses; but there were some little drawbacks: it was populous with vermin, it had a dirt floor, it was in no respect cleanly, and there was a family of goats in the only bedroom, and two donkeys in the parlor. Outside there were no inconveniences, except that the dusky, ragged, earnest eyed villagers of both sexes and all ages grouped themselves on their haunches all around us, and discussed us and criticized us with noisy tongues till midnight. We did not mind the noise, being tired, but, doubtless, the reader is aware that it is almost an impossible thing to go to sleep when you know that people are looking at you.'

"And in his notes he wrote that 'Slept on the ground in front of an Arab house. Lice, fleas, horses, jackasses, chickens and, worse than all, Arabs for company all night.' Sorry about that last bit Mr. Farki."

"Don't worry," he laughs, "I'm used to it by now. Typical American journalist. Sorry about that last bit, Lord Ian."

"*Touché, mon brave, touché.* Now Mr. Farki, what do we make of this? From *Al-Jazeerah*, no less. Dated 6 May 2010. It reads: "Illegal Israeli Settlers Torch Mosque South of Nablus":

> A group of illegal Israeli settlers entered the mosque at Al-Lubban Al-Sharqiya, gathered flammables, and set them alight in the early hours of Tuesday morning. Head of the local council of Al-Lubban Jamal Daraghma said residents living adjacent to the mosque heard cars approaching the building at 3 a.m. Residents said the group tore curtains from the walls and threw several copies of the Qur'an into a pile on the mosque floor and set it aflame.

> The village is surrounded by three illegal Israeli settlements; Eli, Shilo, and Ma'ale Levona, built on Palestinian lands and the abutting illegal communities consumed more than 30 percent of the village lands, confiscated to build the settlements.

> The Israeli Tel Aviv daily *Yedioth Ahronoth* quoted the mosque's imam as saying that residents were waiting for the investigation of the Palestinian police but noted the history of settler antagonism in the village.

"It happens all the time," says Mr. Farki. "Not usually mosques, but orchards and groves. The settlers will never have enough until it is all theirs."

I pull out another cutting from the same *Yedioth Ahronoth*: "Palestinian president Mahmud Abbas on Tuesday blamed hardline Jewish settlers for a fire that gutted a West Bank mosque, saying it threatened US-brokered efforts to revive the peace process... 'President Abbas condemns the burning of the mosque in Lubban ash-Sharqiya by extremist settlers and said the responsibility for this criminal attack lies with the Israeli government because the Israeli army protects the settlers,' his office said in a statement."

By now we are in the center of the village and easily find the mosque by finding the minaret. It is still covered with rudimentary scaffolding and most of the repairs appear to be complete. Mr. Farki leads me to a group of workers, and one of them takes us to a half open door across the street. Inside are two other men. Greetings all round. As the eyes adjust to the darkness it seems we are in a barbershop. Only Mr. Farki speaks English and he's busy speaking Arabic and soon voices are raised in the Arabic way: all friendly enough, I've learned it's just the way they talk to each other.

In the corner a tiny raised TV is blaring out a daytime soap opera. None of the women on screen are wearing headscarves and most of them are crying. The men on the TV are shouting at each just as loudly as they are in the barbershop. Mr. Farki sees me looking at the images and tut-tuts "Abu Dhabi" before rejoining the decibels. From the street a young boy arrives with tea. A few minutes later he returns with four brown paper bags. Soon we are all scooping up hummus, mtabbal and falafel with pita breads. No one seems to draw breath, even in mid-mouthful. I am reflecting: amazing really, here we are, a Jordanian and two Brits, one even a woman, turn up unannounced in this tiny village in nowhere-in-particular, find a random local, he brings us to meet more random locals and in no time we are all eating together like long lost friends. Mr. Farki stands up, taps his watch and says we should go. "Don't tell them where we are going next," he says rather unnecessarily. "As if..." I reply.

In the car juddering back down along the dirt track I ask him what all that was about.

"Israeli settlers," he says, "taking over the olive groves. They come in the night and cut down the trees. Some of the trees are hundreds of years old. Then their militia prevent the farmers going there. The farmers have lost heart anyway. It's their families' land going back to Turkish times. It's so sad they cannot bear to look."

"Militia?"

"Yes, unofficial of course. Each settlement has a militia to police itself and keep the Palestinians out. The militia go on raids together. If you see a white four-door pick-up truck with Israeli plates it will be militia."

"But why? Why cut down the trees? Isn't a bit self-defeating?"

"It's an old Ottoman law dating from empire days. If the land is not used for three years the owner loses it. The Turks wanted the farmers to grow crops so they could raise taxes. Now Israeli settlers cut down the trees so the owner cannot use the land, then they fence it to stop him going there. If he tries, they punish the village. That's what the mosque fire was all about. That's what they were telling me."

"A punishment?"

"Yes, the settlers bulldozed two fields and fenced them but did not patrol them. Then they discovered the villagers had cut through the fence and planted some citrus crops, just so the land was used. Some of the olive trees the Israelis tore down were five hundred years old. As punishment they set fire to the village mosque."

"Who are they?"

"The biblical fundamentalists. The militia. They are the same."

"And the police?"

Mr. Farki just gives a short laugh and shakes his head. "There is no justice here. We say Wild West not West Bank. The Orthodox Jews just wear these people down. You've seen them, they are simple folk. The Jews just push, push, push. They know there is no law. There is no one to stop them."

It's only a short drive to our next stop, the archaeological site of Shilo, but we cannot drive all the way there. Politics again. The site is now part of the Shilo settlement and as such off limits to Mr. Farki and his would-be Chevrolet. I say that I thought he had a Jordanian passport; he says he does, but the problem is the car—it has white Palestinian number plates, and only cars with yellow Israeli number plates are allowed anywhere near, let alone in, a settlement. He drops me a few hundred yards from the entrance, tells me they will have been watching him stop and us get out. We agree he'll go back to see his new friends at al-Lubban and I'll call him to pick us up here when I've had a look at what Mark Twain saw.

What Mark Twain saw was: "About daylight we passed Shiloh, where the Ark of the Covenant rested three hundred years, and at whose gates good old Eli fell down and 'brake his neck' when the messenger, riding hard from the battle, told him of the defeat of his people, the death of his sons, and, more than all, the capture of Israel's pride, her hope, her refuge, the ancient Ark her forefathers brought with them out of Egypt. It is little wonder that under circumstances like these he fell down and brake his neck. But Shiloh had no charms for us."

Apart from the unpleasantness on arrival, the archaeological site is a wonder to behold, and not the pile of rubble and rubbish that Mark Twain saw. At the Visitor's Center one is given coffee and cakes and invited to watch a video. The twenty-minute video explains the biblical rather than actual version of events. The storyline is that in 1165 BC the Ark of the Covenant was buried here until it was lost in a fire three hundred and sixty-nine years later. The visitors are then invited to follow a tour around the site.

Dozens of young Judaic enthusiasts from around the world are digging their summer holidays away as they have been here these last forty years. Vast inroads have been made into the ground. Everywhere one sees sifters sifting and diggers digging while supervisors supervise. Flow charts and clipboards and cameras and tripods abound. After fifty years they still haven't found any evidence that the Ark was ever there or that there had even been a fire which finished its spell there. I ask a young sifter where she is from. New York. Has she, have they, after all this ferreting around found anything, Ark-wise, fire-wise? No, but we will.

Sorry, but highly unlikely. It seems churlish to point out to one so young and bright and bushy tailed but biblical scholars have now placed the traditional version of the ten commandments*—and we saw on the road to Damascus that there are three other versions spanning hundreds of years—as coming from several hundred years after Moses had his one-to-one with his God. Moses' chances of actually putting them in an Ark would appear to be a somewhat fanciful; almost as fanciful as the one-to-one with his exclusive god actually happening in the first place, and almost as fanciful again as him blatantly ignoring his god's own second commandment when describing said ark.

Of course it's a myth, and nothing wrong with that; everything right with that. The Bible** frequently uses the Ark motif to indentify divine emotions which cannot be explained any other way. What has always intrigued mythologists most about the Ark is why it suddenly just disappeared from Judaic folklore. It was last seen in Solomon's Temple and after that it is not mentioned at all—curious considering its pivotal function prior to that. The Ethiopian Jewish tradition has it that one of Solomon's sons and the Queen of Sheba brought it there. The Book of Revelations suggests it is in the Temple of God in Heaven in a vision. The South Africans, Zimbabweans, Yemenis and Irish all claim they have it, while the Knights Templar swear they took it to Languedoc in France. A stately home in Warwickshire in England is also thought to be a possibility. I can hear Mark Twain laying claim to it now: price of entry a

---

* Of the 417 commandments, only a single one of the 417 has found ministerial obedience; multiply and replenish the earth. To it sinner & saint, scholar & ignoramus, Christian & savage are alike loyal. *Notebook, 1893*

** The Bible is a drug store. Its contents remain the same; but the medical practice changes. The world has corrected the Bible. The church never corrects it; and also never fails to drop in at the tail of the procession and take the credit of the correction. *Europe and Elsewhere*

dollar, first prize one viewing, second prize two viewings. Roll up! Roll up!

At the top of the archaeological site is a covered viewing platform. It has a commanding view of the countryside around. The new highway, busy with traffic, snakes through the valley below. They land is green and fertile. On every hilltop is a village. I dig out the map to check where we are, and where al-Lubban is. Then the names on the map ring a bell from the *Al-Jazeerah* article: Eli, Shilo, and Ma'ale Levona. These are the villages on the hilltops, settlements all, that sacked the mosque.

There is no issue so divisive in Israel and no issue so detested in Palestine as the settlements. For liberal Israelis the settlements are an affront on any number of levels. For secular Israelis they are highly subsidized stumbling block to any peace deal. For poorer Israelis they are a massively expensive waste of welfare resources. For financial Israelis the heavily discounted mortgages are a source of constant foreboding.

For biblical Israelis, like the settlers in Shilo, there is ample biblical justification not just for establishing themselves on the lands of Judea and Samaria but also for driving the unbelievers out. In fact, Shilo is a good example of the process. After the 1967 Six Day War the Defense Secretary, Moshe Dayan, declared: "We have returned to the hills, to the cradle of our people's history, to the land of the patriarchs, the land of the Judges and the stronghold of the Kingdom of the House of David. We have returned to Hebron [the site of the tombs of the patriarchs Abraham, Isaac and Jacob, and their wives, and King David's first capital] and Shechem [where Abraham had erected an altar and where Joseph was buried], to Bethlehem [King David's birthplace] and Anatot [Jeremiah's birthplace], to Jericho [as conquered by the Israelites as they entered Canaan under Joshua] and the fords of the Jordan at the city of Adam." He didn't need to mention the other, more poignant conquest: East Jerusalem with the Old City at its center, David's second capital and the site of the First and Second Temples and the capital of the Jews for a thousand years before Christ.

Shilo-ites didn't need reminding or prompting. Sponsored by Gush Emunim, a messianic Judaic organization that believes that as a result of the Six Day War the Jews had unwittingly delivered to themselves the speedy delivery of the long awaited second messiah, they set about settling. All they had to do is meet their god halfway: occupy and build on the land promised to the "children of Israel" in the Hebrew Bible and their god will speed up the messiah process.

You cannot fault their gusto. After Dayan they were told by Ariel Sharon, speaking on Israel Radio, that: "This land is ours; God gave us the title deeds. Grab more hills, expand the territory. Everything that's grabbed will be in our hands. Everything we don't grab will be in their hands." They were only obeying orders (Dayan and Sharon have some form together: in the 1953 Qibya massacre Dayan told Sharon to "blow up some outbuildings and get out". In his autobiography Sharon writes: "The orders were clear. Qibya was to be a lesson. I was to inflict as many casualties as I could." He subsequently massacred sixty-nine Palestinians in their houses.)

I am so close to the settlement at the archaeological site I just have to have a nose around.

"Can we wander up the settlement?" I ask a wonderfully wholesome girl with sparkling blue eyes. Her badge calls her Sophia.

"And can I take photographs?" asks Gillian.

"Of the village, yeah, sure," she says in an East Coast accent. "We got nothing to hide. Wait. Mum!"

"Yeah!" It's mum out the back.

"You going up?"

"Yeah. Five."

"Give these guys a ride!", then to me: "that's my mom, Nancy, it's a hike up there in this heat. I guess you'll want to see the new synagogue? They're coming from all over."

"Well, yes, and just a look around, you know. Have you been here long?"

"I was born here. 1990. My parents came in, like, 1974. They're from New York."

"Oh really, I know it very well. Whereabouts?"

"Brooklyn. Not sure exactly where."

"Well, well, I was there only a few months ago. I'm working on a project that started in a church in Brooklyn Heights. Have you heard of Mark Twain?"

"Oh yeah, he's really cool. He, like, hated this place. Don't blame him back then. Now the Arabs hate *us*. They are taught to hate us. It's so sad."

"Could be the land. Taking their land."

"Oh, this is our land. It's in Judges. And Joshua and Samuel," she says cheerily. "Here's mum."

Mum is indeed Nancy and we clamber into her old Suzuki Vitara. "Sophia says you're from Brooklyn."

"It's Soph-eye-ah, and yes we *were*. Now we're from here."

She came here as part of an archaeological dig in 1974, her husband connected with his biblical brothers ("we are all children of Israel after all"), and he stayed. She followed him two years later. She's not a woman of many words; brusque and bigoted, with no subtext, no grace, no subtleties, nothing in between the lines. She drops us at the new synagogue. "There are four other synagogues in Shilo, mikvas for men and women."

"Wow!" I say insincerely. "And for how many folk?"

"We got two thousand in the village."

"Sounds more than a village."

"Six births per household. That's the average. We got four."

"And do you get paid per birth?"

"Oh yeah. OK?" she gestures us to leave.

I take a look around the new synagogue but I'm afraid to say they don't mean much to me. We passed a shop half way to here and I drift down for an ice cream or something cold and to have a nosey. The social hierarchies of an American suburb are maintained: mobile homes at the lower level, detached one- or two-bedroom houses at mid level and on the hilltop three- or four-bedroom houses. Each house and garden is as prim and proper as one would expect; only the cars are older and shabbier than you would expect. I notice that each drive has a pile of wheels and tires and that the cars are bashed about and pockmarked.

Outside the shop, resting in the shade, an older man is sitting watching the world go by. We fall into conversation. Lionel came here six years ago, brought by his three children and in-laws already living here as he was alone and it was easier all round to have him nearby. Rather than where? Chicago, Highland Park. He lives in one of the mobile homes at the lower level. How is it? Not bad, not home, best thing is his grandchildren. How many? Fifteen—and countin'.

"So what you doing? We don't get many foreigners up here."

I tell him.

"Syria, Lebanon? I ain't been anywhere since I got here. There's a bus to Jerusalem. Been there once or twice. Where you staying?"

"In Ramallah. Twenty miles away. Capital of Palestine now, they say. You've been there I guess?"

"Nope. We don't go there. They don't come here. We reckon they'll stone us or kidnap us if we go to an Arab town."

I think back to Balata only twenty miles the other way. It's hard to imagine Shilo and Balata are even on the same planet—or rather that their mentalities are on the same planet. A beaten-up old Subaru drives past. The driver waves, Lionel waves back. "That's Miriam, she runs the dry cleaner. Everyone knows everyone."

I ask about the cars, like that old Subaru, all dents and pockmarks—and about the spare wheels and tires.

Lionel laughs, and says "I shouldn't really laugh. The local Arab kids sprinkle down tacks and nails at night. To give us flats. Down at the entrance, they don't dare come in. Every morning there's a sweep-up rota before the six a.m. bus to Jerusalem. That's bullet proof, the bus, you know. The rota man sweeps up the tacks, but sometimes one or two don't get picked up and folk get flats. Once in a while they organize a spare tire run into Jerusalem."

"And the dents? Looks like hail stones."

"Oh, that'll be the catapults. They're getting pretty good. Use ball bearings mostly. Sometimes they break a window, mostly not. You get used to it." Another car drives up, an old Toyota Corolla. "That'll be my ride," says Lionel.

Gillian joins me under the tree to see off the afternoon heat. Random scribbles from my notebook that afternoon: Chevy (real) truck w/bumper sticker "The Bible says it—I read it—that settles it". Stocky Orth w/automatic across his back. Sounds of babies thru open windows. All wear relig clothes—not all full h/bangers. So relig, irrelig hatred of Arabs, not unlike t/Christians w/Muslims in Leb. Hitchhiking around sett t/norm—everyone stops. Ad for local elections. Buses to Jer. + TA via other setts. Setts like mini-Israel. Old joke: Jews like everyone else only more so—so setts like Israel only more so? Construction sites around, no freeze ref Jer Post piece? Every boy curls hair, girls long skirts. Susp looks from every passer. No recycling. No solar or roof water tanks. Odd as all else so mod?

It's time to go, time to call up Mr. Farki. A second after realizing that I have left my mobile phone in his car console I remember he cannot come and collect me anyway. We walk back towards the synagogue in the hope of passing Nancy's car—and so finding her house—and seeing if I can call from there. No need—after half a minute a white four-door pick-up truck pulls up. A darker man, about thirty, asks what we are doing.

I explain. He laughs and says in the settlements they have the highest percentage of mobile phones per person in the world. Why so? Because we always keep one free and use it just for emergences. I call Mr. Farki on his non-emergency phone and we agree to meet at the entrance in ten minutes.

"Wait," says my new friend, "I better clear it. Jump in I'll take you there." He makes a call on a VHF ICOM radio identical to the one on *Vasco da Gama*. I see he uses Channel 67, which sailors use for the coastguard. He talks in Hebrew to another man then says to me: "What car and color is it?"

"It's a white Daewoo with Chevrolet written on it."

"So is it a Chevrolet or a Dae-woo?"

"Daewoo. Either, both, neither. Chevrolet. White."

"It's a white Chevrolet," says Gillian patiently.

In a couple of minutes we are at the entrance. Another truck is already there and they talk to each other on the radio again. My new friend says we can wait in the other truck till the Arab arrives. My Arab arrives a few moments later; I've never been so pleased to see an Arab in my life.

"Where next Twain effendi?" says Mr. Farki.

"A bar," replies Twain effendi.

Actually we head back to the Grand Park Hotel in Ramallah, shower and change and then repair to the bar there for a debrief.

There are about half a million Israelis living in over one hundred and twenty official settlements, mostly in the West Bank but also in the Golan Heights and East Jerusalem. Some are just military outposts, others proper cities of between thirty to fifty thousand people. There is supposed to be a halt on new settlements and a freeze on expanding existing ones, and it's clear to see that the latter restriction is being blatantly ignored. It seems, coincidentally or not, that the settlements have been established on the Starbucks cluster principle. The consensus is that about half the settlers are biblically inspired, as at Shilo, and that half are financially inspired by the offer of cheap housing and generous subsidies. As a generalization it is deemed that the former are predominantly ex-American, the latter ex-Russian, and that opposition to the whole idea is predominantly ex-European; as the media here implies, a gener-alization, but one derived from facts on the ground.

Everyone agrees that as has already happened in the Sinai and Gaza when— if—there is ever a peace agreement, most of the settlements will have to become part of the new state of Palestine. In Gaza the operation to pull the settlers out provoked a storm of protest from the religious-right but enough of them were mollified by an average compensation of $250,000 that they eventually left peacefully. It also has to be said that most of the settlers in Gaza were financially rather than biblically motivated, and the West Bank settlers won't be so open to open checks. The Israeli media suggests that pretty much all of the ex-Gaza settlers then re-settled in the West Bank knowing there would be cheap housing in the short term and the prospect of a further payout down the road.

Mr. Farki says that while from an Arab view the settlements are humiliat-ing and provocative, from a Muslim view there is some sympathy for the idea of fulfilling ancient prophecies, even if they are Toranic and not Koranic. What irritates the Arabs most is the feeling that their noses are being rubbed in the dirt, that the humiliation and provocation of the Wall and the settlements are not done by uncaring invaders who know no better, as would have been the case with the Ottomans, but as a deliberate policy either by a right-wing religious coalition with a land grab agenda or by a left-wing coalition that can only be held together by pandering to the biblical fundamentalists.

The region's problems unresolved, we set off the next morning for Bethel and Jerusalem. On the way we pass a shiny new compound with soldiers at the gate. Alongside it is a flattened building. Mr. Farki says that is Yasser Arafat's mausoleum and the pile of rubble is his old HQ which the Israelis kindly flattened for him.

We compare notes about Yasser Arafat. The old terrorist never made the leap to statesman when he had the chance offered to him on a plate. In fact he threw the food off the plate at every opportunity. He did succeed in amassing a personal fortune of $300 million—the IMF reckons total embezzlement over his lifetime was $900 million, while *Forbes* magazine had him down as the sixth richest despot in the world. We see this as pretty disgusting, but Mr. Farki points out that many Arabs think "well done!", that you'd be a fool not to steal all that money if you had the chance.

≈≈≈

Bethel has now become the rabbi-ridden settlement of Beit El, twice the size of Shilo and no doubt just as sanctimonious. In Mark Twain's time it was "a shapeless mass of ruins, which still bears the name of Bethel. It was here that Jacob lay down and had that superb vision of angels flitting up and down a ladder that reached from the clouds to earth, and caught glimpses of their blessed home through the open gates of Heaven.

"The pilgrims took what was left of the hallowed ruin, and we pressed on toward the goal of our crusade, renowned Jerusalem."

But there was rough riding ahead:

The further we went the hotter the sun got, and the more rocky and bare, repulsive and dreary the landscape became. There could not have been more fragments of stone strewn broadcast over this part of the world, if every ten square feet of the land had been occupied by a separate and distinct stonecutter's establishment for an age. There was hardly a tree or a shrub any where. Even the olive and the cactus, those fast friends of a worthless soil, had almost deserted the country. No landscape exists that is more tiresome to the eye than that which bounds the approaches to Jerusalem. The only difference between the roads and the surrounding country, perhaps, is that there are rather more rocks in the roads than in the surrounding country.

(Ten years earlier Herman Melville had made the same journey. He wrote: "Judea is just one accumulation of stones—stony mountains & stony plains; stony torrents & stony roads; stony walls & stony fields; stony houses & stony tombs; stony eyes & stony hearts.")

The road up to Jerusalem now is concreted, as are the buildings that line it for the last ten miles. Two of Mark Twain's memories live well today: the "fragments of stone" and the "tiresome" and monotonous landscape. Rubble and rubbish is the defining motif of Palestine. There seems to be no concept of finishing a construction and then clearing up afterwards. Even brand new hotels are surrounded by rubble and rubbish. No wonder one recalls the images of Palestinian youths throwing rocks at Israeli forces; they did not have to bring their ammunition with them, just to bend down and the arsenal is to hand. Twain's other observation on the landscape near Jerusalem is also apt today, although whereas he saw scrubland desolation, rubble and rubbish we see concrete desolation, rubble and rubbish. At least he was spared the swerving, blaring, darting, incessant traffic. Now it is tiresome not just to the eye, but to the nerves as well.

Two hours later the Excursionists had arrived! "At last, away in the middle of the day, ancient bite bits of wall and crumbling arches began to line the way—we toiled up one more hill, and every pilgrim and every sinner swung his hat on high! Jerusalem!

"Perched on its eternal hills, white and domed and solid, massed together and hooped with high gray walls, the venerable city gleamed in the sun. So small! Why, it was no larger than an American village of four thousand inhabitants, and no larger than an ordinary Syrian city of thirty thousand. Jerusalem numbers only fourteen thousand people."

Our entrance to the eternal city is somewhat less joyous; in fact, we are the cause of a mini-riot at the Wall/Fence. The traffic leading up to the wall starts several hundred yards from it. When he can drive no further we say our sad goodbyes to the redoubtable Mr. Farki and set off on foot towards the wall. This still being Palestine there are no pavements, just roadside rubble and rubbish, so we walk and wheel our luggage squeezed in alongside the stationary traffic. It is stiflingly hot, made worse by the lack of shade and the heat and fumes from the cars and vans. There are no signs so we just follow the jam, then suddenly, fifty yards before the first checkpoint one lane becomes three and the cars rush into their new positions. An old van catches the end of his fender around my luggage strap and accelerates away dragging the bag behind him. I shout "Stop! Stop!" and the bored drivers respond to the sudden excitement by a mass blowing of horns. Suddenly the scene changes from routine resignation to furious maelstrom. As I catch up with the van the Israeli loudspeakers crack into life with shouted instructions—in Hebrew—and two soldiers rush forward with automatics pointing straight at me. They are shouting and pointing, so I shout back in English but this makes them even more jumpy. I am hoping they've got their safeties on as they seem somewhat over-agitated. The soldiers and loudspeakers and guns are enough to cow the drivers back into silence. One driver gingerly winds down his window and tells us to go through an unmarked barrier to our left just outside the car zone.

We walk away wth our tails between our legs and repeat in reverse the galvanized turnstile routine we went through at Janin. Incredibly the whole process is still done entirely by camera—inhuman on at least two levels. Emerging the other side of the Wall/Fence we see Jerusalem up close and personal, and like Mark Twain before us feel we have reached a holy grail—of some description.

7: Jerusalem

A chap needs a bit of luck every now and then. Mine came in a double dose. I was rather dreading having Bruno be our Ferguson again, especially in Jerusalem where a properly trained guide is essential. Two days ago I had received an email from him saying the IDF had messed up his conscription relay and he had to go training with his unit somewhere near Haifa. Very sorry, etc. Then yesterday another email, this one from his father, Prof. Fornaciari—who is also our biblical bouncing board—saying he had just heard about Bruno messing us about. Very sorry, etc. Did we want him to find a replacement? And did we want to use Bruno's now vacant room in his attic? The answers were no thanks and yes please.

Mark Twain makes no mention of visiting the American Consul in Jerusalem, Dr. Hedley J. Smith, but I would be surprised if he had not done so. Until the internet it was pretty much standard practice for roving correspondents far from home to touch base with their embassy or consulate; partly to let them know they were around and partly, actually mainly, for an informal briefing on politics and gossip. It is, of course, quite possible that in the summer heat the consul had taken his leave and a one-month break would require several weeks either side for travelling.

Anyway it is a tradition I like to maintain and whenever working abroad I always seek out the ambassador or consul and pop into the embassy or consulate for a briefing; which with a bit of luck usually means popping out to lunch for a briefing. I had been told at a reception for a UN cultural delegation—not UNESCO, another one whose acronym escapes me—at the British Embassy in Damascus about the unusual diplomatic arrangements in Israel: while all the Israeli government departments are in Jerusalem, the British embassy, like all the other embassies, is in Tel Aviv and we have a consulate-general in Jerusalem. Why so? Well, as the UN woman rather gleefully pointed out, there is a raft of UN decrees refusing to recognize Jerusalem as the capital, and as all UN members have chosen to comply, all the embassies are still in Tel Aviv. And so why the consulate-general in Jerusalem? Because as Palestine is not yet a state but is clearly blinking brightly on every diplomatic radar screen the British need a presence there, and so the consulate-general in Jerusalem is effectively the British Embassy in Palestine.

That was over a month ago and today I'm meeting Our Man in Jerusalem, the British consul-general Richard Makepeace. Over a fine lunch at the American Colony Hotel—also the HQ for the Quartet's Middle East diplomatic mission and occasional residence of former prime minister and envoy Tony Blair—we compare notes. I ask Richard where he had been before Jerusalem.

"I was Ambassador to Sudan, then Abu Dhabi, before that number two in Cairo."

"All heavy with British diplomatic baggage," I suggest.

"Quite so," he replies, "but none heavier than here. Sometimes I think wistfully how easy it must be for an ambassador from an obscure northern European country which has had no say in the world." Rather like, I think wistfully to myself, Britain is on its way to becoming.

I tell him the rather startling news that I have become so fed up with rabid Zionists bending my ear about being British that if I think my interlocutrix is so inclined I tell them I'm Australian.

"I don't think I could get away with that!" he replies, "but how come?"

"If they know my name they will start with, "Now you are a lord, you must realize that the British Mandate... and off they go on a long tirade about how we did them down and sided with the Arabs before and during independence. At first I fought back, reminding them that the second half of the Balfour Declaration..."

"Ah, the dreaded Balfour Declaration!" Richard sighs.

It's worth spending a short while revisiting this source of all woes. In 1917, when Britain and France ran the diplomatic world, an idea whose time had come—that finally the Jewish Diaspora should have their own land—had gathered enough momentum for it to be discussed by heads of state. Leading the charge in Britain were Lord Rothschild and Chaim Weizmann, later to be the first president of Israel. The British foreign secretary was Arthur James Balfour, later the first Earl of Balfour. They all shared the dream of a homeland for the long scattered Jews; Rothschild and Weizmann for obvious reasons, Balfour because, like his prime minister Lloyd George and slavery abolitionist William Wilberforce, he was a Protestant Evangelical who believed the messiah would be more likely to pop back if the Jewish race converted to Christianity and were ready and waiting for this messiah in Israel.

Balfour wrote to Lord Rothschild that

> His Majesty's government view with favor the establishment in Palestine of a national home for the Jewish people, and will use their best endeavors to facilitate the achievement of this object, it being clearly understood that nothing shall be done which may prejudice the civil and religious rights of existing non-Jewish communities in Palestine, or the rights and political status enjoyed by Jews in any other country.

The Zionists seized on this letter, promoted it to a Declaration, and in an early example of Middle East selective memory syndrome promptly ignored the second half—about not upsetting the indigenous Arabs—and have done so, visibly done so, ever since.

Back to lunch. "Then the Israelis say that the point of the British Mandate from 1922 was to implement the Balfour Declaration," I continue. "I politely point out to them that 'No it wasn't' and that anyway if it had been they can rest assured we would have stuck to all of it and not just the half of it that they have chosen to remember."

"And anyway any feelings of being let down are nothing compared to how the Arabs must feel after how we deceived them. You know about the McMahon letters?" asks Richard.

I do. In 1915 the Ottoman Turks had sided with the Germans in the First World War and as a diversion the British urgently needed to stir up trouble elsewhere in the Ottoman Empire. The obvious solution was to encourage Arab nationalism in its southern provinces. McMahon was the British governor general in Cairo and through him the British made specific written promises for post-Ottoman Arab independence after the war, promises it had no intention of keeping. Quite, in fact, the reverse.

"If we hadn't made all these promises the world would be a far happier place," says Richard. "It's easier for them—and us—to blame the sins of our forefathers."

"Well actually my grandfather sat at the same Cabinet as Balfour. He was responsible for Ireland but that, as they say, is another story."

"The anti-British sentiment is something that's turned on and off. Mainly comes from the older Israelis. There's a lot of rewriting of history from younger writers, more objective from a distance, more favorable to us," Richard says.

"Well if you are a last word merchant, you can always remind them that if it wasn't for the British Eighth Army stopping Rommel and the Nazis round the corner in North Africa there wouldn't be an Israel anyway. That normally shuts them up."

"You have been in the wars," he quips. Off record we gossip and background through the menu; Richard's good work will continue when he joins the Prince of Wales at the Oxford Center for Islamic Studies.

Long lunch—and longer siesta—over, it's time to catch up with Mark Twain again. There is no denying the sense of excitement—and after the long hot ride through the desolation, the sense of relief too—that he felt as he entered the old walled city: "Just after noon we entered these narrow, crooked streets, by the ancient and the famed Damascus Gate, and now for several hours I have been trying to comprehend that I am actually in the illustrious old city where Solomon dwelt, where Abraham held converse with the Deity, and where walls still stand that witnessed the spectacle of the Crucifixion."

The Damascus Gate is still the main entrance to the Old City from the north. Dating in its present construct from Roman times and rebuilt along similar lines after every subsequent sacking and conquest—and the Old City has had fifty such visits of one kind or another—it has a classic city defenders' entrance. On entering under the arch one is forced to turn sharp left, then sharp right, the idea being to block the flow of any attack and to disadvantage the usually right-handed spear throwing attackers and advantage usually right-handed sword waving defenders. One would have thought at some stage over the centuries a general would recruit a platoon of left-handers and send them in first, but apparently not.

The old drawbridge leading up to the Gate is now a footbridge, thronged on either side by hawkers whose families have held their pitches for genera-tions. Instantly one sees the character of Jerusalem today as people rush by: satin-coated rabbis and beige-robed imams, crocodiles of gawky tourists, Lonely Planet-ed backpackers, earnest Christian pilgrims, children selling cigarettes and chewing gum, black-turbaned Shia mullahs, old Arab women sweeping the streets, younger Arab women in full black abayas patiently heaving bags of shopping, Coptic monks topped by black zucchettos, subcon-tinental Muslims topped by white taqiyahs, booted and suited ultraorthodox Jews—white heads and black hats down against the world, Jordanian men in keffiyehs and igals, Greek Orthodox priests in a hurry of swirling black cloaks, older Israelis wearing kippahs, Franciscan friars swaying along otherworldly, money changers waving banknotes, barrow boys shouting a clear passage, taxi drivers touting for rides, Israeli border guards in green and semi-automatics, Israeli police in blue and semi-automatics, black-hooded Armenian priests, Sudanese women in jellabiyas, Iranian women in chadors, young Palestinian women in tight jeans and tee-shirts excused by elaborate hijabs, Australian teenage girls unaware in hot-pants and Cistercian nuns sporting white coifs.

Mark Twain does not mention his hotel in *The Innocents Abroad*, but does so in his notes: "Loafed all the afternoon at the Mediterranean Hotel."

In an era when hotels were as scarce as tourists, the Mediterranean Hotel was a Jerusalem institution. It actually moved location three times in the nineteenth century and the Excursionists stayed in the middle version, the one on El Wad Street just in from the Damascus Gate. In the twentieth century it moved for the third time and was incorporated into the New Imperial Hotel and later spun off into the Petra Hostel. The latter now claims that Mark Twain stayed there; he did not.

Due to detective work done by the excellent London-based Palestine Exploration Fund we know that in 1867 the hotel was in the swankiest part of a not very swanky city, next to the consulates of the British and Austrian empires and the Turkish pasha's residence. If there were any rich locals they lived nearby.

The hotel had 23 rooms. The main building had two stories: a courtyard level, which had guest rooms for the lower orders along one side opposite the kitchen and lounge, plus a second floor where the smarter guests, the *effendi*, stayed. It is not known if our man, a mere hack rather than a well heeled pilgrim, stayed with the lower orders down below or with the *effendi* up above. I expect the former which is why we didn't hear about it.

The Excursionists' hotel has had an interesting recent history. Early in the twentieth century it became a private, unmarked synagogue. After the Israeli take-over it became a series of apartments and the main one, in what had been the reception area, was taken by Ariel Sharon in the mid-1980s. Nothing remarkable in that perhaps, but the house is right in the middle of the Muslim quarter, and provocative as ever, Sharon had Stars of David carved into the lintels, surrounded the windows frames with razor-wire and hoisted a gigantic Israeli flag on the roof. This was just a Sharon Jerusalem forerunner: he is widely acknowledged as firing the spark that lit the second intifada when against all advice, commonsense and plain good manners he and his disciples swaggered around the Temple Mount in 2000. If you are ever short of a way to make a Muslim laugh, just remind them that George W. Bush called him "a man of peace". Best not to point out to the laughing Muslim the equal absurdity of Sharon's lifelong adversary, embezzler Yasser Arafat, winning the Nobel Peace Prize.

After his stroke in 2006 Sharon's wife Lily gave the apartment to Ateret Cohanim, a political Zionist property company with an agenda to buy the Arabs and Christians out of the Old City. Funded largely from the United States via its office in New Jersey it is indulging in what the liberal Israeli press call a self-inflicted virtuous circle, whereby the inflated prices with which it tempts non-Jewish owners to sell ensure house price inflation for the benefit of existing American-Jewish investors.

Sharon's flag still flies on the roof, but the entrance to the building is now sinister and secretive in its anonymity: unpainted wooden doors, CCTV cameras, swipe card readers and video buzzers. I want to have a quick look around, to say hello to the old Mediterranean Hotel and sit in the lounge where Mark Twain smoked his narghile. To that end I am part of this wonderful circular telephone conversation:

Woman: "Shalom."
Ian: "Ateret Cohanim?"
Woman: "Ken." (Yes)
Ian: "May we speak English?"
Woman: "No way."
Ian: "Is there someone there who speaks English?"
Woman: "No."
Ian: "Will there be someone there later who speaks English?"
Woman: "You have to contact us first in writing."
Ian: "Ah, you seem to speak English. It's a very quick question."
Woman: "No way." Click.

Back then, the next morning, Tuesday 24 September 1867, the New Pilgrims started their tour of the Old City. It is not clear if they used one of the caravanserai dragomen, Abraham or Mohammed, or hired a specific Ferguson better versed in the subtexts of Jerusalem. I borrowed the British consulate-general's excellent guide, a Palestinian Christian (it's important in Jerusalem to establish race and religion early as it affects every moment), Saed Mrebe, to be our Ferguson for the next few days.

⁓

The complexities of race and religion here are even more baffling now than they were in Mark Twain's day. He wrote: "The population of Jerusalem is composed of Moslems, Jews, Greeks, Latins, Armenians, Syrians, Copts, Abyssinians, Greek Catholics, and a handful of Protestants. One hundred of the latter sect are all that dwell now in this birthplace of Christianity. The nice shades of nationality comprised in the above list, and the languages spoken by them, are altogether too numerous to mention. It seems to me that all the races and colors and tongues of the earth must be represented among the fourteen thousand souls that dwell in Jerusalem."

The Turks were generally tolerant of non-Muslims and always recognized Jerusalem's significance to the other monotheist religions. The Turkish view was you were free to worship but worship wasn't free. The British were even more open to all comers and didn't tax them either, but after 1948 the newly installed Jordanians behaved disgracefully, sacking the synagogues and using the Orthodox churches as stables and sheds. (The only synagogue to survive was the above-mentioned Mediterranean Hotel building where the private, unmarked synagogue escaped the Jordanian bulldozers.) Jerusalem today has an almost Lebanese layer cake of sects and sub-sects of the three monotheist religions, and as man invents new ones to add to those he has already invented no doubt they will find their way here too. There's nothing like a one-and-only-god to encourage countless splinters groups and nowhere like Jerusalem to attract them as pilgrims, including, of course, our own New Pilgrims. There's even a well-known psychiatric condition known as the Jerusalem Syndrome, when ordinary pilgrims, a long way from home and sated with Jerusalem's religious connotations, somehow convince themselves that they are the reincarnated* Jesus or the next Christ or Messiah or Prophet.**

Twain was less impressed with the local government: "Rags, wretchedness, poverty and dirt, those signs and symbols that indicate the presence of Moslem rule more surely than the crescent-flag itself, abound. Lepers, cripples, the blind, and the idiotic, assail you on every hand, and they know but one word of but one language apparently—the eternal "bucksheesh." To see the numbers of maimed, malformed and diseased humanity that throng the holy places and obstruct the gates, one might suppose that the ancient days had come again, and that the angel of the Lord was expected to descend at any moment to stir the waters of Bethesda."

* I have never seen what to me seemed an atom of truth that there is a future life, and yet I am strongly inclined to expect one. *Mark Twain, a Biography*

** Prophesying was the only human art that couldn't be improved by practice. *The International Lightning Trust*

Since the 1967 Israeli victory in the Six Day War, the Old City, along with all of East Jerusalem, has joined West Jerusalem under Israeli jurisdiction. All of Twain's complaints have been addressed: the streets are amazingly swept and the rubbish amazingly collected considering the souk and alley character of the Old City. All of the street lights work. The electric cables and water pipes are all safely tucked away and color coded. There are no beggars of any description. And it's completely safe, with no fear of mugging or even pick-pocketing. The safety comes at the price of "security": armed policemen and CCTV cameras are everywhere—disconcerting, but unavoidable in the circumstances of what is happening on the other side of the Wall/Fence a few miles away. As the liberal Israeli press likes to say about living in this quasi-warzone, paraphrasing Bill Clinton, "it's the Occupation, stupid."

Mark Twain started his tour of Jerusalem, as do most tourists today, with a visit to the Church of the Holy Sepulcher—"the place of the Crucifixion, and, in fact, every other place intimately connected with that tremendous event, are ingeniously massed together and covered by one roof—the dome of the Church of the Holy Sepulcher.

"Entering the building, through the midst of the usual assemblage of beggars, one sees on his left a few Turkish guards—for Christians of different sects will not only quarrel, but fight, also, in this sacred place, if allowed to do it." Later, in the same vein, he added: "All sects of Christians have chapels here, and each must keep to itself and not venture upon another's ground. It has been proven conclusively that they can not worship together around the grave of the Saviour of the World in peace."

It's a shame that no one told Twain about the Status Quo of 1853 as he would have loved the story. As he said, "different sects will not only quarrel, but fight", and even when Salah al-Din was sultan there were so many fights between the Christian sects that he gave one Muslim family the keys to the church and put another Muslim family in charge of the door. These families still are key- and door-holders to this day. By 1853, just before the Excursionists' visit, the Turks had had enough of the endless squabbling, rounded up all the sects and laid down the Status Quo. This gave each sect specific, unique, times to perform their liturgies and maintain the common areas—each being responsible for a part of the church. The Turks introduced a two-tier sect system with the Greek Orthodox, Roman Catholic and Armenian Orthodox sects in the premier league and the Syrian Orthodox, Syrian Catholic, Coptic sects and their splinter groups in the lower league. Where Twain noted that "one sees on his left a few Turkish guards", one now sees on his left a few Israeli policemen. Brawls break out every year; the latest one was one Palm Sunday when an Armenian cleric was late in clearing space for the Greeks. When the Israeli police arrived to separate the brawlers, the brawlers united and started brawling with the police—who under a separate agreement are not allowed to enter unless invited by one of the top three sects.

An amusing aside, pointed out by every Ferguson on the way in, is the story of the ladder. As one enters the main doors up high on the right there is a small six-rung wooden ladder resting on a high level ledge under a window. It has been there since 1852. Why so? Because responsibility for cleaning the ledge was not specified in the Status Quo and none of the sects wants to take on the burden of owning it and upsetting the apple cart. A less amusing aside is that, as our Christian guide Saed points out: "the Status Quo has ruined the church as a place of worship. There are so many compromises on the services, what's in them, how long they take, how big can be the procession, which way the procession must wend, how noisy can they be. Now they are all show, but no good even as a show."

The Easter weekend sums up how it works, and how it doesn't work. Each of the top three sects has been given a day—Good Friday, Easter Sunday and Easter Monday—when each has supremacy for the day in turn. But the Status Quo forgot to apportion the Saturday and so all three started barging in on each other's services, and worse. The Israelis have now banned all services on Easter Saturday due to the unruly behavior of the rival sects. Worse for Saed as a practicing minority Christian is that his own religion in its highest place of veneration is a laughing stock among all his majority Muslim friends who worship with dignity as a united faith—at least here in Jerusalem and Palestine.

Mark Twain visited all the usual attractions in the Church of the Holy Sepulcher, and with an increasing degree of cynicism. This is a fine section of *The Innocents Abroad*, as if he had recovered from the dreariness of the endless desert, had had a good lazy loaf around at the hotel and, refreshed and recovered, finally had something meaty to get his teeth into.

On entering "before you is a marble slab, which covers the Stone of

Unction, whereon the Saviour's body was laid to prepare it for burial. It was found necessary to conceal the real stone in this way in order to save it from destruction. Pilgrims were too much given to chipping off pieces of it to carry home.

"Entering the great Rotunda, we stand before the most sacred locality in Christendom—the grave of Jesus. Stooping low, we enter the vault—the Sepulcher itself. It is only about six feet by seven, and the stone couch on which the dead Saviour lay extends from end to end of the apartment and occupies half its width. It is covered with a marble slab which has been much worn by the lips of pilgrims. This slab serves as an altar, now. Over it hang some fifty gold and silver lamps, which are kept always burning, and the place is otherwise scandalized by trumpery, gewgaws, and tawdry ornamentation."

He then touched upon two interesting stories with more recent developments—and once more they are stories he would have loved retelling: "The chapel of the Syrians is not handsome; that of the Copts is the humblest of them all. It is nothing but a dismal cavern, roughly hewn in the living rock of the Hill of Calvary." The Syrian Orthodox chapel is indeed in a sorry state. The Syrians were generally discouraged by the Jordanians in the inter-Arab fallout after the Six Day War and could not even get past the first hurdle—permission to restore it. The Israelis gave them permission straight away but then the Syrians came up against the Armenians. Under the terms of the Status Quo the Syrian Orthodox chapel falls under the Armenian Orthodox remit. The Syrian Orthodox now have the funds to restore their chapel but the Armenians won't allow them to do so, as the Status Quo says all repairs must be approved and carried out by the Armenians and can be charged back to the Syrians. This the Syrians refuse to do and so they have to pray every Sunday on the dirt floor in front of a charred altar surrounded by bare and damp walls.

Mark Twain touched on the Copts: here is what happened to them. The ancient Egyptian sect, itself one of the earliest Christian sects, is one of the longest standing in Jerusalem but has always been the poorest and, as Twain said, the humblest. In Easter 1970, while they were praying on the Sunday, the Israeli army arrived and cleared out half their space by evicting their monks from the adjoining convent and installing Ethiopian monks in their stead. Why so? Well, firstly Egypt had been the ringleader of the Arabs in the Six Day War just three years previously and the Copts were an easy revenge target, and secondly Israel had already welcomed boatloads of Ethiopian Jews, many rumored to be of dubious Jewish provenance, and saw the strengthening of the Ethiopian community as a whole as a positive development. Of course, the Israelis and Ethiopians deny the whole fandango but the fact is that the last chapel you pass through on the southern entrance to the Church of the Holy Sepulcher is solidly Ethiopian.

Now the Copts aren't giving up without a fight. On a still disputed part of the roof a Copt monk has to sit at all times to maintain the claim. One blistering hot summer afternoon in 2002 a Copt monk moved his chair some eight inches towards the Ethiopian side to find better shade. An Ethiopian saw the transgression, rounded up his brother monks and a full-scale fistfight between the competing sects over the insult left eleven monks hospitalized and the Jews and Muslims stupefied all over again.

Back to Mark Twain's visit: "We were shown the place where our Lord appeared to His mother after the Resurrection. Here, also, a marble slab marks the place where St. Helena, the mother of the Emperor Constantine, found the crosses about three hundred years after the Crucifixion. According to the legend, this great discovery elicited extravagant demonstrations of joy. But they were of short duration. The question intruded itself: 'Which bore the blessed Saviour, and which the thieves?' To be in doubt, in so mighty a matter as this—to be uncertain which one to adore—was a grievous misfortune. It turned the public joy to sorrow.

"But when lived there a holy priest who could not set to simple a trouble as this at rest? One of these soon hit upon a plan that would be a certain test. A noble lady lay very ill in Jerusalem. The wise priests ordered that the three crosses be taken to her bedside one at a time. It was done. When her eyes fell upon the first one, she uttered a scream that was heard beyond the Damascus Gate, and even upon the Mount of Olives, it was said, and then fell back in a deadly swoon. They recovered her and brought the second cross. Instantly she went into fearful convulsions, and it was with the greatest difficulty that six strong men could hold her. They were afraid, now, to bring in the third cross. They began to fear that possibly they had fallen upon the wrong crosses, and that the true cross was not with this number at all. However, as the woman seemed likely to die with the convulsions that were tearing her, they concluded that the third could do no more than put her out of her misery with a happy dispatch. So they brought it, and behold, a miracle! The woman sprang from her bed, smiling and joyful, and perfectly restored to health.

"When we listen to evidence like this, we cannot but believe. We would be ashamed to doubt, and properly, too. Even the very part of Jerusalem where this all occurred is there yet. So there is really no room for doubt."

They continued their tour of the sham relics—the Pillar of Flagellation, where they had to push a stick through a curtain to feel it: "He cannot have any excuse to doubt it, for he can feel it with the stick. He can feel it as distinctly as he could feel any thing"—and the piece of the True Cross: "The Latin priests say it was stolen away, long ago, by priests of another sect. That seems like a hard statement to make, but we know very well that it was stolen, because we have seen it ourselves in several of the cathedrals of Italy and France." They inspected the Prison of Our Lord with its stone stocks and the Tomb of Adam,* where Twain was pleased "here in a land of strangers, far away from home, thus to discover the grave of a blood relation. True, a distant one, but still a relation. The fountain of my filial affection was stirred to its profoundest depths, and I gave way to tumultuous emotion. I leaned upon a pillar and burst into tears. I deem it no shame to have wept over the grave of my poor dead relative. Noble old man—he did not live to see me—he did not live to see his child. And I—I—alas, I did not live to see him. Weighed down by sorrow and disappointment, he died before I was born—six thousand brief summers before I was born. But let us try to bear it with fortitude. Let us trust that he is better off where he is. Let us take comfort in the thought that his loss is our eternal gain." They saw, too, the altar for the Roman Soldier who declared "Surely this was the Son of God" and where "in this self-same spot the priests of the Temple beheaded him for those blasphemous words he had spoken."

Twain was particularly fond of St. Helena, the first Christian emperor Constantine's mother, and of her tireless exploits. In the grotto which is the Chapel of St. Helena he saw where "Helena blasted it out when she was searching for the true Cross. She had a laborious piece of work, here, but it was richly rewarded. Out of this place she got the crown of thorns, the nails of the cross, the true Cross itself, and the cross of the penitent thief. When she thought she had found every thing and was about to stop, she was told in a dream to continue a day longer. It was very fortunate. She did so, and found the cross of the other thief." Then they visited the Chapel of the Invention of the Cross—"a name which is unfortunate, because it leads the ignorant to imagine that a tacit acknowledgment is thus made that the tradition that Helena found the true Cross here is a fiction—an invention. It is a happiness to know, however, that intelligent people do not doubt the story in any of its particulars." Nor did they overlook the column that marks the center of the earth where "Christ said that that particular column stood upon the center of

---

* After all these years, I see that I was mistaken about Eve in the beginning; it is better to live outside the Garden with her than inside it without her. *Adam's Diary*

the world. If the center of the world changes, the column changes its position accordingly. To satisfy himself that this spot was really the center of the earth, a skeptic once paid well for the privilege of ascending to the dome of the church to see if the sun gave him a shadow at noon. He came down perfectly convinced. The day was very cloudy and the sun threw no shadows at all; but the man was satisfied that if the sun had come out and made shadows it could not have made any for him. Proofs like these are not to be set aside by the idle tongues of cavilers. To such as are not bigoted, and are willing to be convinced, they carry a conviction that nothing can ever shake."

He continued to marvel at St. Helena and her industry: "She traveled all over Palestine, and was always fortunate. Whenever the good old enthusiast found a thing mentioned in her Bible, Old or New, she would go and search for that thing, and never stop until she found it. If it was Adam, she would find Adam; if it was the Ark, she would find the Ark; if it was Goliath, or Joshua, she would find them."

But Twain's mood changed when he saw the altar in the Greek Orthodox chapel which traditionally represents the place where Jesus was crucified— the point at which the Jesus of history and the Christ of faith meet. Now he dismisses all he has already seen: "One is grave and thoughtful when he stands in the little Tomb of the Saviour—he could not well be otherwise in such a place—but he has not the slightest possible belief that ever the Lord lay there, and so the interest he feels in the spot is very, very greatly marred by that reflection. He looks at the place where Mary stood, in another part of the church, and where John stood, and Mary Magdalene; where the mob derided the Lord; where the angel sat; where the crown of thorns was found, and the true Cross; where the risen Saviour appeared—he looks at all these places with interest, but with the same conviction he felt in the case of the Sepulcher, that there is nothing genuine about them, and that they are imaginary holy places created by the monks."

But here at the Greek altar the pilgrim "fully believes that he is looking upon the very spot where the Saviour gave up his life. He remembers that Christ was very celebrated, long before he came to Jerusalem; he knows that his fame was so great that crowds followed him all the time; he is aware that his entry into the city produced a stirring sensation, and that his reception was a kind of ovation; he can not overlook the fact that when he was crucified there were very many in Jerusalem who believed that he was the true Son of God. To publicly execute such a personage was sufficient in itself to make the locality of the execution a memorable place for ages.

"It is not possible that there can be any mistake about the locality of the Crucifixion. Not half a dozen persons knew where they buried the Saviour, perhaps, and a burial is not a startling event, any how; therefore, we can be pardoned for unbelief in the Sepulcher, but not in the place of the Crucifixion. The crucifixion of Christ was too notable an event in Jerusalem, and the Hill of Calvary made too celebrated by it, to be forgotten in the short space of three hundred years.

"I climbed the stairway in the church which brings one to the top of the small enclosed pinnacle of rock, and looked upon the place where the true cross once stood, with a far more absorbing interest than I had ever felt in any thing earthly before. When one stands where the Saviour was crucified, he finds it all he can do to keep it strictly before his mind that Christ was not crucified in a Catholic Church. He must remind himself every now and then that the great event transpired in the open air, and not in a gloomy, candle-lighted cell in a little corner of a vast church, up-stairs—a small cell all bejeweled and bespangled with flashy ornamentation, in execrable taste."

Sorry Sam, I know this one was from the heart, and you are certainly right about the "small cell all bejeweled and bespangled with flashy ornamentation, in execrable taste", but more recent developments have suggested—I nearly said "proved" but only charlatans do that around here—that the crucifixion was probably nearby but not where it seemed to you back then. Of course "probably" is the word because as with so much of Jesus' life we can only be imprecise about His death. It is beyond the scope of this book retracing your footsteps to attempt a treatise on all the latest biblical and archaeological research but considered opinion now places the crucifixion next to the most likely place of burial, in a space nearby now called the Garden of the Tomb. It is fair to say this theory is roundly disputed by interests vested in keeping the two at the Church of the Holy Sepulcher.

Irrespective of the rights and wrongs of the case, and the only certainty about the case is its uncertainty, the Garden of the Tomb is a wonderful sanctuary from the intensity of the religious claims and counter-claims and tawdry commercialism of the Old City of Jerusalem. Situated just beyond the walls and close to Damascus Gate, it is a walled garden, a cross between an English country garden and a Japanese ceremonial garden. Apart from whichever space has the better claim to the crucifixion and tomb it has by far the better claim as a place of spiritual serenity; it is in fact the very opposite of the schoolboy squabble that is the Church of the Holy Sepulcher. Tour groups are few and thoughtful, the Fergusons more knowledgeable, the entrance is free with payment by gift box and the volunteers—all on secondment from the softer side of England—tend the garden and tomb.

Sitting there doing nothing one afternoon I hear the following from the leader of an American group. She is wearing a flowery frock and straw hat and is a double, or treble I suppose, for the tennis playing Williams sisters but with a northern East Coast accent: "As we leave the likely tomb questions arise. The tomb is empty now; was it empty three days after the crucifixion? Was it Jesus who died here and did His bones remain—did He really die just a man? Or was it Christ who died here and did His body leave the tomb with his spirit—did He die the Son of God? If the Christ died here—and we here today all believe He did—did His body *really* leave? This is, you might say, the coalface of Christian belief.[*] The go/no-go area. If his body left, where did It go? To heaven, yes, so is heaven a place, or a state of mind—a state of bliss, timeless bliss? If it's a place where is it? Up in the sky? When the gospels were written what did the sky mean? Was there a beyond-the-sky if you will? Christ said "the Kingdom of Heaven is within you"—did He mean heaven is right here and right now and not somewhere else? If so, is it of this world or the next? It must be this world. Perhaps this is the main question for us, for us here and now. Heaven in this world. And the gospellers, were they writers of facts of time and place as we would expect a correspondent to be, or were they writing in parables and allegories as folk then would expect a scribe to be? I say to you: faith[**] is stronger than belief. We can't know what happened back here when Jesus died so there is nothing real to believe, but we can have faith that Christ lives in us now." I write it down immediately and I'm sure it's accurate in spirit but cannot capture the timbre of sincerity and joy. What remains is the silence of the group when she finishes, a theophany they share in stillness next to their Christ's last home on earth.

[*]   If the man doesn't believe as we do, we say he is a crank, and that settles it. At least nowadays, because now we don't burn him. *Following the Equator*

[**]   There are those who scoff at the school boy, calling him frivolous and shallow. Yet it was the school boy who said, Faith is believing what you know ain't so. *Following the Equator*

Mark Twain finished his chapter on the Church of the Holy Sepulcher with: "History is full of this old Church of the Holy Sepulcher—full of blood that was shed because of the respect and the veneration in which men held the last resting-place of the meek and lowly, the mild and gentle, Prince of Peace!"

The next day the New Pilgrims continued their tour of Jerusalem, as do most tourists today, with a walk along the Sorrowful Way, now more commonly known as the Via Dolorosa. The route is a harmless enough invention by the Franciscans in the thirteenth century as a way of incorporating all the major sites in the Old City into a coherent one-way route. It purports to follow the path that Jesus took as He carried His cross from Pontius Pilate's court to Golgotha, but even the most enthusiastic Biblicist would doubt that Jesus' route was quite so scenic as portrayed. A further spanner has been thrown in the Via Dolorosa's works by recent discoveries which seem to suggest that Pontius Pilate actually stayed that year in the Jaffa Gate citadel on the opposite side of the Old City rather than Antonio's Fortress where the Via Dolorosa starts.

Irrespective of that, the Excursionists started on the Via Dolorosa opposite Antonio's Fortress, famous for its lookout tower, built by Herod the Great and named in honor of Mark Antony when he was emperor seventy years before the crucifixion. The prefect of Judea was Pontius Pilate, and like all Roman prefects he lived in the capital Caesarea Maritima rather than provincial Jerusalem, which was peaceful enough except at times of Jewish religious holidays. This was one of those times: Passover, and one of the times it was prudent for the prefect to move with his soldiers to Jerusalem. The Romans despised the Jews with their litigious religion but were always wary of a roused mob; and at Passover the litigious religion and the occupation had previously proved a catalyst for the mob to rampage against Rome. Not totally dissimilar, you may construe, from the Ramadan mob railing against their occupation now.

The New Pilgrims back then—and we today—start opposite Antonio's Fortress because the building itself was destroyed in the sacking of Jerusalem in 70 AD—destroyed by Titus to give his Roman forces easier access to sack the Temple. The Franciscan Monastery of the Flagellation lies to one side of the courtyard and The Monastery of the Condemnation to the other. Both churches were rebuilt in the twentieth century and both sympathetically designed with the spirit in mind. The former has wonderful acoustics and the monks encourage pilgrim groups to sing in there. Every Friday the monks lead a procession from there along the Via Dolorosa and we are lucky enough to be in the right time and place. We are also lucky enough for Saed to have arranged for us a private visit to the Franciscan archaeology collection in the convent behind—and there doubly lucky to meet the Custos, the local head of the order whose title gives us the word "custodian".

We have become fond of the Franciscans in the Holy Land. They seem to be the only recognizably practicing *Christian* sect here. It is partly their love of their churches—any rebuilding is only allowed after extensive archaeology—partly the simplicity and elegance of the new commissions—the lapse at Nazareth aside—and partly their patience in dealing with busloads of irreligious visitors.

Our feeble fondness for them is more than offset by the hatred felt for them by all the Orthodox sects: the Greeks, the Armenians and the Syrians. The Franciscans are unfairly held as being descendants of, and therefore responsible for, the crusades; only in the sense that St. Francis of Assisi was a Latin monk could one stretch and see their point. The mistrust and loathing goes back a long way: up to the point of the Muslim invasion of 638 AD the Greek Orthodox had held the lucrative Christian franchise in Jerusalem. At first the Muslims tolerated them but the toleration turned to persecution when in 1009 AD an unbalanced caliph began sacking the churches and beheading their hierarchies. The surviving Christians finally turned to Rome for help when the Seljuk Turks—the forerunners of the Ottomans—arrived fifty years later. Pope Urban II called for a crusade to free the holy places for the Christian pilgrims. The call was obeyed and the armies of the First Crusade arrived in Jerusalem in 1099. Latin Christians massacred the Muslims and expelled the Orthodox Christians. The latter have never forgiven and forgotten but all the evidence we have seen now suggests their Christianity* is driven by greed and bloody mindedness, and there's no reason to suspect it was any different a thousand years ago.

Twain then reels off the "stations" along the Via Dolorosa. "We passed under the 'Ecce Homo Arch,' and saw the very window from which Pilate's wife warned her husband to have nothing to do with the persecution of the Just Man. This window is in an excellent state of preservation, considering its

---

* I bring you the stately matron named Christendom, returning bedraggled, besmirched, and dishonored, from pirate raids in Kiaochow, Manchuria, South Africa, and the Philippines, with her soul full of meanness, her pocket full of boodle, and her mouth full of pious hypocrisies. Give her soap and towel, but hide the looking glass. *A Salutation from the 19th to the 20th Century,* 31 December 1900

great age. They showed us where Jesus rested the second time, and where the mob refused to give him up, and said, 'Let his blood be upon our heads, and upon our children's children forever.'"

All the stations on the Via Dolorosa are as he described them but, as one would expect, his comments tend to be pithier than any guide would dare: "We crossed a street, and came presently to the former residence of St. Veronica. When the Saviour passed there, she came out, full of womanly compassion, and spoke pitying words to him, undaunted by the hootings and the threatenings of the mob, and wiped the perspiration from his face with her handkerchief. The strangest thing about the incident that has made her name so famous, is, that when she wiped the perspiration away, the print of the Saviour's face remained upon the handkerchief, a perfect portrait, and so remains unto this day. We knew this, because we saw this handkerchief in a cathedral in Paris, in another in Spain, and in two others in Italy. In the Milan cathedral it costs five francs to see it, and at St. Peter's, at Rome, it is almost impossible to see it at any price. No tradition is so amply verified as this of St. Veronica and her handkerchief."

He carried on station by station in this vein but then at some length described the House of the Wandering Jew. He also retold the legend dating from the thirteenth century: "when the weary Saviour would have sat down and rested him a moment, [the Jew] pushed him rudely away and said, 'Move on!' The Lord said, 'Move on, thou, likewise,' and the command has never been revoked from that day to this." Somehow in the last one hundred and sixty years the House of the Wandering Jews has disappeared from the guides" itinerary, nor on examination can any records be found of it every having been here.

The Via Dolorosa leads to the Church of the Holy Sepulcher and Twain's account finishes where it had started. The guide then takes them to three more sites—of far greater significance now than then—where worship the Armenians, the Muslims and the Jews.

The Armenian Cathedral of St. James had just been extensively renovated when Twain visited it. We feel it is the most beautiful of all the cathedrals in the Old City, with its altars in each apse and numerous chapels and minimal pews. For services there are no pews at all and rich carpets are laid across the floor. The lighting is wonderful—hanging candelabras just above head height lighting the areas which the directed sunlight from the dome miss lighting.

The Armenians were at one point recently felt to be an endangered species in Jerusalem but have since recovered in a way to make Twain's journalistic whiskers twitch with mirth. After the Israeli victory in 1967 space was needed in Jerusalem for the influx of religious Jews and it was felt that the Armenians were the most vulnerable—and compared to Latin and Greek communities, the least visible politically—sect. Pressure was applied on them to leave: rents raised, permissions denied, ID papers hard to renew. But good old TLUC rode to their rescue! When the Israelis admitted a million Russians they also unwittingly admitted a considerable number of Christians masquerading as Jews. At the time the arrangement suited both sides: the Israelis desperately wanted white immigrants and there were millions of Russians not about to say no to free housing and much more besides in the land of milk and honey. These new Israeli Christians jumped at the chance of practicing their Russian Orthodoxy again, and found the Armenian version of Orthodoxy more in keeping with their own and generally less avaricious than the Greek. Thus the Armenian congregation has recently prospered.

The plot thickens further: it has now emerged that not only are there an estimated three hundred thousand Russians without Jewish mothers, or even grandmothers, but many of these have Muslim—although long lapsed Muslim—forefathers on the *male* side. The right-wing press is up in arms and the more militant rabbis are on the warpath.

For modern Israelis the crowning glory of today's Jerusalem is the Wailing, now called Western, Wall Plaza. In spite of the claims by Dayan and Sharon and any number of Zionists of whichever religious-right persuasion that history has now reunited with itself, the Jewish hold on Jerusalem over the last three thousand years has been tenuous to see the least.

Historically the Israelites (they weren't called Jews until the arrival of the Romans) emerged as an organized tribal society around 1200 BC. They established a kingdom around 1000 BC, with a capital in Jerusalem, after driving out the Canaanites, another bronze-age civilization which had established itself in the region in the third millennium BC. Some Palestinians now claim to be the descendants of these Canaanites, and therefore outbid the Israelites in terms of Jerusalem descent and so rightful land ownership—but the claim is muddy at best. (Some also claim to be descendants of the Philistines from Philistia and that by quirks of etymology and nomenclature now just happen to be called Palestinians from Palestine and therefore they outbid the Israelites in terms of Holy Land descent—a further claim in unclear water—but around here a claim has to be disproved as much as proved to be taken as true. Proving a negative and disproving a positive are popular parlor games for those hereabouts with selective Levantine memory syndrome.)

The First Temple was built in Jerusalem in the reign of Solomon in around 950 BC. The Israelites believed then the Temple was not just the center of their religion but also the center of the earth, as indeed the literal brigade still do believe today.

Four hundred years of religious and political independence followed until the Israelites were invaded and conquered by a succession of civilizations from the east; first by the Assyrians in 722 BC, then more disastrously by the Babylonians, who in 586 BC destroyed the First Temple and sent the Israelites into exile to Babylon. In 538 BC the Babylonians were defeated by the Persians, who allowed the Israelites to return from exile and the Second Temple was built in Jerusalem.

The next invaders came from the west. The Persians were defeated by Alexander the Great in 332 BC, and for three hundred years Jerusalem was ruled by the Greeks. The Israelites adapted to Greek rule then successfully rebelled in 164 BC when the Temple was converted into a pagan temple to Zeus. They re-consecrated the Temple and for one hundred years governed themselves until the usual rivalries between opposing sects made them vulnerable to the next great power in the region, the Romans, who conquered Jerusalem in 63 BC.

The Romans installed a client king, Herod the Great. Herod undertook many great building projects during his forty-year reign, including re-building the Second Temple. After his death, his three sons did not rule as capably as their father and the real—rather than the proxy—Romans took control. The real Romans were heavy-handed and unpopular. When an uprising broke out between 66 and 70 AD, the Romans destroyed the Second Temple and carried its treasures back to Rome. A further revolt in 135 AD against the Emperor Hadrian led to even more violent reprisals from the Romans, who this time aimed to crush the troublesome, quarrelsome Jews for once and for all. The Jews were forced out of Jerusalem and thousands were murdered, exiled or sold into slavery.

I mention all this because one often hears in Jerusalem today that the Israelites in one form of another have an unbroken claim to Jerusalem; they don't. By my reckoning they have "only" been in government here for seven hundred years out of the last three thousand and until 1967 not at all in the preceding eighteen hundred years. Perspective, whether historical or human, is not a strong point in Middle East today.

The period prior to the 1967 Six Day War victory was perhaps the most galling of all for the Jewish people. Israel held West Jerusalem but the historically symbolic Old City was part of East Jerusalem and had been held by the Jordanians since 1948. The Jordanians behaved without magnanimity or good grace, sacking the synagogues and driving the Jews out; again, one might feel, *plus ça change* now the sandal is on the other foot.

When victory came in 1967 the first priority was to re-establish Jerusalem as a Jewish holy site, and the Israelis—citing as everyone else had cited before them "To the Victor, the Spoils"—bulldozed the old Moroccan Sharaf quarter (there are still thirty thousand Moroccans in the Shu'fat refugee camp five miles away behind the Wall/Fence) to make way for the new Western, ex-Wailing, Wall Plaza. It is now a vast and functional series of terraces leading down to the Wall itself. Non-Jews are welcome having donned a kippah or scarf. Men must use the main part to the left and are in the shade, women are backed into a corner on the right side in the sunlight. Women are not allowed to pray aloud as the Jewish god declared that "a women's voice is indecent".

Supplicants insert written pleas or prayer into the cracks. In a wonderful example of space-age technology meeting stone-age theology supplicants can now fax or email their pleas or prayers to the rabbis, along with their credit card numbers, and the rabbis undertake to insert their messages in the cracks of Herod's old wall.

Taking their cues from the Church of the Holy Sepulcher there are frequent rows between the sub-sects. The ultraorthodox have the franchise to worship next to the wall and are keen to maintain their sacred space there at the expense of lesser worshippers. Scuffles frequently break out as unseen dividing lines are crossed. Sometimes the women in the cattle pen next door get uppity and pray aloud or wear men's kippahs—and then have chairs hurled at them over the dividing wall. Any couple trying to worship together are strong-armed apart. (Most non-resident worshippers arrive at Dung Gate by coach. In the ultraorthodox coaches the men sit at the front, the woman at the back. All ultras assume they have right of frontery on secular buses, too, and scuffles to maintain the privileges they have granted themselves are not infrequent.)

I know it's not going to worry them one jot, but Judaism—at least as shown to the world here in the epicenter—is fast shaping up to be my least favorite religion. In Western countries we don't really notice the practice of Judaism very much; as a minority religion it just gets on with it in the background. But here, where it is a highly visible majority religion, one sees at first hand, as in the Talmud: Kethuboth 11b, what a nasty piece of work it can be: it is sectarian (Blessed art thou o Lord for not having made me a heathen...), racist (... or a slave...), sexist (... or a woman), elitist, wrathful (Pour out thy wrath, o Lord, on...), overbearing, intolerant and vindictive. The Jewish quarter today is newly rebuilt and has a totally different feeling to it than the souks and alleys of the Christian, Muslim and Armenian quarters. It is largely residential; the architecture is in scale with the other quarters but obviously modern; Middle Eastern motifs are subtle to the point of absence; the stone at least is local, or locally colored; shops are few and in malls; cafés fewer and off-street; streets are paved for cars and sidewalks; there are few non-Jewish tourists and that's the way they like it; Arabs are excluded by law and that's the way they like it too. It has the air of an out-of-term university: empty cloisters, museum and library doors swipe card-closed. It's not a bag of laughs and isn't meant to be. Earnest is a word that springs to mind.

Mark Twain then visited the Muslim holy sites. We assume his Ferguson for the day was a Christian and unfamiliar with the mosques mentioned: "Up to within a year or two past, no Christian could gain admission to the mosque or its court for love or money. But the prohibition has been removed, and we entered freely for bucksheesh."

As a result *The Innocents Abroad* has the Muslim holy sites confused: what Twain calls the Mosque of Omar is in fact the Al-Aqsa Mosque and what he calls Al-Aqsa is in fact Temple Mount. Irrespective of that they come in for the full Twain treatment: "The great feature is the prodigious rock in the center of its rotunda. On this rock the angel stood and threatened Jerusalem, and David persuaded him to spare the city. Mohammed was well acquainted with this stone. From it he ascended to heaven. The stone tried to follow him, and if the angel Gabriel had not happened by the merest good luck to be there to seize it, it would have done it. Very few people have a grip like Gabriel—the prints of his monstrous fingers, two inches deep, are to be seen in that rock to-day. In the place on it where Mahomet stood, he left his footprints in the solid stone. I should judge that he wore about eighteens.

"The inside of the great mosque is very showy with variegated marble walls and with windows and inscriptions of elaborate mosaic. The Turks have their sacred relics, like the Catholics. The guide showed us the veritable armor worn by the great son-in-law and successor of Mahomet, and also the buckler of Mahomet's uncle."

Twain then touched on the nub of the trouble for religious folk today: the Muslims built the Temple Mount right bang on top of the Jewish Temple. "Every where about the Mosque of Omar are portions of pillars, curiously wrought altars, and fragments of elegantly carved marble—precious remains of Solomon's Temple.

"At that portion of the ancient wall of Solomon's Temple which is called the Jew's Place of Wailing, and where the Hebrews assemble every Friday to kiss the venerated stones and weep over the fallen greatness of Zion, any one can see a part of the unquestioned and undisputed Temple of Solomon, the same consisting of three or four stones lying one upon the other, each of which is about twice as long as a seven-octave piano, and about as thick as such a piano is high. But, as I have remarked before, it is only a year or two ago that the ancient edict prohibiting Christian rubbish like ourselves to enter the Mosque of Omar and see the costly marbles that once adorned the inner Temple was annulled.

"These pieces of stone, stained and dusty with age, dimly hint at a grandeur we have all been taught to regard as the princeliest ever seen on earth. These elegant fragments bear a richer interest than the solemn vastness of the stones the Jews kiss in the Place of Wailing can ever have for the heedless sinner.

"Down in the hollow ground, underneath the olives and the orange trees that flourish in the court of the great Mosque, is a wilderness of pillars—remains of the ancient Temple; they supported it. There are ponderous archways down there, also, over which the destroying "plough" of prophecy passed harmless. It is pleasant to know we are disappointed, in that we never dreamed we might see portions of the actual Temple of Solomon, and yet experience no shadow of suspicion that they were a monkish humbug and a fraud."

The Temple Mount is today the most contentious issue in a rat's-nest of contentious issues between Jews and Muslims. For the Jews it is the holiest of sites, really the holy of holies, the very site of those two Temples. For the Muslims it is the third holiest site, up there but not the big one. Muslims believe that the rock was taken from the Garden of Eden and that the indentation in it was caused when Mohammed's foot touched it while on his way up to heaven. The attendant indentations are caused by the angel Gabriel holding the rock back.* One day, Resurrection Day in fact, the rock will be united with the Ka'bah in Mecca. (Christian pilgrims during the crusader era saw Jesus' footprint in the same indentation, also left while *en route* to heaven.)

The nastier Jews are very dismissive of Muslim claims to the site being holy on the grounds of unlikelihood: as if the whole story of Mohammed's footprint could possibly be true! Unlikely, it has to be said.

It is too easy for the secular to poke fun at the literal interpreters. The latter can own slaves, but only if they buy them in neighboring countries (Leviticus 25:44); they can sell their daughters (Exodus 21:7); but they must refrain from homosexuality (Leviticus 18:22); they cannot worship if they have a sight defect (Leviticus 21:20); cannot have contact with a woman while she is in her period (Leviticus 14:19-24); cannot work on the Sabbath, on pain of death (Exodus 35:2); cannot plant two crops in the same field (Leviticus 19:19); cannot eat shellfish (Leviticus 11:10); cannot touch dead pig-skin— so no basketball or soccer (Leviticus 11:6-8); cannot curse, on pain of stoning to death by the whole village (Leviticus 24:10-16); cannot sleep with their in-laws, or be burnt to death (Leviticus 20:14); cannot have a haircut around the temples (Leviticus 19:27).

Our own experience of visiting the Temple Mount is instructive of the mess that is the Holy Land today. Saed is a Palestinian Christian but looks identical to the far more numerous Palestinian Muslims. The guides know their way around Jerusalem but even he doesn't know which access points the Israelis are going to allow into the Temple Mount area today. There are supposed to be three possible ways in but, like checkpoints in the West Bank, they change and open and shut for no obvious reason—although the reason is always "security". The idea is to discourage visitors from seeing the Temple Mount and I have to say that if I was not writing this book... after the third entrance is blocked by heavily armed Israeli police I would have quit too.

Saed makes a phone call. Word has obviously spread around the Ferguson Telegraph and a sizeable group is re-assembling back at the first gate we tried. It is now just before 1.30 p.m. when the gate reopens after lunch. Saed says

---

* I have been on the verge of being an angel all my life, but it's never happened yet. *Mark Twain's Autobiography*

the Israelis have taken down the shade and it is as hot and enervating as we wait there as it has been for the last hour traipsing around the Old City's back alleys trying to find a way in. Beside us a large sign says, "According to Torah Law entering the Temple Mount area is strictly forbidden due the Holiness of the Site. By order of the Chief Rabbinate of Israel."

At 1.40 p.m. the gate opens and in we all go. We are near the rear and see the Israelis close this access point for the day. I tell Saed, "Now I know what it feels like to be a Palestinian."

As we enter the Temple Mount more problems lie ahead. The Muslim at the gate has decided to only allow Muslim visitors in today. Why so? He won't be drawn. There is shouting and wailing and gnashing of teeth. Eventually a compromise is reached. Groups with Muslim guides will be allowed in. Saed quickly sets us up with a fellow Ferguson and we join that small group. The tour is horrible as following us everywhere are angry-looking clerics ensuring we infidel dogs to do not defile their holy ground.

Back on planet earth, over Arabic coffee in the Muslim quarter, I complain to Saed, "This is really stupid. You would think that after all the bloody mindedness of the Israelis it would be good PR—if nothing else—for the Muslims to say—like Muslims do everywhere except it seems in a mosque: "Welcome!" Show up the Israelis for behaving as they do. Instead of which some imam somewhere has decided to enter a bolshiness competition with the opposition. It's such bad leadership."

Saed looks into his coffee and says, "My friend, now you *really* know what it feels like to be a Palestinian."

Mark Twain left Jerusalem with the words: "Jerusalem is mournful, and dreary, and lifeless. I would not desire to live here." Today he might say: "Jerusalem is quarrelsome, and ill-at-ease and frantic. I would not desire to live here." I agree. A visit to the scene of the accident before it happens is always memorable, but get out quick before the brakes fail.

8: Bethlehem, then Home

The Excursionists left Jerusalem at 8.00 a.m. on Wednesday 25 September. Their first stop was to visit the Tomb of Lazarus, he of the dead-risen persuasion, in what was the biblical village of Bethany (whose name has been borrowed by dozens of towns and villages, schools and baby girls around the English-speaking world) and is now the teeming Palestinian suburb of al-Eizariya (whose name translates as Place of Lazarus in Arabic).

The way the Wall/Fence twists and turns through East Jerusalem as it scoops up settlements and suburbs and cuts through Palestinian land and villages makes it confusing to know from a distance which town is in Israel and which is in Palestine. Al-Eizariya is clearly visible one and a half miles away in a dip in the concrete as one surveys the view from the Mount of Olives. Unfortunately or not, al-Eizariya happens to be in Palestine and this calls for another fun visit through the Wall/Fence. The only consolation is that our favorite Ferguson, Mr. Farki, will be waiting the other side for us and will guide us from there to Jericho, the Dead Sea and on to Bethlehem.

Media friends have warned us that this is a particularly unpleasant checkpoint as al-Eizariya is rumored to be on the short list, with Ramallah, as the future capital of any Palestinian state—and the Israeli government rumor is that al-Eizariya is riddled with "potential terrorists". Better by far, the wisdom goes, to travel there on a Jerusalem daytrip tour coach heading to the Lazarus Tomb site and then on to Bethlehem; the travel agency is responsible for making sure no Palestinians sneak on board, and the coaches generally go through the Wall/Fence on the nod. My plan is to get off the bus at al-Eizariya, tell the tour company that we'll make our own way back, meet up with Mr. Farki and pick up Mark Twain's trail again all the way to Jaffa. This is indeed the Home Run.

(Actually, and I hope you don't mind, but for the first and last time I'm going to deviate from the Excursionists' route. They left Jerusalem for

Bethany, Jericho, the Dead Sea, the Mars Saba monastery and Bethlehem and then returned to Jerusalem for a second time. After two more days here they then left for Ramla and rejoined the *Quaker City* at Jaffa. It's not clear why they detoured to visit Jerusalem again but for me to do so means two more trials through the Wall/Fence, adding several hundred miles to the journey and losing Mr. Farki before strictly necessary. So after Bethlehem I'm going to go directly to Ramla and Jaffa.)

As we find every time we move, travel around Jerusalem was considerably quicker in Mark Twain's day than it is now. He "stopped at the village of Bethany, an hour out from Jerusalem". Lucky he, what with the traffic and checkpoints before the Wall/Fence and the wait at the Wall/Fence it takes us all morning to reach al-Eizariya. If Twain had better transportation at least I hope to see better housing: "It is fearfully ratty, some houses, mud, 6 ft. square, and others holes in the ground, all windowless."

"They showed us the Tomb of Lazarus. I had rather live in it than in any house in the town. And they showed us also a large 'Fountain of Lazarus,' and in the center of the village the ancient dwelling of Lazarus. Lazarus appears to have been a man of property. The legends of the Sunday Schools do him great injustice; they give one the impression that he was poor. It is because they get him confused with that Lazarus who had no merit but his virtue, and virtue never has been as respectable as money.

"The house of Lazarus is a three-story edifice, of stone masonry, but the accumulated rubbish of ages has buried all of it but the upper story. We took candles and descended to the dismal cell-like chambers where Jesus sat at meat with Martha and Mary, and conversed with them about their brother.

"We could not but look upon these old dingy apartments with a more than common interest."

Sadly the housing is better only in the sense that the concrete will last longer than the mud. Rubble and rubbish abound; we must be back in the West Bank. The tomb itself is standard issue biblical invention—or not. Lazarus may well have lived there, he may well have died there, he may even have been re-born there but, like Mark Twain, one visits the site without much conviction after all the other hoaxes of Christendom. At least it was not discovered by St. Helena, so there is a chance it may be genuine.

What is genuine is my advice not to visit it with a tour group; even more genuine advice is not to visit it at all. Access to the tomb is via a tiny doorway off a busy unshaded street. As you wait—and wait and wait, this is a one at a time job—traffic blares and fumes beside you. Unsightliness abounds. When your turn arrives you have to bend double to enter the stairwell then clamber down two dozen uneven steps. A product liability lawyer would set up shop next door. In the depths there is a tomb, Lazarus' or an imposter's, and the smell of dank and damp. If I were Lazarus I would have preferred to remain dead than to come back to this hovel.

I tell the tour coach driver we want to disembark now and make our own way back; I had arranged to reunite with Mr. Farki at the Abber Hotel nearby the Tomb an hour ago. Problem. We are on the crew list. The tour company is responsible for checking us out of Israel and checking us back in. No one-ways. Why not? The driver, an old Palestine hand who looks North African, laughs and shrugs. "Israel! Like to make problems for us."

A phone call later Mr. Farki arrives and they argue the toss. The bus is now full again, full of tourists on a short temper leash, tourists who left their hotels five hours ago and have so far seen only traffic and checkpoints, concrete ugliness, rubble and rubbish and a dismal tomb. Now there seems to be another delay, this one caused by two of their own. I turn my back squarely to the rumbles and grumbles, like the chap at the front of a long bank queue who is taking more than his fair amount of time. Gillian is somewhere in the shade.

A deal is reached. Mr. Farki will fax a photocopy of our passports to the tour company with a note in Hebrew saying we both have runny tummies and had to go and find a doctor. Must have been something we ate. Mr. Farki, the driver and I shake hands on this unlikely sounding solution. I turn round to wave an apologetic goodbye at the tourists but goodwill time for the whole day out expired three hours ago and I'm met by looks of ice and fire.

"Thanks Mr. Farki. Let's rewind and start again. I read this place was being considered for the future capital of Palestine."

"It is."

"But compared to Ramallah it's, well, horrible. The Wall/Fence goes right by it. There's a terrible atmosphere. Even in the tourist coaches people look at you with hatred."

"Only the Israelis want the capital here, do you know why?"

"Not unless you tell me."

"Because when the Jordanians were here they responded to the Israelis evicting the Palestinians from Israel by evicting the Christians from here. There were never many, but enough that the Israelis can say 'OK, we asked some Muslims to leave, but you did the same to the Christians in al-Eizariya.' But it will never happen."

"The capital?"

"Not here, it can only be Ramallah."

"It's as grim as we've seen. I can't believe it has a future. Unlike its most famous son. Time to move on."

"Jericho?"

"Jericho."

Jerusalem rises 2,500 feet above sea level; Jericho lies 850 feet below sea level. Using all ten fingers and thumbs that means a descent of 3,350 feet. They are only fifteen miles apart. As the Taoists say, "The Journey is the Reward." It is one of the most dramatic drives one will ever see. There is a fine new road that swerves gently from side to side as it swoops down through the valleys of gigantic dunes. The landscape changes from lunar to Mercurial to Venusian. We have Mr. Farki's Daewoo Chevrolet's aircon maxed and the outside temperature is 41°C. It can't be much less inside.

About half way down to Jericho the road rises and one crests a high dune and the surroundings become barren and aimless as one takes one's first view of the Dead Sea. A minute later the road drops down past the Sea Level sign. Even after several rises and falls above and below sea level it still seems spooky to us sailors who spend most of our time bobbing up and down on Neptune's bounty. Bedouin camps line either side of the road. Pick-up trucks have replaced camels; off-road motor bikes have replaced donkeys;* aluminum cladding has replaced canvas. I don't suppose it was a bag of laughs back in the romanticized days of David Roberts' paintings; it looks like hell now. The Bedouin live like nomads without the fun of nomading. Mr. Farki blames the Israelis, but then he would. If he won the lottery he'd suspect an Israeli plot.

---

* I believe I would rather ride a donkey than any beast in the world. He goes briskly, he puts on no airs, he is docile, though opinionated. Satan himself could not scare him, and he is convenient—very convenient. When you are tired riding you can rest your feet on the ground and let him gallop from under you. *The Innocents Abroad*

When he tells us dismissively that many Arabs are certain that 9/11 was a Jewish plot to discredit the Muslims I have a sneaking feeling one per cent of him suspects it might just be true. To change the subject I read Mr. Farki Mark Twain's passage from *The Innocents Abroad* on what we are seeing now:

"We had had a glimpse, from a mountain top, of the Dead Sea, lying like a blue shield in the plain of the Jordan, and now we were marching down a close, flaming, rugged, desolate defile, where no living creature could enjoy life, except, perhaps, a salamander. It was such a dreary, repulsive, horrible solitude! It was the 'wilderness' where John preached, with camel's hair about his loins—raiment enough—but he never could have got his locusts and wild honey here."

Once the land levels, sprouts of green palms mark small oases. On the smaller hills around are settlements, again highly contentious. There are now twenty-six settlements around this part of the Jordan Valley and like all settlements they blossom and bloom at the expense of everyone else: the *Jerusalem Post* estimates that 75 per cent of all water resources in the West Bank are used to service them. Especially here, when all around is barren beyond description, the lush verdant hilltop settlements look particularly provocative, deliberatively wasteful; intentionally so, no doubt.

There is a new part of the old city of Jericho and we go there for lunch and to sit out the early afternoon heat blaze. There is nothing much here. Poor old Jericho has always been impossible to defend, the first town after the desert the invaders reach from the east and the first town the invaders from the mountains reach from the west. But the constant invasions, the last two by Jordan in 1948 and by Israel in 1967, have not wiped Jericho out—far from it, as it claims, along with Damascus, to be the oldest constantly inhabited city of the world. Mark Twain had little to say of it except: "Camped near old square tower (Middle Ages, no doubt) and modern mud Jericho, garrisoned by 12 men, Bedouin war."

The old square tower is still there, albeit now not in the center, the buildings are shabby and concrete—and this being Palestine are surrounded by rubble and rubbish. But the most interesting part of modern Jericho is the garrison, now itself largely rubble, ankle deep in rubbish, no longer even able to muster a dozen men at arms and only at war—with Israel—as a fantasy. However, there is an interesting modern story to tell and a story to appeal to Mark Twain's love of decisive action.

A story should have a beginning but in the case of Middle East politics it is hard to pinpoint at which point tit became tat and goes on to become tit again.

But for the sake of brevity let's start in mid-2001 during the second intifada. A Hamas suicide bomber walked into a luxury Park hotel in Netanya and blew up thirty Israeli guests. The Popular Front for the Liberation of Palestine (PFLP) claimed the glory. In retaliation Mossad assassinated PFLP Secretary-General Abu Ali Mustafa and in retaliation for *that* the PFLP's Ahmet Saadat assassinated the Israeli Tourism Minister Rehavam Ze'evi—the latter a particularly unpleasant racist and bigot, but not the only one of those in any given Israeli government.

It did not take the Israelis long to find out where Saadat and his gang were hiding: in Yasser Arafat's HQ building in Ramallah. They already had Arafat's compound surrounded as part of Operation Defensive Shield and they demanded Arafat hand the killers over. Eventually a deal was brokered in Washington as a part of the endless peace talks that the gang would be held in the jail in Jericho under British and American guards. For good measure the Israelis tried them *in absentia* in a military court in Ramallah and sentenced them to various terms of hard labor.

Fast forward four years and the imprisoned killer/hero Saadat was elected an MP in the Palestinian elections. The Israelis claimed he did not even know he was standing and they may very well have been right. The election was won by Hamas, who claimed that its first priority was the release of Saadat and his associates from Jericho. Actually that was their second priority: the first was blowing Israel off the face of the earth, or as they more charmingly put it, "the overdue destruction of the infidel Zionist entity, too long a cancer in our midst". Even this second priority was too much for the Israelis who were already unhappy enough about Saadat's gang being in what was portrayed in the Israeli media as an Anglo-American holiday camp with no evidence of any hard labor. It also did not help that photographs of the jail, the old British barracks dating from the time of General Allenby's Egyptian Expeditionary Force, showed an attractive clinker built residence, with a/c units much in evidence. It helped even less that the inmates were always on *Al-Jazeerah* complaining about Zionist imperialism. And now they were about to be released! Operation Bringing Home the Goods was duly launched. (I've applied to the Israeli Army to be Officer Commanding, Operation Thinking Up Silly Names but so far have not yet heard back.)

Early on the morning of 14 March 2006 the American and British guards left the compound on convenient errands in Jericho, U-turned further down the road and headed for an agreed Israeli checkpoint. This was the signal for Operation Bringing Home the Goods to hit the road. Within an hour the barracks were surrounded by 100 troops. Other troops joined, helicopters joined, tanks joined, bulldozers joined. The bulldozers started tearing down Allenby's old walls and the Apache helicopters fired into the compound to create a bit of the old shock and awe. Inside the jail 200 prisoners and guards trembled and took cover as best they could. When the onslaught stopped the Israeli commander offered safe passage to anyone who wanted to leave. The prison officials and guards—and many of the prisoners—came out in their underpants with hands held high. Saadat and his gang, and sixty-five other prisoners took over the armory. Saadat wasted no time in calling *Al-Jazeerah*: "Our choice is to fight or to die. We will not surrender. We are not going to give up, we are going to face our destiny with courage." But by nightfall he chose to face his destiny with discretion rather than courage and led the prisoners out, again in their underpants with hands held high but this time with Israeli film crews recording their humiliation. In all fairness to *Al-Jazeerah* it was on their news straight away. There were riots all over Palestine and Tony Blair had to lie again to the House of Commons, this time about the disappearing monitors.

There is, of course, an important archaeological site at Jericho, known as Tel El-Sultan, but it strains the imagination to see that it was once a city. As Twain put it: "Ancient Jericho is not very picturesque as a ruin." Quite so, in fact it looks to the uninitiated like a pile of dried mud, which in a reductionist sense is exactly what it is.

Twain recounts the old biblical myth: "When Joshua marched around it seven times, some three thousand years ago, and blew it down with his trumpet, he did the work so well and so completely that he hardly left enough of the city to cast a shadow."

The famous battle scene has biblicists and mythologists baffled, although archaeologists are certain it never happened as there was no city at the time of Joshua's famous trumpet voluntary. Numerologists insist the significance is in the number seven which has well-known occult layers of meaning.

To recap: Every day for six days Joshua ordered his priests to blow their rams' horns while other priests and soldiers carried the Ark of the Covenant once round the city walls. Then on the seventh day the priests marched seven times around the city. That done Joshua ordered the soldiers to shout and the rams' horns (the famous trumpets) to blow and the city walls came tumbling down. The soldiers then marched into the city and massacred every man and woman, young and old, yea verily even all the oxen, sheep and asses.

Mr. Farki found an inscription in Hebrew declaring the site of the city to be from 8000 BC making it the oldest city in the world. There is evidence of a sacking in around 2300 BC, a rebuilding thereafter and a final destruction by fire in 1600 BC. When Joshua's retinue arrived there were no walls to blow down nor—bad luck for him and the boys—residents to massacre. The city was repopulated in around 700 BC but slowly abandoned as residents gravitated towards the site of the new city, where we just had lunch, after that.

It's only a few miles from the dead city to the Dead Sea and we set off musing about the number seven. Mr. Farki knows it plays an important part in the Sufi mystical tradition and somehow would have the same Abrahamic roots as the Joshua story. All very interesting but I must say I am looking forward to having a float in the Dead Sea, what Mark Twain called "a funny bath".

There's not much funny about it now. There didn't seem to be too much funny about it then either: "The desert and the barren hills gleam painfully in the sun, around the Dead Sea, and there is no pleasant thing or living creature upon it or about its borders to cheer the eye. It is a scorching, arid, repulsive solitude. A silence broods over the scene that is depressing to the spirits. It makes one think of funerals and death.

"It was a funny bath. We could not sink. You can lie comfortably, on your back, with your head out, and your legs out from your knees down, by steadying yourself with your hands. You can sit, with your knees drawn up to your chin and your arms clasped around them, but you are bound to turn over presently, because you are top-heavy in that position.

"If you swim on your face, you kick up the water like a stern-wheel boat. You make no headway."

One of the other Excursionists wrote in his diary that "Mr. Twain rode his horse in and fell off it." Mr. Twain's explanation for this unfortunate mishap: "A horse is so top-heavy that he can neither swim nor stand up in the Dead Sea. He turns over on his side at once." Oh dear, Mr. Twain.

The shore from which they swam, on the north-west corner of the Dead Sea nearest to Jericho, has now been nastily developed into a hellish resort for Russian mud-bathers. Let me explain. The Wall/Fence and the checkpoints have effectively killed off the casual floater visitors from Jerusalem—only fifteen miles away—who used to make up the bulk of the tourists. In fact, hardly any foreign tour groups come because of the Wall/Fence's unpleasantness and reputation for delays. Fine, you might think, nice empty Dead Sea in which to float. Not so. All around Jericho are settlements, settlements on every hilltop. Something else I hadn't realized until this afternoon: the houses on the settlements are arranged in a spiral around the hilltops, like wagons in a circle, as if to say to outsiders: "Just you try!" There's not a lot for the settlers to do except pop down to the Dead Sea and have a float.

First they have to go through another wall of sorts: the entry to the resort. Gillian resents the fact that there's a resort here at all, and so does Mr. Farki. Her objections are on the grounds of tastelessness, his on the grounds of illegality. I find it hard to disagree with either of them. Someone has just fenced off a fine piece of shoreline, put in some turnstiles, bought some hideous old disco CDs and enormous ex-disco speakers, made a gift shop out of a tent, inserted a beer stall and numerous loungers and sat back and counted the money. You can tell you are back in Israel—even though of course you aren't—by the almost Parisian standards of rudeness, by the scowls and snarls. It's bad enough for us but Mr. Farki has to endure looks of racial indignation as well.

As these settlements are disproportionally populated with Russians, it's mostly Russians who staff it and who float—even the one thin one floated. There are signs in Russian everywhere and those are Russian voices ordering more food and beer—and covering themselves in mud.

"Disgusting!" says Mr. Farki.

"I never thought I'd hear you agree with a European Jew," I say.

"How so?"

"They all hate the Russians. Think they're gross."

"They're peasants," says Mr. Farki. "And they've got a much better deal from the Jews than the Palestinians."

"But they are Jews," I say.

"Some are; some aren't."

I look over at the family opposite and have to agree. She is disgustingly fat and covered in mud—as if that was going to do her any good. He is thin except for a pot-belly, balding with a bad haircut and has a nasty habit of picking his nose and swallowing the snot. The two children are running around out of control, which only encourages the mother to shout at them, and they, seeing that they are being noticed at last, are encouraged to run around screaming even more.

I ruminate to poor Mr. Farki who clearly can't wait to leave—and we will when I've finished this beer. I bore him thus: "Imagine you were sitting up there in some deadbeat town in the Ukraine, in a horrible one-bedroom Soviet-era flat on the twelfth floor, you and the wife and the four kids, elevator broken, garbage collection out of the window, power on and off at someone's whim, odd jobs for cash when you are not waiting in line, when an old friend pops in. Hey Comrade, he says, you remember that old farmer whose great-grandmother knew someone who was a filthy Jew? Yes, I remember, you say. Well, it seems these Jews have got their own country now and need to fill it up. Looking for anyone who will admit to having even the remotest Jewish connection. You can say you are her descendant. Why would I want to do that? you ask, imagine the shame. Are you joking? he says, it's sunny all the year round, you get a free house with lots of other Russians around, they give you money and everything. There's even a lake nearby. But I can't swim, you say. You don't have to, he replies, it's a special lake—you just float in it. I'm going, he says, you should too, bring your family. What about your Lyudmila and the kids? you ask. They're coming too he says and my brother Sergei the strangler. The prison is forging Jewish grandmother papers for all the worst prisoners, your old friend says, sees this as a good chance to offload them."

"I hate this place," says Mr. Farki thinking out loud. "Everything is unnatural. You can't sink in the water. It's below sea level. It stinks of bad eggs. I hate these people too. Israel does not belong in the Middle East but we have to accept it now. But Russia? Why should they be here on Arab land? Half of them aren't even Jews. And Arabs living like Russians peasants in refugee camps."

"Sounds like you want to leave," I say.

"Sorry, I know it's on the list to visit. Aren't you going for swim?"

"You must be joking, swimming here? I might meet Avigdor Lieberman!" I empty the beer. Mr. Farki laughs. The Russian Lieberman would just be another bigoted dolt if he weren't Israel's Deputy Prime Minister and Foreign Affairs Minister. Born fifty miles from here he'd be a high-up in Hamas, calling for Israel's destruction instead of a high-up in Israel calling for Palestine's destruction. Both Hamas and Lieberman are products of democracy. Terrifying.

"So we can leave?" Mr. Farki asks hopefully.

"Is the pope Catholic?" I reply.

"What do you mean? Of course he's Catholic."

"I'll explain later."

In the car I am reading a *Jerusalem Post* I found lying on someone's old lounger at the resort from hell. I come across this story about an Israeli company called Ahava who make cosmetics featuring Dead Sea minerals and claim they are made in Israel, when in fact they are made in the West Bank/Occupied Territories/Palestine. I read the piece aloud to Gillian and Mr. Farki:

A call to boycott Israeli-made Ahava products in a Maryland beauty supply store backfired last week when pro-Israel activists countered by purchasing the shop's entire Ahava inventory.

When the Jewish Community Relations Council of Greater Washington found out that the pro-Palestinian group Sabeel DC had organized a protest and boycott call at Ulta in Silver Spring last Saturday, the organization sent out an action alert urging supporters to visit the store and buy Ahava.

"They cleaned the shelves out. It was the best Ahava sales weekend the store has ever seen. They had to order an expedited shipment," said Arielle Farber, director of Israel and International Affairs for the Community Relations Council. "The greater Washington community is not going to stand for this campaign to delegitimize Israel."

Rona Kramer, a Maryland state senator, was among those answering the Community Relations Council call. When she heard of the boycott, she though "it's a good opportunity for the community to show its support for Israel."

Faith McDonnell, another area pro-Israel activist, was moved to show up on Saturday morning because she figured many members of the Jewish community wouldn't be able to come due to observance of Shabbat.

"'There were a lot of Christians who were standing with the Jewish people and Israel on this," McDonnell said.

The Sabeel DC Metro chapter that organized the action said it was held on Saturday morning to take advantage of the large crowds attending a farmers' market held by the store.

Paul Verduin, who coordinated the Saturday event and was one of 12 participants, said he wasn't disappointed by the outcome, which saw Ahava sales boosted.

"We operate under the concept of witness. We're trying to testify to the fact that Ahava is one of the products being sold in the US claiming to be an Israeli product when it is made in the West Bank," he said, saying that Sabeel is a nonviolent organization that seeks a "just peace" between Israelis and Palestinians.

In his letter announcing the boycott, Verduin described Ahava products as "made by West Bank settlers from natural resources stolen from the Palestinian people."

"That's right," says Mr. Farki.
I read again:

In a statement on the subject, Ahava countered that "the mud and materials used in Ahava cosmetics products are not excavated in an occupied area. The minerals are mined in the Israeli part of the Dead Sea, which is undisputed internationally."

Further, it states that Mitzpe Shalem, a West Bank kibbutz where Ahava products are produced, "is not an illegal settlement."

"They are all illegal," Mr. Farki pipes up.
I continue:

Ahava North America CEO Michael Etedgi told *The Jerusalem Post* that despite boycott actions in California, New York and Texas as well as in Washington, DC, business has not suffered, nor has he heard from any company that plans to stop selling Ahava as a result.

Verduin said that his Sabeel chapter intended to carry on with its efforts. "We will continue this until the Occupation stops," he said.

Outside the car the countryside... well, it cannot really be called countryside, the landscape, the wilderness "is not of this earth".

Often over the last weeks my heart has often gone out to the Excursionists and their caravanserai as they traversed the barren, arid Samarian scrubland

and now this Judean desert, swaying through the liquid heat, squinting against the dazzling whiteness, holding high their parasols almost in desperation, jaded by the endless repetitiveness of the desolation, by the constant thirst and the unrelentingly discomfort. But even by the standards of what they have endured before, this must have been like riding through the very hell of Hades.

"I cannot describe the hideous afternoon's ride from the Dead Sea to Mars Saba. It oppresses me yet, to think of it. The sun so pelted us that the tears ran down our cheeks once or twice. The ghastly, treeless, grassless, breathless canyons smothered us as if we had been in an oven. The sun had positive weight to it, I think. Not a man could sit erect under it. All drooped low in the saddles. John preached in this 'Wilderness!' It must have been exhausting work. What a very heaven the messy towers and ramparts of vast Mars Saba looked to us when we caught a first glimpse of them!"

〜〜〜

And so they are even to us in Mr. Farki's dodgy Daewoo. The Excursionists' ride through the breathless canyons must have taken them five, or even six, hours. It takes us half an hour and we give up on with the faltering a/c and open the windows, partly, as I explain to a reluctant Mr. Farki, "to get the real caravanserai experience". It is more than unusual to travel through absolute nothingness but we see only sky, air and rock, empty of life, as if it had never rained. The road was a track in the dust and either side of it someone had laid forlorn way poles.

When we first see the monastery of Mars Saba it is as incongruous as it is later to become magnificent. The first sighting is from about half a mile away as the car crests a mound: two desert-colored Byzantine towers rise up from the rim of a *wadi* and then disappear as the car falls into the next dip. Moments later the full extent of the architecture, the achievement of it all, becomes clear. Up close the wadi is actually a cliff face and the multi-floored monastery is somehow etched onto it as if in defiance of all known laws of gravity and reason. One is reminded instantly of a smaller version Potala Palace at Lhasa in Tibet, but the view of that is always looking up at the massive lower fortifications and buttresses; here one approaches the monastery from the side elevation and arrives at it from above. Standing on the lip of the cliff face we see Mars Saba falling away carelessly below in a tumble of inter-layered vertical connecting walls, blue domes, earthen cupolas, Hellenic crosses, spiraling cell doors and windows, shaded balconies and a host of random staircases. It's hard to determine if it was all built at once by a divinely inspired genius or it is the creation of a Disney cartoonist or has grown organically, as it were, over the centuries as hermits left their caves for the safety of a structure—and hermits in caves became monks in cells.

It is, of course, the latter. In the early Byzantium period it was not unusual for supplicants to follow John's example and seek salvation through asceticism in the Wilderness. The shelter of cave dwelling as a hermit followed naturally and as caves tend to come in clusters, building a surrounding wall around them for safety—and the company and discipline of congregation—was the next progression. As enlightened hermits attracted their own devotees the congregations needed an organized structure and by the time Mars Saba was founded, in about 550 AD, there were already fifty or so monasteries in this John the Baptist desert part of the Holy Land; there would later be as many as one hundred and fifty; now there are nine, of which Mars Saba is the most prominent and permanent. It cannot however claim total permanence from 550 AD: in 614 the Persian army invaded and massacred all four hundred monks in residence; their skulls are still neatly arranged in the Chapel of the Cross cave in Mars Saba, as neatly arranged as the prayer cushions in an Anglican church in the English shires. Within two weeks of the Persian massacre other hermits from nearby caves came to bury the dead, preserve the skulls and revive the monastery.

In Mark Twain's time all monasteries were open to pilgrims and travelers, and as he wrote: "The convents are a priceless blessing to the poor. A pilgrim without money, whether he be a Protestant or a Catholic, can travel the length and breadth of Palestine, and in the midst of her desert wastes find wholesome food and a clean bed every night, in these buildings. Pilgrims in better circumstances are often stricken down by the sun and the fevers of the country, and then their saving refuge is the Convent. Without these hospitable retreats, travel in Palestine would be a pleasure which none but the strongest men could dare to undertake." He should have added Orthodox too, whether Greek, Syrian or Armenian—and it was Greek in the case of Mars Saba.

For himself, "I have been educated to enmity toward every thing that is

Catholic, and sometimes, in consequence of this, I find it much easier to discover Catholic faults than Catholic merits. But there is one thing I feel no disposition to overlook, and no disposition to forget: and that is, the honest gratitude I and all pilgrims owe, to the Convent Fathers in Palestine. Their doors are always open, and there is always a welcome for any worthy man who comes, whether he comes in rags or clad in purple."

Not so today. Firstly, of course, there has been a massive decline in Christianity as a whole in the region. In Twain's time there were about half a million people in the Holy Land; one reads estimates of a quarter of them being Christian—and devoutly Christian too. Today, although the population has increased twentyfold the number of Christians has declined to about five per cent—and many—most—of those are lackadaisical in their worship. Secondly, religious intolerance has increased as every headline will aver, partly because the Muslims associate Zionism with Judaism, partly because Judaism associates Islam with terrorism and partly because the Christian bloc has fractured into increasingly acrimonious factions. And thirdly, the whole concept of monastic life sits at odds with the way we live today; it is no longer a variation on home life—and for most it was a variation with practical material advantages—but a complete repudiation of how humans are living and how human consciousness is evolving.

All of which brings me to the current dilemma as I say goodbye to Mr. Farki and Gillian at the gate of Mars Saba. It is no longer possible to just arrive, Excursionists-style, at a Greek Orthodox convent and ask for shelter—or even a visit. As we have observed before, the Greek Orthodox Church in the Holy Land has gone off on a seemingly unChristian tangent in its attitude to pilgrims, visitors and even to itself. As I write there has been a *coup d'état* in the Greek Orthodox Patriarchy in Jerusalem with the extant patriarch under house arrest and the current patriarch, a Greek, fighting off an Arab insurgency among his flock.

Sin-wise* the problem has been sevenfold: a combination of wrath, greed, sloth, pride, lust, envy and gluttony—but especially greed. The fully titled "Patriarch of the Holy City of Jerusalem and all Palestine, Syria, beyond

* A sin takes on new and real terrors when there seems a chance it is going to be found out. *The Man that Corrupted Hadleyburg*

the Jordan River, Cana of Galilee, and Holy Zion" has accumulated massive holdings over the centuries and the temptation for a bit of asset stripping has become too much. While it was bad enough to sell church land to property speculators in Tel Aviv for apartment construction, it wasn't such a good idea to get caught selling church-owned property in Jerusalem's Old City to right-wing Zionist settler groups like (but not) Ateret Cohanim. It gets worse. Recently it has come to light that the patriarchate has been selling land in East Jerusalem to proxies for the Israeli government for more settlements on land the Palestinian Christians—and all Palestinians—hope will be part of a future Palestinian state. The scandal has now gone diplomatic with the Greek, Israeli and Jordanian governments, the Greek Patriarchy in Athens, the Israeli Supreme Court and the Palestine Authority all trying to protect their positions. Meanwhile the extant patriarch, languishing behind bars in Jerusalem, has been demoted to a monk and refused criminal immunity by the Greek government—under pressure from Israel, Jordon, Hamas and common decency—after he sought voluntary repatriation for himself and his burgeoning bank account.

So back to my dilemma. For a non-Orthodox to stay, or even visit, at Mars Saba one needs written permission from the patriarchate in Jerusalem but in view of all the shenanigans they have not replied to my phone messages, then emails and lastly a registered letter. Cold calling didn't work either. Meanwhile in Jerusalem I heard that convents like Mars Saba are so disenchanted with the patriarchate that they are rowing their own boat. I decide the only option is to arrive alone (as the Muslim Mr. Farki and the female Gillian certainly won't be allowed in) with copies of the correspondence and appeal to their better selves. If unsuccessful I am to call Mr. Farki and Gillian and they'll come and fetch me; it is as we say goodbye we realize there is no cell phone signal in the middle of the Judean desert. Oh, for the simplicities of a caravanserai parked on the doorstep.

I need not have worried. The gate opens and particularly hirsute monk ushers me in unspoken in a swish of black robes. I am led down the first of many staircases to a courtyard and the refectory off it and gestured to sit. All the windows are wide open and a hint of a breeze cools the air. It is about four in the afternoon and a shadow dissects the room. After ten minutes a young monk, in his late twenties, arrives and says, "Yes?"

I introduce myself and explain about Mark Twain and the patriarchate. I show him the correspondence but he just glances in their direction. I start to explain who Mark Twain was but he holds up his hand—he knows. He looks at me intently and I'm disarmed by his kind eyes and fear my explanation must seem a rush from another world.

"My name is Father Spiro. How long do you want to stay?" he asks softly.

"Well I'm following Mark Twain's footsteps, so one night if possible, just as he did."

"I hope you are not too hungry," he smiles by way of acceptance. "We live simply." Outside bells chime.

He shows me to the room—up a dozen steps—one is always going up and down steps in this place. Fr. Spiro is in his early forties, not late twenties, and has been here for fifteen years. He visited once with a pilgrim tour from Thessalonica and decided then and there to change his life, to "find God for myself, directly". And the English? He was a teacher in Greece and now he reads the Bible[*] in English—the proper King James version I'm pleased to report—as well as in Koine Greek.

The room, really a small cell, has stone floors, whitewashed walls broken up by a Greek Islands blue dado, a homemade bedstead, a dozen blankets for a mattress, coarse sheets and an embroidered cushion for a pillow, an empty shelf, a window, and a lantern. There's a stool, a desk—homemade like the bedstead, two candles and a box of matches. Fr. Spiro sees me looking at them and laughs: "There is no electricity. And this is one of our luxury cells for visitors."

～

When Mark Twain stayed here there were seventy monks; now there are twenty. He was at first shocked by their life choice, then the next day apologetic for being shocked—of which more later. "They wear a coarse robe, an ugly, brimless stove-pipe of a hat, and go without shoes. They eat nothing whatever but bread and salt; they drink nothing but water. As long as they live they can never go outside the walls, or look upon a woman—for no woman is permitted to enter Mars Saba, upon any pretext whatsoever.

---

[*] During many ages there were witches. The Bible said so. The Bible commanded that they should not be allowed to live. Therefore the Church, after eight hundred years, gathered up its halters, thumb-screws, and firebrands, and set about its holy work in earnest. She worked hard at it night and day during nine centuries and imprisoned, tortured, hanged, and burned whole hordes and armies of witches, and washed the Christian world clean with their foul blood. Then it was discovered that there was no such thing as witches, and never had been. One does not know whether to laugh or to cry. *Europe and Elsewhere*

"Some of those men have been shut up there for thirty years. In all that dreary time they have not heard the laughter of a child or the blessed voice of a woman; they have seen no human tears, no human smiles; they have known no human joys, no wholesome human sorrows. All that is lovable, beautiful, worthy, they have put far away from them; against all things that are pleasant to look upon, and all sounds that are music to the ear, they have barred their massive doors and reared their relentless walls of stone forever. They have banished the tender grace of life and left only the sapped and skinny mockery. Their lips are lips that never kiss and never sing; their hearts are hearts that never hate and never love; their breasts are breasts that never swell with the sentiment, 'I have a country and a flag.' They are dead men who walk."

I presume Twain and the New Pilgrims stayed in the same row of "luxury cells" as I am staying in and at least observed the same regime as I'm following now. Fr. Spiro has told me I've missed the one meal of the day, always bread and salt, boiled vegetables and feta cheese, which they take at midday "when the sun is at its fiercest". They only drink water. He told me the monks were resting in their cells now.

❧

"I'll say good night." It was twenty to five. "Do you wish to join us for morning office?"

"Yes," I reply, "I'd like that very much. And to join in everything else that you do while I'm here."

"Very well. The church bells ring to wake the monks. A hand bell will sound outside our door to wake you too."

It's too early to sleep and anyway I have the day's travels to wash away. I climb down to the communal washing area, aware that even bare foot my rubbing trousers are making far too much noise. Back in the cell I am writing down these notes and thoughts, waiting for it to be dark enough to enjoy the excitement of lighting a match to light the lantern and candles. There are adjustments to be made: the feeling of a sudden vacuum and empty space after all the activity at Jericho and the Dead Sea, then a feeling of having to fill the space, and then living in the peace of having nothing to do, nowhere to go, no need to plan, no one to talk to, no questions to answer, no reason to rush, no past to recall and no future in which to escape; just, being here, sitting quietly, doing nothing.

Ding-dong-ding-dong; ding-dong-ding-dong. The sleep is deep, the ringing is urgent and from high above the cell. When we first wake up our different faculties wake up in turn: first the universal feeling of existence, then the memory, then the shared intelligence and then the egoic mind. Mind wants to know what time it is so it can start bossing me around. I strike a match and see it's one o'clock and lie back down and fall asleep as the ringing from the campanile continues outside. Ding-dong-ding-dong; ding-dong-ding-dong. The ringing is now from right outside the door. The struck match shows one thirty. Still back to doze if not to sleep. Ding-dong-ding-dong; ding-dong-ding-dong. This time the bells from the campanile above again, joined now by other flatter sounds from closer bells. Five to two. Can prayers really start at two? They do; at two all the bells in the monastery ring in unison, if not in harmony, the storm before the calm.

I regret to report that I fall back to sleep but with every intention of getting up "soon". "Soon" turns out to be just before five. In the cold and darkness I struggle into the clothes and feel my way down to where the sound of monastic chant and murmur is coming. The soft scent of frankincense guides me in.

One enters directly into the nave; there is no narthex, the space in which the non-Orthodox normally must wait. The basilica is lit by four lanterns resting on a high sill around the northern and southern walls and a dozen candles around the *horos*, the chandelier above the nave. The effect is to light the rim of the dome and the icons above eye height across the walls. The iconostasis, at the eastern end of the nave remains practically unlit. Below that the light is dim and flickering so the black-robed monks cannot be individually discerned, only heard as a mass, as it were.

The liturgy is heavily ritualized with breaks in the chanting, the noiseless swinging of frankincense in censers and ringing of hand bells. All chant and pray together in the biblical Koine Greek and all pray together facing the east, the monks behind the priest. One cannot help considering what a massive error it has been for the Catholic Church to reduce the language of their liturgy to everyday speech and have the priest turn towards the congregation and not towards God, thereby turning the sacred and the mystical into a sort of humdrum business convention. The Orthodox tradition is still with purpose another world, one beyond the analytical mind to dissect and justify, an artificially created parallel universe which invites its devotees to forsake their egos and join the Godhead in a state of presence leading to transcendence.

This similarity between the Eastern Orthodox tradition, with which I am not familiar, and the Vedantic tradition, which is more home ground, became clear at first light, just before six o'clock. The monks have by then been at prayer for four hours, filling the monastery with the same chants and prayers and murmurs that its walls have heard, apart from the two-week Persian incursion, every morning for the last 1460 years. The early light shows the Christ Pantocrator—the creator of the universe—in the dome. Below that and above the iconostasis hang three large icons of Father, Son and Spirit—not three gods but God as Three, very intentionally mythological and therefore available, with devotion and discipline, charity and compassion, to human comprehension—even if, by the terms and conditions of Reality, ultimately ineffable.

We shall never know if Mark Twain saw or maybe even heard any of this liturgy, although he could hardly have missed the constant, and seemingly random, peeling of bells; it is not mentioned in *The Innocents Abroad*, or in his notes, or articles for the *Alta California*, or as far as I can tell subsequently at all. However, his stay at Mars Saba did have an effect on him. When he arrived he commented rather acidly about the monks as quoted above and yet the next morning he was moved to observe:

"These hermits are dead men, in several respects, but not in all. There is something human about them somewhere. They knew we were foreigners and Protestants, and not likely to feel admiration or much friendliness toward them. But their large charity was above considering such things. They simply saw in us men who were hungry, and thirsty, and tired, and that was sufficient. They opened their doors and gave us welcome. They asked no questions, and they made no self-righteous display of their hospitality. They fished for no compliments. They moved quietly about, setting the table for us, making the beds, and bringing water to wash in, and paid no heed when we said it was wrong for them to do that when we had men whose business it was to perform such offices.

"We fared most comfortably, and sat late at dinner. We walked all over the building with the hermits afterward, and then sat on the lofty battlements and smoked while we enjoyed the cool air, the wild scenery and the sunset. It was a royal rest we had."

He does not elaborate on why these "dead men who walk" should now be seen differently, but my instinct is that he not only came across charity at Mars

Saba, as he acknowledged, but he also came across love, and came across it for the first time since the Holy Land tour started. I'm imagining that the Holy Land Semites whom Mark Twain came across are very much, deep down, the same Holy Land Semites one comes across today. Now although the Semites, Jewish or Muslim, have many fine qualities—hospitality, honesty, generosity, courtesy—I cannot really say that love, in the Christian sense, is among them. My feeling is that when Twain came across pure, unconditional, unsentimental love at Mars Saba he was taken aback by the experience.

I think it's fair to say that the evolved liturgy and symbolism notwithstanding, the Eastern Orthodox tradition is far closer to the original message of Christianity than the Western one; if nothing else the language of prayer is the same. Our Western understanding of the Trinity as mentioned above, for example, has lost all its original mythological and mystical flavor and has become a barren intellectual concept to be argued this way and that in the same evolved language in which the revised message is heard. Jesus himself was after all a Galilean Hellenic Jew, and the Greco-Roman Jew Paul took his version of the meaning of Jesus' life, turned into the sacrifice of Christ's death and took the message that became Christianity to a Hellenized gentile world. Neither Jesus nor Paul were unreconstructed Semites. It's a short leap from self-sacrifice to universal-love, a longer leap from Pauline Christianity to Eastern Orthodoxy but given time the connection is there. The quality of Love after all transcends time; Love is perfect kindness, also timeless. What Mark Twain experienced was descended directly from Christ's message of love—and in the Holy Land would have come as much a shock for him then as it has for me here at Mars Saba now. I would only suggest to Sam that it is *because* they live as hermits and without ego that he found Love here, and not *in spite of* them living like hermits as he implies; a sort of TLUC in reverse.

I suspect that Twain's love bells were easily rung. Here in Mars Saba the message was of impersonal love: Thou shalt love thy neighbor as thyself, the Golden Rule. He was also open to personal love and a year later met and two years later married Olivia, sister of one of his Sinner shipmates. It was "love at first sight" and so it stayed until Olivia's death thirty years later. In Paris, two months before visiting Mars Saba, he had made a special effort to see the tombs of the legendary lovers Abelard and Héloïse; he even wrote a skit on their romance in *The Innocents Abroad*. These lovers were an early example—from the twelfth century—of the new Western idea of love between two people who willing chose each other—rather than having the state, church or family choose each one for the other. From then we also find for the first time the romantic tragedy *Tristan and Isolde*; it was a time when troubadours sang of "what the eyes had made welcome to the heart", when Guillaume de Lorris wrote of "noble and gentle hearts". In these sound bite days we might say it was the triumph of libido over credo.

Time to move on. All concerned left early to reach Bethlehem before the desert furnace made traveling intolerable, the hardy Excursionists and their caravanserai at five, the soft Saxon Daewoo-ers and their faithful Fergy at seven. Twain left with the words: "Our party, pilgrims and all, will always be ready and always willing, to touch glasses and drink health, prosperity and long life to the Convent Fathers of Palestine." I'm trying to avoid saying "I'll drink to that," but I'll drink to that. Then: "So, rested and refreshed, we fell into line and filed away over the barren mountains of Judea, and along rocky ridges and through sterile gorges, where eternal silence and solitude reigned."

<hr/>

The rocky ridges and sterile gorges are now a particularly depressing part of Palestine. The Judean desert actually ends about fifteen miles west of Mars Saba and then one is upon the outskirts of what certain parties would like to call Greater Jerusalem. There is desolation here, but of the human kind, abandoned concrete shells, rusted cars, the obligatory rubble and rubbish. This used to be near from where Palestinians commuted to Jerusalem to work, but since the Wall/Fence have been prevented from doing so. It's a forlorn, listless, forgotten corner of Palestine, without the enormous aid dollars keeping north of Ramallah buoyant and without the Russian one-way tourism that keeps Jericho with its head above the below-sea-level water.

I ask Mr. Farki if any of the Palestinians we see loafing about can get into Jerusalem to find work. "In theory yes, in practice very few. There are qualifications. You have to be married and have a family, you must be over forty and never involved in any political activity. Unofficially it helps if you are a Christian. Half the population is under twenty and if you are over forty it's hard not to have been involved somehow in the two intifadas. It means they can pick and choose."

"But if I was an Israeli," I reply, "I would, say fair enough. We have profiled suicide bombers and seen that they are unmarried, under forty and politically active. So we'll just let in those who, demographically, are unlikely to blow us up. What's wrong with that?"

"What's wrong with that is that the desperation it brings just breeds more suicide bombers."

"So I finish off the wall. You have to admit that the wall and the profiling have stopped the suicide bombers."

"If you say so. All I have to admit to is that it's a mess. Both sides are in the wrong," Mr. Farki replies.

"Or in the right. That's the problem."

"And anyway," he says, 'the Israelis started the suicide bombing."

We are soon just short of Bethlehem and the magic spell of Mars Saba is wearing off. Mark Twain "reached the Plain of the Shepherds, and stood in a walled garden of olives where the shepherds were watching their flocks by night, eighteen centuries ago, when the multitude of angels brought them the tidings that the Saviour was born.

"The Plain of the Shepherds is a desert, paved with loose stones, void of vegetation, glaring in the fierce sun. Only the music of the angels it knew once could charm its shrubs and flowers to life again and restore its vanished beauty. No less potent enchantment could avail to work this miracle."

Mr. Farki has no idea where the Plain of the Shepherds was or is; Twain's description could apply to any of the abandonment around here, and by then we are in Bethlehem.

Well, Bethlehem looks abandoned too. We have no problem parking the car, always a bad sign, prosperity-wise. We park in a side street next to the Church of the Nativity; all the fronts of all the souvenir shops are boarded up. As soon as we open the door a guide is offering his services.

"It's dead town, Mr. Farki. The Wall/Fence again?"

"Yes, it's the Wall/Fence again."

Opposite the Church of the Nativity is Manger Square, now a fully concreted commercial center but, according to models at the Palestine Heritage Center nearby, where the Excursionists and their caravanserai would have stopped on their quick visit to Bethlehem. On one side of it is a newish white building called Peace Center, kindly donated by Sweden, as Sweden is often kind enough to donate ivory towers to good causes. Our old amigo TLUC showed up again when the Israeli Army thanked the Swedes very much for their foresight and commandeered the Peace Center as its HQ during the 2002 Siege of Bethlehem during the Al-Aqsa, or second intifada.

~~~

After the faux-religiosity at the Church of the Holy Sepulcher Twain was expecting the worst at the Church of the Nativity and he wasn't disappointed.

"In the huge Church of the Nativity, in Bethlehem, built fifteen hundred years ago by the inveterate St. Helena, they took us below ground, and into a grotto cut in the living rock. This was the 'manger' where Christ was born. A silver star set in the floor bears a Latin inscription to that effect. It is polished with the kisses of many generations of worshiping pilgrims. The grotto was tricked out in the usual tasteless style observable in all the holy places of Palestine.

"As in the Church of the Holy Sepulcher, envy and uncharitableness were apparent here. The priests and the members of the Greek and Latin churches can not come by the same corridor to kneel in the sacred birthplace of the Redeemer, but are compelled to approach and retire by different avenues, lest they quarrel and fight on this holiest ground on earth."

I don't believe he was there long enough to see the inter-denominational cleaning routine. If he had, he would have been amused by its absurdity. This is what happens. The church is divided up into three chapels, one for each denomination of Greek Orthodox, Roman Catholic and Armenian Orthodox. Under the Greek Orthodox chapel is Christ's manger and a fourth tiny chapel has been built there. This they share. They have a strict rota system for masses in the manger chapel. After each mass priests from the two absent denominations have to decontaminate the chapel and its surrounding areas in preparation for whomsoever's turn is next. Why so? Because either of the other sects would surely have left heretical dust behind in their semi-pagan service in the sacred space.

Down in the manger this morning the Armenian Orthodox are holding a mass. Two Greek Orthodox priests are waiting in their chapel above, one with a multicolored fluffy duster, the other with a purple plastic soft broom. A Franciscan friar is leaning on the gatepost of the Roman Catholic chapel with a broom in his hand. The house-husband in me can't help noticing that they are all brooms and no pans.

After the mass an Armenian cleric climbs the few steps up to floor level and carries his icons to a cupboard and locks them away in it. He then walks over to his own ground-floor chapel, right next to the Greek one, pulls a rope and rings a bell three times. All eyes now turn to a door leading into the Catholic chapel. Presently the friar arrives with his long wooden broom. The two with brooms now start sweeping where the Armenian priest has just walked, while the one with the fluffy duster is now fluffy-dusting the venerable old stone pillars which the Armenian has just walked past. A minute later all three descend to manger level and, out of sight, presumably sweep and fluffy-dust away down there. The whole process takes ten minutes during which time a queue of several hundred flustered and impatient tourists has built up. Now one might have thought that at some stage over the last thousand years and more one of the patriarchs might have said to the other: "Hey guys, this is a bit daft. If we have to clean up after each other's non-existent mess six times a day why don't we each chip in a few euros a week and get a cleaner?" but alas, no.

Now, when the cleaner priests have finished buffing up the manger the crowds are allowed in but it is such a tiny space that it is entry Noah's Ark-style only. Sensibly enough there's a one-way system. There's a glitch, however. Tourists who have employed Fergusons are allowed into the manger through the exit—they follow their guide to the exit, he tips the security men, and the guide shows them down to the exit. In the manger this causes total logjam. Eventually a gaggle of breathless visitors stagger out up the stairs. Within moments from both the official entrance and unofficial exit more of them meet in the manger middle—and so the slow and tiresome procedure repeats itself.

Sadly here even the normal helpful and cheerful Franciscans have been supping at the same bloody-minded cup as the Greek Orthodox. One can have sympathy for the Franciscans. Presumably they joined for spiritual reasons and they have been sent here, to this most deeply unspiritual place. I presume this is a hardship detail, a kind of penance.

But we can have some sympathy. If the Church of the Holy Sepulcher, where Jesus is supposed to have died, is the least spiritual place the writer has ever visited, then the Church of the Nativity, where Jesus is supposed to have been born, comes a close second. Maybe it's all these "supposeds"; even the most unquestioning cleric must have heard by now that modern investigations have placed the birth and death elsewhere, close by but still elsewhere, and once the authenticity has been lost only the pretence remains. And one imagines a young Franciscan friar did not join to pretend.

At least now one is spared the horrors of "the troops of beggars and relic-peddlers" who plagued Mark Twain's visit to this and all the other holy sites. After leaving the Church of the Nativity he wrote that "You can not think in this place any more than you can in any other in Palestine that would be likely to inspire reflection. Beggars, cripples and monks compass you about, and make you think only of bucksheesh when you would rather think of something more in keeping with the character of the spot."

The next day he was more reflective about the irony involved with feeling unholy in a holy site: "It does not stand to reason that men are reluctant to leave places where the very life is almost badgered out of them by importunate swarms of beggars and peddlers who hang in strings to one's sleeves and coat-tails and shriek and shout in his ears and horrify his vision with the ghastly sores and malformations they exhibit. One is glad to get away. Shrunken and knotted distortions, with scarred and hideous deformities, and the discordant din of a hated language, and then see how much lingering reluctance to leave could be mustered.

"We do not think, in the holy places; we think in bed, afterwards, when the glare, and the noise, and the confusion are gone, and in fancy we revisit alone, the solemn monuments of the past, and summon the phantom pageants of an age that has passed away."

～

It's time for us to leave the spiritual tackiness and material depression of Bethlehem behind, but any positive feelings about saying goodbye to either of these are tempered by also having to say goodbye to Mr. Farki. He drives us to the Wall/Fence and we both bring out the profusions: his of gratitude and mine of appreciation, and both of ours for the memories of our time together against the official nonsense from both sides in this faux-war zone of Palestine. I promise to send him a copy of this book. One day he will reach this very sentence and will read: *As-Salami Alaykum*, Farki effendi—may peace be upon you, your family and your country.

Time to put way the hankies and move on. Mr. Farki drops us at the Wall/Fence crossing point at Bayt Jala. We are becoming dab hands at the push and shove at the turnstiles and masters of the art of obsequious posing for the cameras. This crossing has large signs in Arabic and English* forbidding those crossing from dropping litter; as a result, underneath the sign is a veritable mound of empty coffee cups, Coke tins, scrunched up cigarette packets and other detritus of minor victories. TLUC? Maybe.

Twain does not say very much about their overnight stop in Ramla except to note that they stayed with "the good monks at the convent". One has the impression—well, one knows, that by now the Excursionists had had quite enough of the rigors of excursioning and were racing, literally horse racing the next morning, to rejoin the *Quaker City* at Jaffa and start the long, slow voyage back to the comfort and certainties of New York.

But the convent at Ramla, actually the Franciscan Church and Hospice of St. Nicodemus and St. Joseph of Arimathea, was of some interest to me as in March 1799 Napoleon Bonaparte stayed there during his Levantine Expedition. He was on his way to meet his first Waterloo at Acre courtesy of my hero, Sir Sidney Smith, of whom Napoleon later said: "That man has cost me my destiny."

There is a sign on the convent door: "By previous Appointment only, Admission", but I ring the bell anyway. Nothing happens, no-one at home. As we are leaving a beaten up old white and rust Toyota Corolla pulls into the driveway and a handsome-looking friar jumps out. "Hi," he says, "can I help you?" On the wall across the street someone has graffitied "No Arabs No Terrorism".

"I'd recognize that accent anywhere," I say.

"Seattle."

"Ah, well I got that wrong."

"You're English? That's not too hard."

"Right first time, and so is my wife here, Gillian."

He had been out on a dry cleaning errand and we follow him into the sacristy. I nearly put my foot in it when he says his name is Friar Engelbert; I'm about to say "like the popular singer Engelbert Humperdink" when he says "like the German composer Engelbert Humperdink." I explain about being here officially in the footsteps of Mark Twain, and unofficially in those of Napoleon Bonaparte. "Not likely bedfellows but they both stayed here."

Fr. Engelbert knows all about them both and shows me a visitors' book signed on Saturday 29 September 1867 by "William Denny Esq., & Co."; Denny was in fact the New Pilgrims' group leader.

---

* To any foreigner, English is exceedingly difficult. Even the angels speak it with an accent. *Pudd'nhead Wilson*

"They probably stayed in some of the hospice rooms. How many were they?" he asks.

"Eight Americans. Twenty odd more in the caravanserai, they'd have stayed outside."

We snoop around upstairs. Napoleon's room is clearly marked, but plain and empty. Above the door are signs in Arabic or Hebrew. Fr. Engelbert reads them both aloud and translates: "Here stayed the Emperor Napoleon. 2-11 March 1799." Ahead lies a long passage with a dozen clean and simple rooms on either side. Fr. Engelbert assumes that the Excursionists would have stayed in these.

We take tea in the refectory and I admire his trilingual skills. He reflects that Arabs and Jews have a lot more in common than a similar language. They greet each other with shalom or salaam, which both, irony apart, mean peace. They are both genetically Semitic. They both seek to regulate all aspects of a person's life, not just their personal faith. Their death rituals are remarkably similar—and obviously have the same source. They both have invented a system of religious jurisprudence—the rabbis' *responsa* is not dissimilar to the imams' *fatwa*. They both worship one god and trace their theology from Abraham—and are more monotheistic than Christianity with its doctrine of the trinity. In the days of Christian supremacy—either crusader or Byzantine—they sided with each other. They both abhor pork, among other dietary restrictions. They both have a day of rest. They both revolve around their families. They both specialize in selective memory syndrome. And they are both quite prepared to resort to terrorism for their piece of the Holy Land, the Israelis against the British and the Arabs against the Israelis.

"That's right," he says, "in 1948 the Jews exploded a bomb in Ramla market killing fifty Christians and Muslims."

"Did many Christians leave then?" I ask.

"Oh yes, many fled," Fr. Engelbert replies. "There were very few Christians here after 1948. The Israelis evicted twelve thousand Muslims and Christians from here and Lydda, now called Lod, at gunpoint. Hundreds died on the forced march to Jordan."

Gillian pours more tea; I ask him more questions. He says: "Everyone talks about the Israeli massacre of hundreds of Arabs, all Muslim this time, at Deir Yassin. But many more died here. This was an Arab city, one of the main ones. Deir Yassin was just a village. The Israeli viewed themselves as freedom fighters, but the Christians must have thought them terrorists."

"It has always been thus," I reply, "One man's freedom fighter is another man's terrorist. The Americans backed the Mujahideen, now they're the Taliban. They also sponsored the IRA bombers for years, thought of them as freedom fighters; the Brits called them terrorists—which is what they were."

I tell Fr. Engelbert about a random paragraph I had read in a *Jerusalem Post* supplement. The Israelis justify the Occupation by abhorring terrorism. When the Israeli were terrorists, when they were shooting and hanging the British, the British High Commissioner summoned David Ben-Gurion to a meeting. Ben-Gurion said that of course he deplored terrorism—but in view of the British occupation, what else could the British expect? Once more perspective and irony in the Middle East run for cover.

The Excursionists rode the final ten miles of the Holy Land Tour at a brisk pace. One senses they could not wait to reach Jaffa and rejoin the *Quaker City*, which they hoped would be lying at anchor offshore.

"We galloped the horses a good part of the distance to Jaffa for the plain was as level as a floor and free from stones, and besides this was our last march in Holy Land. These two or three hours finished, we and the tired horses could have rest and sleep as long as we wanted it. As we drew near to Jaffa, the boys spurred up the horses and indulged in the excitement of an actual race—an experience we had hardly had since we raced on donkeys in the Azores islands."

Mark Twain did not dwell too long in person, or too much in prose, in Jaffa. He saw "the noble grove of orange-trees; we passed through the walls, and rode again down narrow streets and among swarms of animated rags, and saw other sights and had other experiences we had long been familiar with."

He didn't see much because there wasn't much to see. By all accounts Jaffa in 1867 was at it lowest ebb. It had recently—recently by Jaffa's standards—been sacked by Napoleon. On its surrender he ordered the beheading of its four thousand inhabitants. So that it wasn't quite the PR disaster it might have been he imported Muslim executioners from Egypt to swing the axe. A visit to the museum shows photographs from around the time of the Excursionists' visit of a cholera-infested shantytown with filthy streets and filthier people.

Almost as a metaphor for Israel, the old port city has been transformed. Jaffa's famous walls have been rebuilt and inside them the streets leveled and cleaned. The port outside the walls is still a touch ramshackle by these standards but not for much longer—it will soon be "upgraded" into a marina with matching boutiques and theme bars. Elsewhere artists have been shipped in to create a colony of sorts and an "olde Joppa"-style hotel is on its way. One is reminded of Covent Garden in London or Les Halles in Paris, a sort of

Disneyfied version of the good old days. It's attractive enough on a peripheral level but at heart it's just another commercial development without a soul.

Two genuine buildings are of interest in Jaffa. St. Peter's Church is the last Franciscan church we will see in the Holy Land and it's almost as if they have saved the best for last. By the time of Twain's visit it had been sacked by Napoleon twice: for the first time on his way north and then for good measure by his army on its retreat south. It was rebuilt in the late nineteenth century by the Spanish in the Spanish imperial baroque style; we could just as easily be in Santiago or Lima. The windows and panels depict Spanish saints as well as St. Peter. The stained glass windows are particularly attractive and what at first appears to be marble around the altar is in fact a paint effect. Today the Franciscans hold masses in all the major European languages and Russian and Polish.

The other building of interest is the old Ottoman municipality building, the Serrani. An imposing three-story building with a façade of four high relief columns, it was the headquarters of what passed for Ottoman rule until the British Mandate in 1923. In early 1948 an Israeli terrorist donned the uniform of a Royal Irish Fusiliers driver and exploded his truck at the entrance. He killed twenty-six people and injured hundreds more. A few months later the Israelis lobbed twenty tons of mortars into Jaffa with the aim of driving the Muslims and Christians out. The aim succeeded: 95 per cent of Jaffa's 65,000 Arabs were ethnically cleansed—and the poor old Serrani was seriously devastated. The building still has the dominant position in Jaffa and has since been restored to better than its former glory and can be viewed inside by appointment.

But this has all happened since Mark Twain's visit. Back then, he finished his notes with a mixture of relief and triumph: "We dismounted, for the last time, and out in the offing, riding at anchor, we saw the ship! I put an exclamation point there because we felt one when we saw the vessel."

We say our goodbyes at the dock in Jaffa. It is a sad moment and brings on a sense of foreboding. Nothing to put one's hands on, just a vacuum in the air, something missing in the heart. I throw a twig of olive into the sea and smile goodbye. We have grown fond of each other these last few months: he battling against the odds, a barometer for the Excursion, looking over his shoulder to see how I'm doing, if I'm keeping up, making sure I'm entering into the spirit of the thing; I, like a bloodhound with a kipper, following him doggedly, uniting with him at all those Holy Land's *plus ça change*-s, enjoying all those TLUCs and ironies together, amazed at how he and the New Pilgrims put up with each other. Above all I've come to love his enquiring mind, his stoic demeanor by day and his set-'em-up-Joe by night; he wields a nifty fountain pen too.

The *Quaker City* set off for Alexandria, Egypt and back through the Mediterranean to New York. *Vasco da Gama* left Haifa for Cyprus and Turkey. Mark Twain returned to fame and on/off fortune and—overall—happiness and serenity. I'm not quite sure what's going to happen to me; it depends on how many people get to read these words.

In Egypt, after a few days reflection, Twain summed up his experience in the Holy Land thus:

> Of all the lands there are for dismal scenery, I think Palestine must be the prince. The hills are barren, they are dull of color, they are unpicturesque in shape. The valleys are unsightly deserts fringed with a feeble vegetation that has an expression about it of being sorrowful and despondent. The Dead Sea and the Sea of Galilee sleep in the midst of a vast stretch of hill and plain wherein the eye rests upon no pleasant tint, no striking object, no soft picture dreaming in a purple haze or mottled with the shadows of the clouds. Every outline is harsh, every feature is distinct, there is no perspective—distance works no enchantment here. It is a hopeless, dreary, heart-broken land.

> Palestine sits in sackcloth and ashes. Over it broods the spell of a curse that has withered its fields and fettered its energies. Where Sodom and Gomorrah reared their domes and towers, that solemn sea now floods the plain, in whose bitter waters no living thing exists—over whose waveless surface the blistering air hangs motionless and dead—about whose borders nothing grows but weeds, and scattering tufts of cane.

Nazareth is forlorn; about that ford of Jordan where the hosts of Israel entered the Promised Land with songs of rejoicing, one finds only a squalid camp of fantastic Bedouins of the desert; Jericho the accursed, lies a moldering ruin, to-day, even as Joshua's miracle left it more than three thousand years ago; Bethlehem and Bethany, in their poverty and their humiliation, have nothing about them now to remind one that they once knew the high honor of the Saviour's presence; the hallowed spot where the shepherds watched their flocks by night, and where the angels sang Peace on earth, good will to men, is untenanted by any living creature, and unblessed by any feature that is pleasant to the eye.

Renowned Jerusalem itself, the stateliest name in history, has lost all its ancient grandeur, and is become a pauper village; the riches of Solomon are no longer there to compel the admiration of visiting Oriental queens; the wonderful temple which was the pride and the glory of Israel, is gone, and the Ottoman crescent is lifted above the spot where, on that most memorable day in the annals of the world, they reared the Holy Cross. The noted Sea of Galilee, where Roman fleets once rode at anchor and the disciples of the Saviour sailed in their ships, was long ago deserted by the devotees of war and commerce, and its borders are a silent wilderness; Capernaum is a shapeless ruin; Magdala is the home of beggared Arabs; Bethsaida and Chorazin have vanished from the earth, and the desert places round about them where thousands of men once listened to the Saviour's voice and ate the miraculous bread, sleep in the hush of a solitude that is inhabited only by birds of prey and skulking foxes.

I'm sure that this enquiring mind would love to know how the Holy Land lies today. Awhile back I resolved that when the re-Tour was over I would spend a few days at anchor off Cyprus writing him a letter, Dear Sam, as an epilogue.

Epilogue:
Dear Sam, being a letter from Ian to Sam about the Middle East as he would find it now.

s/y *Vasco da Gama*
At anchor
Ormos Pissouri
Cyprus

Dear Sam,

Goodness gracious! That was some endurance test we did back there. The Holy Land is not for the faint of heart, nor for the correct of politic. Religion red in tooth and claw, culture suspended for the duration, old civilizations newly uncivilized, a place where old souls cry and new souls swagger—not your favorite place then, not my favorite place now.

I left a week ago, almost exactly one hundred and forty-three years after you did. A week is a good time for reflection; events and impression are still fresh, just the immediacy of coping with all that the Holy Land throws at you has dampened down enough to allow reflection to take place. I thought you might appreciate a letter, a think piece, a Sitrep, hack to hack as you might say, about how it's all turned out since you waved Jaffa goodbye.

You won't be surprised to hear that the Holy Land has lost none of its intensity: whereas you saw desolation and serfdom, I saw arrogance and desperation; whereas you saw religious skullduggery and barbarity, I saw religion politicized and so doubly dangerous; whereas you wished the British and French Empires would sink the Ottoman Empire, I saw how the British and French Empires' broken promises have left only broken dreams.

I thought it might be helpful to summarize succinctly the history of the Holy Land from when you left towards the end of 1867 until now. I'm going to approach this from a British point of view for several reasons. Firstly, of course, I'm British and can't do much about that. Secondly, it has to be said that the British are largely responsible for the *unholy* part of the mess in which the Holy Land finds itself today. Thirdly, in an area where there are twelve sides to every coin it makes for a more consistent summary to plant one's feet in a particular patch of ground and keep them there.

When you were in the Greater Syria province of the Ottoman Empire you met some ultraorthodox Jews in Tiberias and some more in Jerusalem. There was also a Jewish quarter in Damascus. "Body-snatchers" you called them on account of their self-righteous and sanctimonious bearing. There were something like ten thousand ultraorthodox Jews living there and this population stayed steady for the next dozen or so years. Like all non-Muslim religions they were free to practice their creed upon payment to the Ottomans for the permits to do so. The Jewish communities were self-contained and, as always, good citizens; they left alone and were left alone.

Meanwhile in Europe, especially Eastern Europe, a groundswell was building in Jewish communities for a permanent Jewish home. The groundswell became an outbreak in the 1880s when the Eastern Orthodox Church in Russia sponsored a series of anti-Semitic pogroms (a Russian word meaning "devastation") banning Jews from the countryside and universities and from urban professions. As a direct result in 1882 seven thousand Jewish refugees fled to the Holy Land. They found, as you had done, a sparsely populated and desolate land, literally dirt poor. The American Consul* in Jerusalem at the time, Saleh Merrill, wrote to Washington that the Holy Land was in long term decline and that "the population and wealth has not increased these past forty years". In spite of this gloomy outlook the newly arrived Jews somehow made their circumstances work as Jews have always done and by the turn of the last century there were twenty thousand Jewish immigrants in what was still called Greater Syria; Palestine as a nation state was an idea whose time was yet to come.

The idea whose time by now had most definitely come was Zionism; Zion being the Hebrew word for Jerusalem, and Zionism came to mean the dream of returning to Jerusalem. It needed an exceptional man to bring together all the ideas blowing in the wind across Middle and Eastern Europe and this nascent Zionism found him in a young and radicalized Austrian Jew called Theodor Herzl. In 1897 he convened the First Zionist Congress in Switzerland and crystallized the idea of a Jewish homeland for the Jewish people.

Over the next fifteen years a further forty thousand Jews settled in the Holy Land and the number of immigrants reached a level where the indigenous Arabs—and most estimates suggest that there were about a quarter of a million

---

* They want to send me abroad, as a Consul or a Minister. I said I didn't want any of the pie. God knows I am mean enough and lazy enough, now without being a foreign consul. *Letter, 1868*

of them—became fearful of displacement. Herzl's activities continued apace as he lobbied around Europe and North America for his dream of a Jewish state in what by now was increasingly being called Palestine.

In 1914 events in the Holy Land were subsumed by events further west. In June a Yugoslav nationalist assassinated Archduke Franz Ferdinand of Austria. The Austrians responded by threatening Serbia. A complex arrangement of imperial pacts and alliances soon led the British, Austro-Hungarian, Russian, German and Ottoman Empires, as well as France and Italy to become involved in an arcane dispute, an involvement that over the next four years was to cost the lives of nine million souls. The world was at war: the First World War. By the time it ended the United States had helped the Allies to victory and the Russian, Ottoman, German and Austro-Hungarian Empires to defeat—and extinction. The waste of lives and the pointlessness of it all devastated Europe. The League of Nations, the precursor of the United Nations, was founded in an attempt to prevent such a human catastrophe ever happening again.

During the war the British made three specific agreements which fundamentally altered the geopolitics of the Holy Land. The background was the need to undermine the war effort of the Ottoman Empire, which had allied itself with the Germans. The British perceived that the Ottoman Empire had a soft underbelly in its sparse Syrian provinces stretching all the way down to Egypt. In 1915, in an effort to encourage an Arab revolt against the Ottomans, the British entered into an agreement with the Arabs that indicated British support for an independent Greater Syria if and when all sides had defeated the Ottomans. This is known as the McMahon-Hussein Correspondence. A year later Sir Mark Sykes of Britain and Monsieur Georges Picot of France met in secret and formulated plans to divide up this same enormous piece of land—also if and when all sides had defeated the Ottomans. This is known as the Sykes-Picot Agreement. Lastly in 1917, partly out of sympathy for the Diaspora, partly out of a Protestant Evangelical wish to hasten the coming of the next messiah and partly as an attempt to persuade the United States to join the war, Sir Arthur Balfour wrote to Lord Rothschild promising British support for what amounted to the state of Israel. This is known as the Balfour Declaration.

These three agreements were made in expediency and with the knowledge that at any given time two of them would have to be... re-aligned. When the League of Nations was formed Britain and France were the dominant powers and set about dividing up the now-defunct Ottoman Empire as per the Sykes-Picot Agreement. But there was an American fly in the imperial ointment.

After the First World War President Woodrow Wilson announced the frankly radical notion that nations should be entitled to self-determination. This was to become American policy. It was both a successful attempt to gain the moral high ground with subject nations and a shot across the bows of renewed post-war European imperialism.

The Europeans had a solution that, for a while, kept all sides happy: the Mandate system, whereby Britain and France ruled the Middle East under a League of Nations Mandate. Under these 1922 Mandates Britain and France would, in effect, foster-care the emerging Arab countries until they were deemed ready to govern themselves; deemed ready, of course, by the foster-carers. It was of course imperialism by the back door so the Europeans were most content, yet it wasn't imperialism so the Americans were more-or-less content, in its way it recognized *de facto* that the Arab countries would at some stage become independent so they were partly content and as for the still unborn Israel, well it was another step towards statehood so they were not uncontent.

Under the Mandate France was to inherit Syria, Lebanon, and the oil-rich area of Mosul in Iraq. Britain was to gain the rest of Iraq and all of Palestine; Palestine at that time included what are now Jordan as well as Israel and the West Bank. Later Britain and France horse-traded some other oil concessions. The British installed a puppet Arab, Faisal, to be King of Syria but he fell out with the French so Britain told him he was now King of Iraq instead. Wasn't life simple in those days? Not so long ago, either.

On the ground it didn't take long for all the sweetness and light to unravel. While France had an easy-ish ride with the Syrians and the Lebanese, the British were overseeing two worlds colliding. The Jews—not yet Israelis—were under the impression that the League of Nations Mandate's main aim was to implement the Balfour Declaration; it wasn't but, as ever, nations believe what they want to believe. Jewish immigrants were arriving in vastly increasing numbers to form their own country so that by 1930 there would be 200,000 Jews in the Holy Land. Interestingly enough Jewish immigration was matched by Arab immigration, the latter attracted into the Holy Land by the new prosperity that the former had engineered.

The Arabs, for their part, did not harbor the secular Western concept of country. Islam did not separate politics from religion and had never paid any attention to separate nations—only the idea of the nation of Islam, the *umma*. Now faced with an influx of foreigners, foreigners of a different race and definitely of a different religion, Arab consciousness stirred and for the first time formed around the idea of "Palestine"——not at this stage as a separate country but as a part of a Greater Syria.

Sensing trouble ahead with the French, the British——in traditional divide-and-rule tactics——divided up and ruled what was then Palestine into what we know think of as Israel and the West Bank on one side and Jordan on the other. The former were given twenty per cent of the land, the latter eighty per cent. Into Jordan the British put another puppet king, Faisal's brother Abdullah, and one whose descendants are still ruling there today.

Throughout the 1930s the British found their Mandate territory to be increasingly ungovernable. They saw a large group of people, the Arabs, who were relatively easy to govern, had vast amounts of oil and who, if left alone to pray in peace, were unlikely to be too troublesome. Furthermore, although they were poorly educated they were immensely charming and hospitable; a bit of a shambles but it didn't seem to bother them. Then the British saw a much smaller group of people, the Zionists, who were motivated by a single agenda, a nation state, and an agenda that they would push and push and push. They were highly educated and no fun, on any level, at all. It was as if a tribe of single-issue lawyers had descended on the British lawn and were rudely interrupting the croquet——and at tea-time. Furthermore the large group was concerned that the small group was taking its land and——as importantly—— practicing a heretic religion and not practicing it discreetly in the *umma*. Culturally too, the Arabs saw their traditional society and its Islam-based values threatened by these new people with new ideas. For the Zionists the Arabs were a primeval and backward people, uneducated, uninquiring, inefficient, dishonest individually, duplicitous collectively with a desert culture and a primitive theology. Then as now the Arabs and the Jews were on different planets.

Time by time the British sympathy moved towards the indigenous people whom they saw as being dispossessed and disadvantaged by the waves of immigration. By the mid-1930s the British lost sight of the Balfour Declaration and its aims and started to side with the oil-rich Arabs and the easy life. Jewish immigration was severely restricted after 1935 and Arab immigration encouraged. Arab riots were ignored, if not actually sanctioned, and Jewish defenses dismantled.

In 1936 the British concluded that the Mandate was unworkable as the Jews and Arabs were so completely incompatible. For the first time a form of two states within Palestine was proposed: one Jewish and one Arab. Unfortunately it wasn't simple to put into place. The land was predominantly Arab with various Jewish settlements scattered within it; in others words neither side had contiguous land that could be neatly divided. Both sides attacked the plan ferociously and predictably: the Jews because it gave them too little and the Arabs because by now they just wanted the Jews out and certainly weren't prepared to give them any of *their* land.

Events now began to turn even uglier in the form of Israeli terrorists and Nazi exterminators. Sam, you won't have heard too much of terrorists or anything about Nazis—or even fascists. These were to come later. The first recognized act of terrorism happened in Russia two years after you left the Holy Land when a revolutionary used a detonation to cause terror to the civilians as a means of achieving the political ends he wanted. His ends, in other words, justified his means.

The Nazis? I'm going to have to write you another letter about the Second World War or we'll run out of pages. It started only twenty-one years after the last one finished and finished six years after that. You'll be pleased, but not surprised, to hear that the Americans and their allies won again and the Germans and their quislings lost again. For now you need to know the Nazis were state-sanctioned political fundamentalists who believed that the Germans were an Aryan master-race and that lesser races should be exterminated. They viewed the Jews as a lesser race and established a plan on a multi-national industrial scale to exterminate the Jews from the planet. There were nine million Jews in Europe at the start of the pogroms; they murdered six million of them. As you can imagine, the effect was devastating for the survivors and for the people as a whole—and tangentially for the world as a whole. The Nazis called this The Final Solution; the Jews called it the Holocaust. It effects on the Holy Land were profound and we will refer to it often from now on.

The first Jewish terrorist attacks were against Arabs, bombs exploding in crowded markets, the sort of outrage I'm afraid to which we have become softened by time—but at the time considered truly outrageous. The British reacted by abandoning any pretence at equanimity; they just wanted out of the whole mess they had created. They offered the Arabs an independent state of Palestine. The Arabs rejected this out of hand; they didn't want a state of Palestine, they still wanted to be part of Greater Syria and, more to the point, they still wanted all the Jews out of Greater Syria—and right now.

Jewish terrorism now turned on the British. It couldn't have come at a more tragic time. The Nazis were sweeping through Eastern Europe with devastating consequences for the Jewish population. The Holy Land was the only obvious escape route, and now that was being blocked by the British in an effort to appease the Arabs and punish the Jews. It was a disaster from every angle, and the more the British tried to restrict the Jews the worse the terrorist attacks became and the tighter the British response to the attacks became. Matters came to a head in 1944: relations between the British and the Jews were so bad that the British refused to bomb German railway tracks to extermination camps in Eastern Europe because the request had come via a Jewish agency thought to be associated with terrorism in the Holy Land. The Zionists responded by assassinating the British Minister in Cairo. The British responded by shutting down all cooperation with the Holy Land Jews, including allowing in fleeing European Jews.

Hopes that peace in Europe would bring peace in Palestine were short-lived. The British assumed their positions as if nothing had happened. The Jews had by now built up a territory that they believed could be self-supporting. The Arabs again took fright at the Jewish success and petitioned the world for their expulsion. The British built up their armed presence to keep the two sides apart. The Jews responded with increased terrorism, targeting British officers and their families. The Arabs rioted on a massive scale. In July 1946 Jewish terrorists blew up the King David Hotel in Jerusalem, the headquarters of the British presence. Ninety-one people, including fifteen Jews, were murdered. By now the world was watching. The British, citing the Mandate's provisions, denied Holocaust survivors immigration to the Holy Land, even diverting some to Mauritius.* More Jewish terror; more Arab riots. The British military and public, exhausted by war in Europe and Empire, just wanted out and in 1947 asked the newly formed United Nations to take the whole mess off their hands.

The UN proposed two solutions, solutions we will refer to again: the One-State solution and the Two-State solution. Under the former all of what is now Israel and the West Bank would be one country. The Arabs would be in the clear majority and the constitution would protect Jewish interests. The Arabs made it clear that although they wouldn't expel any Jews already *in situ* they weren't prepared to accept any more. After the Holocaust the Jews demanded as an absolutely minimum condition unlimited Jewish access to the Jewish homeland. The One-State solution was clearly unworkable and was dropped forthwith.

---

* Apparently, there has been only one prominent event in the history of Mauritius, and that one didn't happen. *Following the Equator*

The Two-State solution, however, clearly showed a way forward. The UN called this the Partition Plan and drew up a map of the Holy Land to determine where would be Israel and where would be Palestine. It wasn't possible to assign particular areas to Jews and Arabs because so many Arabs had moved into the newly prosperous Jewish areas; any state of Israel therefore was bound to contain a large Arab population. Jerusalem was to be a UN-administered international zone. When finally drawn the map showed that Israel was granted sixty per cent of the land but over half of that was the Negev Desert. Moreover, most of the land in the new Israel would still be Arab-owned. The population of Israel would be 850,000: 500,000 Jews and 350,000 Arabs.

The Partition Plan could be said to offer rough justice; everyone lost—the Arabs had to accept an alien invasion and the Jews had to accept a significant and probably troublesome Arab presence. It's at this point we come across a phenomenon that has run consistently throughout Middle East peace negotiations from the Partition Plan to today: the Jews always say "yes", the Arabs always say "no". The Jewish—actually I think we can now start calling the wandering tribe Israelis—the Israeli tactic is to take whatever is on offer, lock it away, build on it and keep demanding more. The Arab tactic is simply to reject outright any proposal at all. Perhaps tactic is the wrong word for the Arab approach as it implies a course of action that has been thought through, an intellectual approach to the situation, whereas their response has always been more cultural and emotional. It is clear that this single-minded, legalistic stance has served Israel well and the more poetic Arab stance has served it poorly; these are material judgments, whether the Israelis have won and the Arabs have lost in the abstract is far less clear.

Lack of intellectual application has also led the Arabs into a series of disastrous decisions in their dealings with Israel. The first came in 1948 when the Arab League—Egypt, Syria, Jordan, Lebanon and Iraq—declared war on Israel the day after Israel declared its independence. Despite being outnumbered four to one the Israelis prevailed. The Arabs didn't just lose, they were humiliated by an enemy that was literally fighting for its existence, inspired by leaders who had fought the British and manned by troops who had survived the Holocaust or who had already built new lives with new families with bare hands in the godforsaken scrubland. At the end of the war the Arabs ended up with thirty per cent less land than they had been offered under the Partition Plan and still had no state of Palestine as the Arab allies merely helped themselves to new land: Jordan grabbed the West Bank and Egypt grabbed Gaza. In addition, the Arabs had lost half of Jerusalem, had enabled Israel to become a contiguous territory and had shown the world that Arabs were better at fighting each other than fighting a common enemy.

The biggest casualty of the war was not Arab pride but Arab refugees. Some 700,000 Arabs fled from, or were pushed out of, Israel. Fled or pushed? Both sides have an interest in re-inventing the truth. The Arab League leaders told hundreds of thousands of Arabs to leave their land, told them that it would only be for a short time before the inevitable Arab victory, when they could return to a Jew-free country of their own. Eighty-five per cent of the Arabs fled, never to return. Furthermore, Arabs leaders exaggerated Israeli atrocities in the hope of stiffening indigenous Arab resolve; it had the opposite effect as the peasants in particular ran for their lives. The Israelis were undoubtedly responsible for ethnic cleansing, either by massacre or forced marches, which led to further hundreds of thousands of refugees. But the reality is probably more mundane. More Arabs fled than were forcibly pushed and when an advancing Israeli unit stumbled across an empty Arab village it moved into the empty houses; after the war if a villager returned to his house he was sent packing. Israel's position ever since has been that responsibility for the refugees should fall on the Arab League countries that started the war in the first place.

It is often forgotten that the war also created 600,000 Jewish refugees when the defeated Arab League countries turned on their own Jewish populations in retaliation for the defeat. The difference was that the Jewish refugees were welcomed wholeheartedly by Israel whereas the Arab refugees, now nearly four million strong, are still helpless in refugee camps scattered across the Middle East, rejected by Israel *and* their Arab hosts. All aspects considered, the Arab League's 1948 invasion was a disaster; the first, as it happens, of many.

Thus, in 1948, Israel became a nation. And over sixty years later, in spite of two major and several minor wars against the Arabs, in spite of endless "peace treaties", "peace initiatives", "peace processes", "peace talks" and "roadmaps to peace", Israel still exists and is still at war—albeit now with just half and not all of its neighbors. And Palestine? That still doesn't exist, although slowly, slowly as the new guard replace the old gangsters there may be... hope. Not only does it still not exist, but its very boundaries are changing by continuing Israeli incursions into it from the north, south and west, constantly shrink- ing the size of any future state. Within that state there are over a hundred Israeli settlements, miniature colonies, with 300,000 Israelis living in what they call the West Bank, the Palestinians call the Occupied Territories and the NGOs and guidebooks call the Palestinian Territories. Only its eastern border, defined by the River Jordan, is secure.

A month ago we were sitting under an acacia tree outside the Buddha Bagel café on the north side of Dizengoff Street in central Tel Aviv. (Sam, you remember those sand dunes just north of Jaffa? That's now Miami-cum-Madrid transplanted to the Middle East. It's the cultural capital, where you'd want to live if you had to live anywhere in Israel; as they say down there, "Jerusalem prays; Tel Aviv plays.") At the base of the tree there's a plaque. I leant forward and read, "And the tree of the field shall yield her fruit, and the earth shall yield her increase, and they shall be safe in their land, and shall know that I am the Lord. *Ezekiel 34:27.* A gift from Larry & Sylvie Aarons, Boca Raton, Fla. 'Despite Impossible Odds'." The religiosity and the generosity seemed to us then to sum up the worst and best in Israel today. Earlier on the way here, just two minutes window-shopping away, was another plaque, this one built into a wall of a bookshop. Under the Hebrew writing in English it read: "To commemorate the lives of 21 young Israelis who died by suicide bombing here on 1ˢᵗ June 2001. 'The soul of man is the candle of God.' *Proverbs 20:27.*"

Looking around the tables at the young, carefree Israelis chatting and laughing, some smoking,* some texting, some flirting, some preening, young souls driven by the light, it seemed *outrageous* that a suicide bomber could just sit himself down among them and destroy their young lives, so full of worth and promise. He would destroy his own young life too, but that life up to then had been so different: religiously indoctrinated to hatred, uneducated, without prospects of any kind, a soul driven by the dark and with not even a vague idea of what he would do with the seventy-two virgins he had been promised in paradise—his reward for killing all those worshipers of the same god with a different name.

Over and over again these past months in Arabic countries and in Israel we have seen how the two sides are so far apart they inhabit entirely different mental orbits. There really is no hope of reconciliation as there was, say, in Northern Ireland where the Protestants and Catholics finally got tired of

* This majestic vice *Tom Sawyer*

blowing each other up and then had a shared base from which to rejoin the world. Neither side here has any idea—and let's face it, not much interest— in finding out how the other side lives, thinks, acts, what they believe in and why, where they want to go, how they plan to get there; nothing. Jew and Arab never socialize with each other; if there is any contact it is always on a ruler/ subject, landlord/tenant, employer/employee basis. Even inside Israel where Israeli Arabs make up a fifth of the population strict caste lines apply.

Further north, east and south of here there is a very different story. If the Israelis have moved ahead of the twenty-first century, the Arabs seem stuck in a fourteenth-century religious quicksand. The latter are having a very unfortunate transition from the medieval to the modern and the faster the modern progresses the more it runs away from them. *Insha'Allah*, "God willing", is not just a phrase you hear all the time but the guiding philosophy, the very stuff of life. The secular Jews—thankfully the vast majority are just that—know very well that Allah—by any name—doesn't exist except as a man-made concept and so there's not much point in relying on his will; better to do whatever needs doing yourself and do it with some man-made expertise. For ourselves, as Gentiles to the Jews and Infidels to the Muslims, we see the gap between the two sides best expressed through education. For the Jews education is not only all-important in itself—to learn what is already known—but as a means of finding out what is new and unknown. For the Muslim masses education means studying the Koran, and studying doesn't mean investigating its different versions or debating hidden meanings or discovering possible insights, it means learning it by rote. Any onward learning is always looking back over its shoulder for Koranic approval.

One could say that ultraorthodox Judaism and fundamentalist Islam are one primitive desert nomad theology versus another but the Jewish people will always be at an advantage because only ten per cent of them take their primitive theology at face value, whereas the Muslims suffer from a ninety per cent take-up, meaning that massively more Jews are always capable of original thought rather than worrying about original sin. If one looks beyond the religious enthusiasts in each culture one can add another meaningful statistic and discount—as a generalization—the female half of the Muslim population in terms of *material* contribution to society.

Lack of education has led to a corresponding lack of opportunity, but opportunity is further hindered by the structure and politics of Arab society. One is either born into a position of stature and influence or one is not. Sideways mobility is the best one can hope for, upwards mobility an alien concept. Whereas Israel is a meritocracy that would frankly frighten privileged people like me, Arab society would wrap its arms around me, respect me for how I was born and politely—always politely—ignore what I have become.

The lack of education and opportunity and the social stagnation have led to a lack of progress in any sphere. It has been well observed that if no Muslims had been born in the last few hundred years the world would be exactly as it is now. For the Arabs this has also led to a debilitating inferiority complex towards the West in general and Israel in particular and may go some way to explain the blatant heart-on-sleeve anti-Semitism one finds on the famous Arab street. The vehemence of this anti-Semitism is shocking to one used to the Western or Christian version—now thank heavens not only deeply unfashionable but practically extinct; neither is it the distorted logic of the Nazi extreme; with the Arabs it feels like pure emotional hatred. The Nazis haven't been forgotten though: *Mein Kampf*, according to the British *Daily Telegraph*, is consistently in the Palestinian bestselling books list.

Where does that leave the young population of the young Israel, the happy souls chatting outside the Buddha Bagel? Looking west—at the West. It seems to me that as if collectively they have said to their neighbors: "Look, we have tried everything. We have offered you our own country, you said no. We have offered you $30 billion, you said no. We have asked just that you recognize us, you said no. We have offered to pull back the settlements, you said no. We have even offered you a thousand of your prisoners for one of ours, you said no. You think we are just another crusade episode that you will eventually defeat, we say get real, this is our home and we're here to stay. If you don't want to live in peace that's up to you. We have built a wall around us and you can't touch us now. Sorry it's messed you up about—but if you will suicide bomb us, what do you expect? If *you* don't want peace, fine, but *we've* moved on.'

Three or four nights later we were back on board *Vasco da Gama* looking through some of Gillian's photographs of the Galilee. They were great and so is the Galilee, but it prompted the question: why is Israel every tourist's least favorite destination? Better rephrase that: Why is Israel every Gentile tourist's least favorite destination? Conversely why is Syria, let's face it politically the bad boy in the Middle East, everyone's favorite destination?

One answer is the rudeness, the brusqueness and a total lack of any form of charm. It is quite unique in the world. People used to complain about Paris but that is really only noticeable because it is in such variance to the rest of France. In Israel it's not just in the center of Tel Aviv but in every corner of the land. Even people in whose interest it is to be welcoming, hotel and restaurant staff for example, are unwelcoming and everyone else actively dis-welcoming. Ask for any help, finding anywhere or with the language, and your askee will not just be unhelpful but actively dishelpful. As for charm, any delightful scene that one comes across, a hilly village, an Alpine meadow, will be spoilt by a bossy official or a snarling roadblock or an officious sign or an authoritarian rabbinical pronouncement. To use Syria as a counterpoint, the very opposite of all these apply: they couldn't be more welcoming and helpful and charming—and bossy signs and officials aren't the Syrian way.

So why so rude? One theory is as follows: the reaction of new Israelis seeing the Holocaust footage of their parents and grandparents being sent off to the concentration camps with no seeming resistance was to vow there would never be such meekness again. They unkindly call the victims "soaps", as bars of soap was what they would become. No more soaps! This is an explanation of the unsettling machismo that even young girls show, swaggering egos buttressed by military conscription which all non-ultraorthodox boys and girls must undertake.

This warrior mentality, this macho posture, this rejection of the feminine principle is profoundly unspiritual—if such a concept can be said to exist. In Israel, one never feels a deeper level of meaning; no coincidences jump out and greet you, ironies prefer to keep their own company and paradoxes are swamped by all that logic. Mystical spirituality is the opposite of patriarchal monotheism and monotheism in Israel is omnitheism and all the more annoying for it—annoying on levels political, cultural, personal, intellectual, decorative, social, demographic, proportional, preferential, culinary, aesthetic, commonsensical, and above all, yes, religious. But one doesn't feel alone, the ninety per cent of Israelis who aren't fundamentalists agree with your assessment of the "body-snatchers" but have had to learn to live with this vociferous, over-self-privileged, self-righteous sanctimonious swarm in their midst.

The Gentile tourists' other grumble is a strange one, the lack of humor. Anyone from the Anglophone world will been brought up on a steady diet of American-Jewish humor full of irony and subtlety—more than this, one's own sense of humor will have been shaped by it. So why is there no humor in

Israel? Maybe it's the first-generation nation-building, maybe the first generation of Jewish immigrants to America were equally earnest and solemn and
it wasn't until there was enough wealth that subsequent generations could
afford the luxury of humor and irony?

So Sam, as a good journalist you will have read about all the effects and
will be asking about the causes. Why no humor? Why no mysticism? Why so
earnest? Why no charm? Why, above all, is it just no fun?

Religion apart, all answers come back to "It's the Occupation, stupid."
The Occupation poisons everything. It has made Israel an unhappy country
because it has split its personality: a democracy, yet one without common
decency, Amnesty International and Human Rights Watch snapping at its heels;
a victim of religious hatred and a practitioner of religious arrogance; a victim
of racism and a culprit of racism; the brave defender and the callous invader;
a lover of children and a conscriptor of youth; aspirationally sincere and
morally suspect; an economic miracle and an international pariah; troubled by
complexes of inferiority and superiority and not knowing whether to praise
itself or blame itself.

The way they treat the Palestinians is disgraceful. Yes, the Palestinians can
be unreliable partners, yes, they have a less literal version of the concept of
truth, yes, they are hamstrung by a backward theology and a chauvinistic
society, yes they are frustrating to deal with, yes, they lack leaders and are
addicted to squabbling, yes they have elevated futile gestures to an art form,
yes, they wish the Israelis would go back to from whence they came, yes, it's
annoying when they throw leavened sandwiches into the reservoirs at Passover,
so the crazier rabbis forbid drinking the polluted water, yes to all these and
more, but where is Israel's sense of magnanimity? What is there to prove by
humiliating them? By impoverishing them? By breaking up their families? By
confining them? Stealing their land? Diverting their water? Why do they treat
Arabs in Jerusalem like undesirable aliens in their own city? Can't they see—as
outsiders do—the moral similarity between what went on in Warsaw and what
goes on in Hebron? Is it really worthwhile having the country on a permanent
war footing, with conscription and all the machismo and hatred that spins off
it? More to the point, is the Occupation worth the lives of these conscripted
young boys and girls? Is it worth being an international outcast, even being
asked not to stamping visitors' passports? What does it say about a society that
accepts state-sponsored torture and squalid refugee camps? What message do
the images of schoolchildren throwing stones at tanks send to the world? Why
is there no one with the vision to break the spell? Could it be that some of the

ultraorthodox Judaic view of Muslims (and Christians) as inherently inferior has seeped through to even modern freethinking Israelis? Could it be that in their bones they still believe that Palestine is "land without a people for a people without a land". Why do they just carry on building settlements and pandering to the religious maniacs who will never rest until Israel is a theocracy? Do reasonable Israelis actually *want* to live in a theocracy? If not, why tolerate those who do while not tolerating those who would live in peace?

Sam, this brings me on to the last part of the letter: we've seen the problems, what are the solutions, where does it all go from here? The following summarizes current thinking, what my friends at the *Jerusalem Post*, the embassy people one meets at receptions and the great and the good who debate and give conferences all call "informed opinion".

The first point is to put the ultimate cause, religious bigotry, to one side as unsolvable. I'm sure you would agree with all the wise souls who have observed that the Israel-Palestine saga should be an easy one to solve. You have two races who cannot live together, races of roughly equal size claiming the same piece of land. Surely it can't be beyond the wit of man to divide the land, give one chunk of it to one race as one state and the other chunk of it to the other race as the other state? Ah, the wise souls continue, then you factor in religion to this utopia and the problem becomes unsolvable.

All true, but this dismissal of religion forgets the fact that if it hadn't been for the rabbis and their interminable man-made laws the tribe of Israel would have disappeared in the great human mix many centuries ago—like all the other tribes of the biblical Middle East have done. Secular Jews never forget this. Over dinner they will tell you that the whole biblical jurisprudence edifice doesn't stand up to any intellectual examination. They reveal gleefully that archaeologists have discounted the Egyptian exile story, cast doubt on the very existence of Solomon and David, claimed that the Israelites of Exodus were actually the Asiatic Hyksos and most shockingly of all have suggested that the "One God" Yahweh actually had a consort, the goddess Asherah. These may very well all be the case, the secularists will say, then remind you again that on an historical level their sectarian religion has kept them intact as a race and, ultimately, delivered them a nation. In one of the few ironies hereabouts the indisputable truth that was shown to be a wayward truth has been forgiven and resurrected as a convenient truth.

The secular Arab view—and yes it does exist—is that their religion*

---

* I am quite sure now that often, very often, in matters concerning religion and politics a man's reasoning powers are not above the monkey's. *Mark Twain in Eruption* doesn't stand up to much intellectual examination either. It sounds patronizing but it's true that secular Muslims are nearly always the better-off and better educated, frequently it has to be said educated in the West. For them to live in Islamic countries is no hardship: they can ignore its restrictions in private with their own kind, and enjoy its benefits in public. Benefits there are aplenty: to live at the top of a respectful, traditional, reverential patriarchy is clearly agreeable, and Islam accordingly delivers a society that is most certainly agreeable to its elite. If the elite by birth happen not to be the elite by brains they can take comfort in the reverence* their birth ensures.

For the masses—not the maniacs but the masses—Islam provides a code for living that informs every aspect of their life, and none in a way harmful to them or others, in fact quite the opposite. It makes sense of the inexplicable capriciousness of life, provides succor for the unfortunate and constancy when all around is unpredictable. Its society is built around families, extended families, tribes and anyone else of Muslim belief in that order; politics are religious and religion political; only recently has the Western idea of an nation state taken hold and even then only as subset of a greater Islamic nation.

Neither the religious nor secular anywhere in the Middle East therefore has any wish to abandon religion—and of course they couldn't even if they wanted to. It suits them all. We have then to accept that if the religions cannot get along, then the societies, having been made by these religions, also cannot get along. One is a democracy and there is every reason to suppose the other may become a theocracy—and not a very pleasant one at that. The demographics between Jew and Arab are now finely poised but even if they tried to live together, given the far greater Arab birth rate the Jews would soon be in a minority. You could say that Israelis are frightened that they would be ethnically cleansed out of any new Palestine, just as they ethnically cleansed the Palestinians out of the new Israel.

Two states are needed. The first problem is that there is no obvious geographic feature around which one can fashion a border. However, if one dusts down Oslo and Camp David accords there are possibilities around Israel keeping its 1948 territorial gains but sacrificing its 1967 gains, especially if Israel wants to avoid the Palestinian demographic time bomb and remain a majority Jewish democracy. The settlements beyond the 1967 line are, in the opinion of non-Israeli international lawyers, quite simply illegal. But here there's a deal to be done, one accepted in principle before: Israel keeps the settlements immediately adjacent to the 1967 border and gives up the rest.

---

* Irreverence is the champion of liberty and its only true defence. *Notes & Journals*

Palestine is compensated for the adjacent settlements on an acre-for-acre basis with land currently within Israel's southern borders.

However queasy some Israelis feel about sacrificing land, most realize that with Iranian missiles on the way Israel will no longer need territorial buffers along its borders for its protection but the diplomatic buffer of non-aggressive neighbors. These neighbors may well have let the Palestinians down repeatedly, shamefully, over the years but politically they know they can only open up to Israel once the Palestine question has been settled; and the Palestinians know this too.

A further advantage of giving up the far-flung settlements, as has already happened in Gaza, is that it neutralizes the Arab claim of the right to return of the 1948 refugees to what is now Israel. Having new Arabs living in Israel and new Israelis living in Palestine flies in the face of the logic of a Two-State solution. There have to be sacrifices made in a best worst-option solution and these are some of them.

So, given God's will and good will, and leaving Gaza and Jerusalem to one side for a moment there may be a map to be drawn. Here the problems really start. The map may be acceptable to Israel but it certainly won't be to Palestine, again for reasons of justice and demographics. The injustice will be that of the Mandatory Palestine it is now proposed that 79 per cent will go to Israel and 21 per cent to Palestine. Why should they accept that? Would you? Geographically, it's easy to forget how very small is the land area to be divided. From the Mediterranean to Jordan is only fifty miles and the Two-State solution proposes that both states squeeze into this space. What we are now calling Palestine already holds four million souls. It is not unreasonable to expect that once the restrictions are lifted, most of the Palestinians in Gaza would want to move to the West Bank—in many cases back to the West Bank. It is also not unreasonable to suppose that many or most of the four million Palestinian refugees and/or guest workers scattered around the Middle East would also want to return once they have their own homeland. Palestine as defined by the 1967 +/- borders simply isn't big enough to hold them and without contiguous access to the sea is simply not viable economically and politically.

The obvious solution to this is to create more land. How so? Well, the informed opinion goes, by absorbing the West Bank into a greater Jordan and Gaza into a greater Egypt. On the face of it there are obvious attractions. Both Jordan and Egypt have space to spare. Both have functioning economies, an infrastructure and political credibility, all lacking in a nascent Palestine. Jordan already has a Palestinian majority and has even had a Palestinian prime minister; many Jordanians already live in the West Bank, which Jordan ran from 1948 to 1967. Many West Bank Palestinians already have Jordanian passports—the only ones they are allowed. An influx of Palestinians would boost the Jordanian economy. An absorption of Gaza into Egypt would be less seamless but Gaza is tiny and it is unlikely that many would choose to stay there if they could join other Palestinians elsewhere. Not that it probably matters that much to them but absorbing Gaza would go some way to assuaging Egypt's dismal treatment of the Palestinian refugees there, a refugee crisis they not only created but refused to ameliorate.

Of course, there are problems galore. Firstly the majority of Palestinians may not want to become Jordanian. The hope of informed opinion is that over the course of the negotiations they will come to see this is the least worst option; it is in fact their only realistic option. For Palestinians there would be autonomy; there would be citizenship; they would be a majority; there is every chance of prosperity; there would at last be peace. They would live in Palestine but it is called Jordan, a country the vast majority of whose citizens are also Palestinian. How the rulers of Hashemite kingdom and their Bedouin constituency would view this influx is a different matter. It was only in 1951 that the young King Hussein saw a lone Palestinian gunman assassinate his grandfather King Abdullah.* The Black September war against the PLO only ended in 1971.

The monarchy can at least console itself that it cannot be outvoted or voted out. It could be—and no doubt will make sure it would be—compensated from international funds, ostensibly for the cost of absorption. But if the British are quite happy with a German royal family why should the Palestinians not be happy with a Jordanian one? After all the years of strife and poverty, surely the Palestinians' first priority would be peace and prosperity, not nominal tribal supremacy?

And lastly to the big one, Jerusalem. There are two Jerusalems, the sprawling new town and the Old City. A slice of the former could be carved out in settlement of a bigger picture but it's the latter that remains the problem. No claim of sovereignty is acceptable to all sides, therefore why not try to have no sovereignty? An exemplum for this already exists right in the center of Jerusalem: the Church of the Holy Sepulcher and its Status Quo. Why not the Status Quo writ large? There is a good chance that as people become more sophisticated the passions arising from the Temple Mount will lessen. The

---

* Assassination of a crowned head of state whenever and wherever opportunity offers should be the first article of every subjects' religion. *Notes & Journals*

hope is that the Status Quo in the Church of the Holy Sepulcher shows that this *will* happen; Christians of all faiths visit the Church of the Holy Sepulcher now no longer out of fervor but out of interest. Is it not unreasonable to hope that in two or three generations people will look on monotheism as today we look on superstition?*

Thus runs informed opinion. I'm not so sure. The first objection is that you cannot force freedom—individual or national—on someone, it has to be taken. The same is true of liberation or independence. The Palestinians will not feel free unless they have won it, not been given it. Being independent is as much about feeling independent as having a legal document saying that you are independent.

An offshoot of this is that while Israel is so overwhelming powerful militarily, and Palestine so correspondingly weak, Israel cannot bomb or bulldoze the Palestinians into accepting what they don't want. Palestine can never win the war; survival is its victory. Israel can provide as much war as it wants but only Palestine can provide peace; thus in the epicenter of the Holy Land the holiest irony applies: the weak have become strong and the strong have become weak.

The second objection is that, as we have seen, grand gesture peace agreements imposed from afar—like Oslo and Camp David—only make matters worse as they give extremists on both sides an incentive to ramp up the terrorism, to form a holy/unholy unofficial alliance to destroy the peace agreement. All of the above informed opinion solution requires a new Oslo or Camp David. At the moment the vehicle chosen is the so-called Quartet, representing the United States, the United Nations, the European Union and Russia. I visited the Quartet headquarters at the American Colony Hotel in Jerusalem. Impressive it is not; not the hotel I hasten to add, which is superb, but the organization itself. The problem starts at the top as it is headed by a totally discredited figure, the ex-British Prime Minister Tony Blair. The inherent arrogance of bringing these foreign bodies to tell the ancient tribes of Israel and Arabia how to conduct themselves is offensive and counter-productive. So is the Quartet's posturing. Surely if they are asking Jordan and Egypt to be part of the solution they should formalize their involvement, and that of neighbors Lebanon and Syria too?

My solution, the millionth solution hereabouts where everybody has their own solution is to just leave well enough alone and let nature take it

---

* Let me make the superstitions of a nation and I care not who makes its laws or its songs either. *Following the Equator*

course. Have we not seen how imported peace agreements from the 1947 UN Partition Plan to the latest pow-wow in Washington to the Quartet's pronouncements only make matters worse?

Israel has not known a day of peace since its foundation, not peace as we know it in the real West. When there hasn't been an actual war, there's been a phony war, or preparations for war, or rumors of war, or the aftermath of war and always a real or imagined state of emergency. The demographics in Israel are changing; the young—and 45 per cent and growing are under thirty—want peace, they don't want conscription and they certainly don't want war.

Over the border, now that Hamas has been sidelined to Gaza, foreign aid is pouring into the West Bank. There is new-found prosperity. Israel has already wound down dozens of checkpoints and outposts and there is good reason to suspect that with every terrorist-free day another will be dismantled. With checkpoints leaving security zones will dissolve. Palestinians can see that peace and prosperity are Pavlovian. As in Israel the demographics are changing fast; youth prevails, change is in the air.

The most obvious problem on the ground are the settlements. They cost Israel a fortune to maintain and subsidize, they are full of unsavory people and are the biggest single obstacle to any... settlement. Why not just leave them and let it sort it self out? Tell them they will no longer live in an armed camp and if they want to leave here's a Gazan style pay-off check. I suspect many will take the money and run. A lot of the biblical brigade will up sticks the moment an unrestricted Palestinian taxi drives up. The rest will just get used it; after all they have a nice house and garden on the top of a hill, which is more they had when they arrived.

The second most obvious problem is Gaza. In theory it is part of Palestine; in practice it is its own worst enemy. Most West Bankers would cast it adrift tomorrow if their best interest were best served by so doing. As long as Hamas is in power there will never be a solution, so why not just set it to one side and let it sort out its own destiny?

The last most obvious problem is Jerusalem. Here I can offer no suggestions with any chance of Realpolitik success. Again we can just hope that time and education will lessen its significance to all concerned. The Byzantines built the magnificent church of Santa Sofia in Istanbul; the Muslims made it into a mosque; now it's a museum. When the Muslims made it into a mosque the Christians were angered; when it became a museum the Muslims were angered. Now, well it just doesn't seem to matter, religiously, to anyone any more—it's just a wonderful museum open to all. Who's to say in some years hence the world will be welcome to visit the Museum of the Temple Mount?

So that's it. Peace is just a dream. Nationhood is as quarrelsome as ever. Religion is as troublesome as only it can be. Hope? No, not on the face of it. And yet, and yet… the old have too much invested in past attitudes and past struggles; too many old scowls on too many old faces. The young on both sides have tasted the new world doctrine—more powerful than religion and politics—consumerism and prosperity. They talk to each other on Facebook and Twitter and see that neither of them are devils. They can read young blogs from students in Ramallah and refugees in Balata, reply from conscription camps in Haifa and kibbutz in the Golan. Their parents' stories of hard times and hard luck are fading fast. More importantly the numbers are on their side, more and more with every election. Hope? I think so, give or take a generation or two.

For now Sam, thank you for the inspiration to make the trip. It's right to leave the last word to you, the last words from the Holy Land in *The Innocents Abroad*, last words we could have sung and danced together:

"The long pilgrimage was ended, and somehow we seemed to feel glad of it."

Very best wishes, from your good friend and fellow hack,

Ian

Acknowledgements and Further Reading

The main source material of course was Mark Twain's *The Innocents Abroad, or The New Pilgrims' Progress: Being Some Account of the Steamship Quaker City's Pleasure Excursion to Europe and the Holy Land*. It was first published, on subscription, by the American Publishing Company in 1869 and cost $3.50 cloth backed. It was to remain his bestselling book during his lifetime. There are many current editions; I used the Penguin Classic version with its useful Introduction by Professor Tom Quirk.

Among academic studies of the book, research by the University of Virginia is particularly useful; see their The Innocents Abroad homepage. Also helpful was the University of California Press' *Traveling in Mark Twain* by Richard Bridgeman and *Mark Twain: The Adventures of Samuel L. Clemens* by Jerome Loving, as well as the University of Chicago's *Mark Twain Abroad: The Cruise of the Quaker City* by Dewey Ganzel.

Well thumbed is the Ron Powers biography, *Mark Twain, a Life*. A real labor of love is David H. Fears' *Mark Twain Day by Day*, a reference work which is just what it says it is.

The main Mark Twain research body is the Mark Twain Project based at the Bancroft Library, University of California at Berkeley. They are digitizing all the material relating to his life and works and making it available for research through their online facility.

Looking across the cabin at the bookshelves I can see the following:

Edward Said, *Orientalism*
Benny Morris, *One State, Two States*
Tom Segev, *Elvis in Jerusalem*
Charles Glass, *The Tribes Triumphant*
Alan Dershowitz, *The Case for Peace*
Brian Sewell, *South from Ephesus*
William Dalrymple, *From the Holy Mountain*
Robert Fisk, *The Great War for Civilization*
Norman Finkelstein, *Beyond Chutzpah*
Mitchell G. Bard, *The Complete Idiot's Guide to the Middle East Conflict*
Karen Armstrong, *Islam* and *The Case for God*,
Christopher Hitchens, *God is not Great*
Reza Aslan, *No God but God*

Once out at sea the politics and religion stay ashore. There are no pilot books for sailing down the Levantine coast but yachtsmen can use the semi-wiki www.noonsite.com or the forums on the Seven Seas Cruising Association's website. As always Nigel Calder's *Boatowner's Mechanical and Electrical Manual*, Tom Cunliffe's *The Complete Yachtmaster*, Jimmy Cornell's *World Cruising Routes* and Peter Bruce's *Heavy Weather Sailing* are close to hand.

Index

248